Dreaming About the Church

Acts of the Apostles of the 20th Century

Walbert Bühlmann

Translated by Peter Heinegg

Sheed & Ward

Scripture references are taken from the Revised Standard Version Bible.

Sheed & Ward TM is a service of National Catholic Reporter Publishing, Inc.

Library of Congress Catalog Card Number: 86-63591

ISBN: 1-55612-061-3

Published by:

Sheed & Ward 115 E. Armour Blvd. P.O. Box 414292
Kansas City, MO 64141-4292

To order, call: (800)821-7926

Contents

1

3

Foreword

Dreaming is probably the most appropriate way to deal with the Church. Merely rational thinking cannot cope with its mystery. Of course, by dreaming I don't mean fantasizing, but rather being open to the Spirit and, on the other hand, being inspired by the Spirit, as it was understood in the Old and New Testament.

What would have become of the young Church back then if it had not lived on dreams. Joseph was warned in a dream not to divorce his pregnant wife, Mary, but to flee with her and her child to Egypt, and—when the danger was past—to return to Nazareth (Mt 1:18-22; 2:13-23). Peter realized in a dream vision that there is nothing unclean and that gentiles too can be well pleasing to God (Acts 10:1-43). In an apparition one night Paul recognized that he was supposed to head not to the interior of Asia Minor but to Macedonia and Greece, and to open up the Church's path to the West (Acts 16: 9f.)

Today too this is how we may dream of the Church's path and mission. The Second Vatican Council traced out a whole new future for this Church. A horizon full of hope opened out in those days before the Church and the world. People breathed a sigh of relief. The "John-event" and the Council seemed, as the Jesus-event had once done, to bring God's Kingdom closer. What came of all that? Why hasn't the promise been kept? Can we ignore the current mood of disenchantment and resignation, or can we come to terms with it? Might not the impulses given

by the Council prevail and—as spring does, again and again—
overcome all resistance?

There were and still are groups of people in the Church, even
structures in the Church, blocking this path. These individuals
were more comfortable in the pre-conciliar situation, which they
would therefore like to maintain, and which they promote in
their concrete activities. They like to identify themselves with
the Church, to act in the name of the Church. But they represent only an obsolete, atrophied form of the Church: Insofar as
they embody pre-conciliar attitudes, they can call themselves the
Church only as a misnomer, a "Church" in quotation marks. Thus
we are called upon—out of love for the Church, for the sake of
the Church, doggedly but not bitterly—to speak the truth with
laughter on our lips, to suffer from this "Church," even to fight
with this "Church," so that the real Church may become ever
truer to the Gospel, to the Council, to the Holy Spirit, not just
in a dream but in reality.

There are two ways to suffer from this "Church." One can
endure it, put up with it, accept it in apathy or even expiation
as a *fait accompli*, silently offering up one's pain to God. Or we
can react, we can move from silence to action, trying every which
way, even if it means taking risks, to battle together with the
Church of our dreams against the "Church" in quotation marks,
so as to change it. That is the point of this book. It aims to give
new hope to all those who are suffering from the "Church," and
to encourage them to carry on the struggle. Merely dreaming,
in other words, is not enough. That would come too cheap. It
would be a downright betrayal not to translate the dream into
commensurate action. The greater we see the Church of Christ in
dreams, the more stubbornly we must fight in and with the human
Church, so that it matches this dream image, this ancient image
that is our goal. Mysticism proves its piety and authenticity only
when it goes beyond egotistical pastimes and masturbation into
politics, making the Church and the world different—and better.
Dreaming of the Church and battling with the Church are two

sides of the same coin, of the same existence in the Church. That is why between the first and last pages of this book, which talks about dreaming, there will be a battle between the Church and the "Church." The reader should not be confused by such sounds of combat. Tensions belong to the growth process of every living organism. The early Church had its share of them.

For that reason it helps to recall some situations from the Acts of the Apostles. It is by no means true that after first Pentecost everything suddenly sprang into movement and a wondrous transformation began. Even then people hesitated to take the daring leap from vision to reality. Think of the story of Ananias and Sapphira, who had to pay so high a price for their half-hearted devotion to the Gospel; or of the complaints of the Hellenist widows who felt they were being neglected in the distribution of bread. People stood in utter helplessness, confronting Jesus' missionary mandate. The Apostles sat tight comfortably in Jerusalem, until they were finally "driven out" by persecution, and so at last commenced spreading the Gospel. The contradiction between theory and practice was already in operation. Then came the bold decision of the Apostolic Council that gentile Christians were free from the Mosaic Law; then Peter's small-minded behavior toward the gentile Christians of Antioch forced Paul to oppose the coward "to his face" (Gal 2:11). But despite all, the breakthrough succeeded and the Gospel won, as the Spirit of God gave his Church no rest, again and again driving it on to act in accordance with Jesus.[1]

Apostolic history is not limited to that early time. One could write an "Acts of the Apostles" for every century. But undoubtedly no issue in this series would resemble the first one as closely as that of our own day. Just as back then the Gospel went on a triumphal march through the whole known world, so the Church in these last few decades has become for the first time a church of the six continents, a world church in the full sense. As there were tensions then on account of the freedom from the Mosaic Law enjoyed by gentile Christians, so nowadays the western Church is finding it hard not to impose western forms of theology, liturgy, and discipline on the young Churches of the other continents. It is even finding it hard to stop inculcating the pre-conciliar fear of sin and hell into western Christians, as opposed to simply proclaiming the God who is "rich in mercy" (Eph 2:4), as Jesus did, and so to acknowledge a "liberation theology" in the best sense, both social and spiritual, not only for Latin America but for all of humanity. But just as back then the Spirit of God made its presence felt over and over again with new initiatives and impulses, so we may assume that thanks to the Spirit's creative power the current stagnation will be overcome and after the present phase of restoration and stabilization in the Catholic Church is done with, the definitive realization of the Council's intentions will take place.

It is our task, through openness to the Spirit and through the shaping of consciousness in the Church, to help this last phase of the Council to dawn, and together to experience and write the 20th century version of the Acts of the Apostles.

Walbert Bühlmann

Part One

Suffering From the Church: Why?
An Analysis

1. The Johannine Spring

Thinking back, it seems like a dream. On the 28th of October, 1958 the Patriarch of Venice, Angelo Roncalli, was elected pope, taking the name John XXIII. After the first jolt of disillusionment and disappointment over this old, roly-poly man with the square head, the potato nose, the floppy ears, the stout chin, generally regarded as a "transitional pope," i.e., makeshift solution, something unexpected happened: At one of his first audiences, for a Jewish delegation, he promptly won the sympathy of those present there and—through the mass media—of the entire world, because, instead of giving an intellectual speech, he chatted in a kindly, human fashion, and said, "Don't be afraid, I am Joseph, your brother!" Suddenly the usual distance between the pope and other people had broken down. And in other ways too he lived like an altogether ordinary person: He invited bishops and relatives to dine with him; he spoke with the employees he met in the corridor or out in the garden; he even joked about himself and the Vatican, so that a book appeared with the sensational title, *A Pope Laughs*,[2] all things that the ceremonial code for popes had previously not allowed.

In John the "kindness and generosity of God" appeared once more (Tit 3:4). Even before the Council defined the Church as a "sign of salvation for all," in his person he made the Church a sign of salvation. Within a few weeks and months he changed the climate in the world and created an atmosphere of hope and amity among Christians, non-Christians, and even atheists.

Two months later, on January 25, 1959, he took the world completely by surprise with the announcement of a Council. He himself repeatedly stressed that this happened under a sudden "divine inspiration," and that he expected a "new Pentecost" from the Council.

After three and a half years of preparation, in which so many hopes were aroused along with a great deal of anxious suspense, the Council Fathers convened for the first time on October 11, 1962. In his opening address the pope, already seriously ill, sounded a note that was decidedly pastoral, optimistic, and nothing short of prophetic. He dissociated himself from the "prophets of doom," who interpreted (and lamented over) everything going on in the Church and the world as "downfall and disaster." He himself saw in everything the "hidden plan of divine providence," which "pursues its own goal down through the course of time and the works of man." He then expressed the view that the Church's teaching was not to be guarded like a treasure in a museum, but "to be explored and explained, as our time demands." He wished to see the image of the Church as authoritarian teacher completed, if not replaced, by the Church as a "very loving, kindly, and patient mother, full of compassion and benevolence toward her children, a mother who would rather turn to the remedy of charity than raise the weapons of severity, because she believes that under present circumstances it is more appropriate to proclaim far and wide the power of her teaching than to condemn." But when, still speaking in the light of a threefold vision, he set forth the prospect of the unity of all believers within the Catholic Church, of unity with all other churches and with all religions, everyone knew that "A great prophet has arisen among us: God has shown his care for his people" (Lk 7:16). And people were convinced that the Church would experience a new Exodus, that a new period of Church history had begun; and they were all glad.

The Council itself proceeded, with its laborious but purposeful procedure, in authentic dialogue between the best bishops and the best theologians, to prepare the texts in which the many accumulated problems were worked up, allowing the Church to make real progress. The new theology, which had hitherto developed only on the margin of the official Church and under continual suspicion of heresy, was now introduced into the Church, and men like Congar, Chenu, De Lubac, and Rahner, who not long before had been removed from their teaching positions and placed under censorship, got their vindication. Whereas all previous Councils had only busied themselves in an introverted fashion with the Church itself, and with its dogmas, morality, and discipline, the Second Vatican Council distinguished itself by opening itself with understanding and sympathy to the "others—" to other Christians, the Jews, non-Christians, and even atheists, who had previously been simply scorned and condemned.

After the death of John XXIII, Pope Paul VI adroitly continued the Council and brought it to an end. Then began the rapid succession of his trips to the other continents, to Africa, Asia, the two Americas, and Australia. After the Apostle Peter came to Rome, no pope had ever crossed the frontiers of Europe. Now in a twinkling the barriers were dropped systematically to signify that the western Church had now become the world Church. This same pontificate also witnessed for the first time the reduction of the overwhelming preponderance of western Christians (in 1900 they still constituted 85percent of the Church's membership). The number of Catholics in the southern continents underwent a specially vigorous increase, so that by the year 1970 51 percent of all Catholics lived in the southern hemisphere. By 1980 this figure had risen to 58 percent. We can now easily predict that in the year 2000 it will be around 70 percent.

The end of the Council brought those sensational meetings with the eastern Patriarchs, the Primate of the Anglican Church, the World Council of Churches in Geneva, and with representatives of the Asian religions. Visits were made and returned that stirred people's attention and made it clear to discerning observers that the Church was going through a quite extraordinary period in its history. The decade from 1958 to 1968 practically resembled a triumphal procession, resounding with hallelujahs and hosannahs. Nowadays one often thinks back to those fine times with nostalgia.

2. The Church vs. the "Church"

In 1968, however, the "Hosannah" abruptly changed into "Crucify him!" The occasion was the publication of the long awaited encyclical "Humanae vitae," which sketched a prophetic view of the ideal marriage, but was known simply as the "pill encyclopedia." The Council had spoken about legitimate birth control and had wished to take a position on the pill, but Paul VI reserved the question for himself. Thus this frail, hesitant man in his lonely responsibility had to make a decision—and then almost broke down in the face of the negative reactions it unleashed. Immediately after the pill came on the market, there was a sudden decline in the birth rate. Paul VI declined too because of the whole affair, and did not recover from it until years later.

For the first time the old proverb, "Roma locuta, causa finita" (Rome has spoken, the issue is decided) was no longer valid. Now the discussion began in earnest, and it ended with the majority even of good Catholics no longer obeying a decree from on high, but their conscience, and hence with their using whatever method of birth control suited them, with peace of mind. For the first time it was not the shepherd but the flock that chose the way. The Church was taking a position against the "Church."

This phenomenon, this kind of schism, now became a typical sign of the period that followed. Across parishes, countries, and the world there sprang up groups of "right" and "left wing" Catholics, "conservatives" and "progressives," believers whose mentality was markedly "pre-" or "post-conciliar"; and the tensions between them grew stronger. To be sure, many pedagogical errors were committed by not measuring out the Council in small doses and judiciously making the laity familiar with it. Instead the Council, with its new liturgy, theology, and discipline, came crashing in upon the people, disturbed many churchgoers in their rhythm, and provoked them to resistance. This was the beginning of the unfortunate polarization that to this day makes life harder for pastors, bishops, and lay people too. One can at any rate be glad that we no longer attack one another with truncheons and rifles, as was frequently the case in earlier centuries.

Along with the split among the laity there was increasing division in the Church between the people and the leadership, between the Church below and the Church above. The "top" of the Church (Rome) should have stood *above* the warring parties, should have coordinated the different groups and charisms, should have fostered mutual understanding and tolerance, should have prudently and single-mindedly led the Church forward on the path the Council had opened up. Instead, more and more, one could not avoid the impression that Rome itself had its doubts about the Council and threw itself on the side of those who sought to tame, legalize, and trivialize the Council. One had to suspect that the ten to eighty constant nay-sayers at the Council were to a considerable extent members of the Roman Curia. Voices were heard from the Curia saying that it would take twenty years to undo the "mischief" that John XXIII had done in the Church. I myself once sat in a Vatican Congregation across from a monsignore who was bemoaning the nasty conditions in the Church. When I innocently objected that John XXIII hadn't complained but had proclaimed a message of hope I was told, "If John XXIII could come back and see the harm he has caused the Church, he would cry his eyes out."

Paul VI was followed—for thirty-three days—by John Paul I, who came into harsh conflict with the Curia because of his statement that "God is not only Father, but Mother too," and because of his unconventional way of speaking, living, and working. There was soon fearful talk of a "relapse" into the era of John XXIII. But for all that there is no need to accept the hypothesis of poisoning offered by D. Yallop in his book, *In the Name of God?* We know, after all, that even back in Venice, Patriarch Luciani had been under medical supervision on account of his heart. We know further that on the evening before the night he died he had a long telephone conversation with his friend, Cardinal Colombo of Milan, in which he poured out his heart to him and spoke of his difficult situation vis-a-vis the Curia. So we have a ready explanation for his heart failure in all the grief it suffered.

Then on October 16, 1978 came the surprising election of the man from a faraway country, Cardinal Karol Wojtyla, who has since stamped his strong "Polish" faith on the entire Church, and who through his unyielding position on many issues has heightened even further the above-mentioned tension and division in the Church.

Thus we have reached the stage of the Church versus the "Church." Is this only an assumption, or even slander? A large part of the Church, to be precise, the alert and alive Christians, were pleased and encouraged, animated and committed. But they became visibly disappointed and weary, frustrated and resigned, because they came to learn that under pressure from the Roman Curia the Council was not keeping its promises. A whole sequence of arguments seems to prove them right.

a) Rome had the ideal competence and authority to interpret and apply the "legacy and mandate of Christ" for the present day—not simply to adhere to tradition in the retrospective sense, but to create it afresh in the prophetic sense. It remains, however, nervously wedded to conventional forms, and continually says "No" to ideas and suggestions from the "Church below." I

have repeatedly gone to the general chapters of various orders
and communities to present "my ideas" to these elite forces. I
have always been pleasantly impressed by the fact that when useful ideas were submitted by individuals or groups, the plenary
assembly would say: "Good, this will be incorporated into the
by-laws," or "The leadership will make a note of that." But in
the Roman Curia spontaneous defensive reactions are the order
of the day. There is immediate fear of the consequences of any
innovation. The staff always invokes precedents and painstakingly
strives to avoid new problems and new solutions. In short, the
Curia clings desperately to the status quo.

And so when lay people in parish councils or regional synods
become active and voice suggestions, in order to commit themselves more strongly to church life, they are bluntly put in their
place and reminded—not, for the most part, by pastors and bishops, but by Rome—that they are only laity and that they should
not clericalize the laity. And when women argue that they really
ought to have somewhat more of a say in the Church, their wings
are clipped by invoking a dogma that is no dogma at all.

One step higher: When religious communities decide, after
mature deliberation, that they would like to reformulate their
mission and their goals, so as better to comply with their founder's
intention in today's world, they are quickly given to understand
that they should stick to the good old ways, that they should not
be setting up a magisterium alongside the Church's magisterium,
and hence they must conform to the higher authority "out of
obedience"—or they risk stirring up, as happened for example at
the general chapter of the Franciscans in 1985, a kind of rebellion.

Yet another step higher: When local churches desire to move
forward, either theologically or pastorally, by taking certain measures, the gate is immediately slammed in their face and they
are instructed that they must subordinate themselves to the entire
Church, i.e., to the Roman model of unity.

The highest step: When in the synods of bishops in Rome a

new spirit of Pentecost and the Council bursts forth, when pastorally minded bishops present realistic analyses, supported by
appropriate concrete proposals, and people in the world outside
are already sitting up, taking notice, and hoping, the concluding
document that comes out a year later once again stifles all hopes,
and everything remains as it was before, as it is prescribed in the
Code of Canon Law, never mind the synods. Thus the synod
bishops and Catholics in general feel a growing sense of frustration and helplessness; they feel they have wasted their effort and
been bullied in the process. The Council was supposed to be the
beginning of a new path, on which the Church must boldly press
forward, since it has defined itself as the people of God on pilgrimage, not staying in the long-established, bourgeois motel of
the Roman Curia.

b) From the fact that the "Church below" carries so little
weight, it follows necessarily that the documents published by the
"Church above" likewise carry little weight. Anyone who reads
them with a somewhat critical mind, and pays heed to the "seis-
mographs" that measure them, the commentaries in ecclesiastical
and theological journals, will almost always come, unfortunately,
back to the same conclusion: that these documents do not give
satisfaction, but that, on the contrary, they beget indignation and
antipathy, and that they strengthen the manifest dissent separating
the magisterium and moral theologians, the magisterium and pastoral theologians, the magisterium and ecumenical circles. This
is no surprise, because these documents are no longer based, as
they were in the Council, on a genuine dialogue with the best theologians, but on handbook theology, on onesided information, on
mystery-mongering, on authoritarian decisions. All this explains
why these documents do not "catch on," do not "go down well,"
are not regarded as help for the way, indeed with time are no
longer read at all, and why Rome with its "good sheep" is becoming a ghetto church. Meanwhile the others say: "We are the
Church of the Gospel and the Council, whereas the one in Rome
is a product of an unreconstructed medievalism, which still goes

on spinning for a while, like a flywheel, but no longer makes anything go."

This broad divergence between the "Church above" and the "Church below," once asserted on the strength of the "sense of the Church" (*sensus ecclesiae*), has since been proved scientifically. In a poll entitled "Catholics 1985" the Allensbach Public Opinion Research Institute detected a decrease in loyalty toward the Pope and the Church. In West Germany barely one out of four Catholics, 23 percent to be exact, views Rome's decisions as important and binding. The others ignore directives from Rome that disagree with their own way of thinking. So it would be correct to say that only a fourth of all German Catholics are "Roman Catholics" in the full sense. Who is to blame for this situation? Is it only the other three fourths, the dissenting Catholics, or might it not be just as much, or even more, the top authority, because it still doesn't recognize the signs of the time?

How far this dissent has spread and flourished can be seen in the latest book by N. Greinacher and Hans Kung (editors), *Where is the Catholic Church Headed?: Against Betraying the Council* (Munich, 1986). This present book of mine offers background information to fill out that picture. It shows the reason why the Roman Curia provokes and unleashes this dissent, instead of obviating it by prophetic conduct.

This current obstructionist behavior on the part of the Roman Curia is not new, it is not simply a post-conciliar phenomenon. It is the extension of a consistent line that began more than 100 years ago when Rome, faced with the critical, autonomous thinking of the modern perşon, could only utter its authoritarian "No," and continually condemned ideas that ended by prevailing anyway. We need only recall Pius IX's *Syllabus of Errors* or Pius X's campaign against "modernism." The Second Vatican Council finally found a way to connect with modern thought, but meanwhile the Curia lingers in its antiquated attitude, with the result that three quarters of all Catholics, in Germany at least, no longer listen to it.

The bishops and bishops' conferences are faced with the ticklish obligation of putting a good face on a bad situation, of giving their official consent for the sake of church unity, and of publicly playing down their conflicts with Rome·as much as possible. Just think, for example, of the poor bishops of the Dutch synod in Rome in 1980. The divided bishops' conference, with its progressive majority and conservative minority, was invited to Rome. They had expectations that the Pope, as an authoritative outsider and discussion leader could bring both groups into dialogue, and help them to reach a solution or at least a compromise. Instead, the bishops were confronted by a group of cardinals from the Roman Curia, who then joined the conservative minority to form a majority and determine the position taken by the concluding document.

c) In order to avoid in advance any such conflicts with bishops, Rome does everything it can to surround itself, on the international level, with a staff of the most loyal, conformist co-workers. Candidates for the episcopacy are scrutinized in their "heart and reins," and if it becomes evident from the Vatican Archives, where all the information about possible candidates is stored, or from the strictly secret investigative process, that a candidate has ever said anything deviating from the Roman line on the subject of *Humanae vitae* or on disconnecting the priesthood from the Church's law of celibacy, or on the ordination of woman, then he is out of the running, whatever fine qualities he may otherwise have. This is how all discussion of new questions is kept at arm's length, instead of authentically grappling with them. Hence the only men who get a chance are, with individual exceptions, only very well-behaved, conservative, absolute party-liners so that the hierarchy increasingly reflects, not the whole, living Church, but above all its right wing, which is identified with the true Church. One could prove from examples such as Holland, Brazil, or the U.S.A. how these "endangered bishops' conferences" have been infiltrated by such elements in recent years

and transformed "for the better," how archconservative candidates have been forced upon a local church despite the express
opposition of laity and clergy. And so a "Church above" is cast
in concrete, and Rome once again feels quiet and secure. The
members of the church meanwhile stand by apathetically. The
Church versus the "Church." The pope's visit to Holland in 1985
clearly pointed this up. Does anyone really believe that unity in
the Church can be compelled in this fashion? People who disdain human dignity and freedom of conscience, which are recognized in the Council document "Dignitatis humanae," are simply
missing the signs of the time. They will eventually realize their
miscalculation.

Nonetheless, the situation is not hopeless. Archbishop Helder
Camara has shown in his book *Conversions of a Bishop* how he
himself became a convert to the poor only in the course of time.
Back in 1955 he had been the chief organizer of the Eucharistic
World Congress in Rio de Janeiro, and had, with help from
the government, erected a grandiose altar on the well-known
Copacabana beach. Afterwards Cardinal Gerlier of Lyon put
his hand on his shoulder and said: "My dear brother bishop, I
congratulate you for the Congress. But I must confess to you that
for me it was a scandal. Here is this triumphalist Church—and a
few kilometers back the hopeless favelas of the poor. You really
must put your organizational talent to work somewhere else, I
mean for helping the poor." Gerlier's words struck home, and
Helder Camara became the man he is today. And so even today
in Brazil one sometimes hears that newly appointed right-wing
bishops, once they have witnessed the lively discussions in the
bishops' conference, "convert" and begin thinking in terms of the
gospel and the people, and no longer so much in terms of the law.

Some of us had a similarly hopeful experience, a surprise in
fact, with the Dutch bishops. We had thought that the conformist
bishops had gotten the upper hand in Holland. There was all
the more amazement, then, when they issued a petition to the
synod of bishops in Rome in 1985, declaring that Rome was still

taking itself much too seriously as the one universal Church and "[looked upon] the local churches only as a necessary extra or even a deviation instead of a treasure" and that for this reason a "disturbed relationship had arisen between the Vatican and the local Churches," a situation due not least of all to the authoritarian system for nominating bishops. Later on we shall hear several more statements in this vein, in connection with the synod of bishops.

In this process of naming bishops the nuncios play a strategic role. I have already pointed out elsewhere,[3] how despite the express wish of the Council and many bishops' conferences, the bastion of the Italian nuncios is stubbornly holding its own. From 1970 to 1980 the number of Italian nuncios was lowered only from 75 to 73: at this rate in 110 years 50 percent of the nuncios would still be Italian. As a President of the State in Africa will build up his dynastic power by appointing people from his own tribe, so Rome seems to have a special reliance on Italian nuncios with their predominantly Roman-legal way of thinking. It must be said, however, that these nuncios, with few exceptions, are looked upon not as sympathetic liaison-men with the universal Church, but rather as curial officials who onesidedly represent and pursue the interests of their system.

d) If we analyze the last nomination of cardinals, on April 24, 1985, we must denounce two ugly features of the list.

First, the Third World does not have an adequate voice. After the appointments of 1983 there was no missing the fact that although Africa and Asia/Oceania were properly represented, with fourteen and fifteen cardinals respectively, Latin America, which has significantly more Catholics than all of Europe, is clearly undersupplied, with only twenty cardinals, while Italy alone has twenty-nine. This time Africa got two new cardinals, Asia got two, Latin America three, but Italy got five and the whole western world twenty-one. Thus the predominance of the western Church is being expanded instead of reduced. Allowance is still not being made for the fact that the Church's center of gravity has long since shifted. Rome seems to refuse to believe the facts of history and to feel a certain fear of the Third World, especially Latin America with its "inflammatory liberation theology."

Second, as with the bishops, most of the new men admitted into the College of Cardinals are conservatives. Since the main task of this body is the election of the pope, this is a deliberate effort to prevent the "John XXIII experiment" from happening again.

Around the time when the labor union movement "Solidarity" was still relatively free to act, I spent three weeks in Poland. I often thought to myself, when they told me about the Polish political system, "Almost like the Vatican!" And when for my part I told people about the Roman Curia, on three separate occasions my interlocutors spontaneously remarked, "Exactly like our system!" In both cases—though, of course, there are many shades of difference—there is a "central committee" made up of individuals who have worked their way up and made a career for themselves through absolute fidelity to the party line. Largely isolated now from the people, they eradicate all opposition and exercise their power. They support and cover for one another so as to keep the system going. They always present the party's opinion, and cannot afford an opinion of their own. They do not learn from the system's mistakes and do not take the advice of experts, because they are convinced they know better on the strength of their ideology or dogma. We may wonder when, where, and how something like a Solidarity movement demanding more of a say, might come into existence in the Church—and what its fate would be.

As I analyze it, the Council has thus far gone through five phases:

—The first phase was that of the *charismatic impulse*, when John XXIII had his sudden inspiration and announced the Council on the spot.

—There followed the phase of *tradition-bound preparation*, when, under the direction of the Roman Curia, schemata, or working papers, were drawn up. The Curia thought and hoped that the conciliar assembly would read them through, retouch them here and there, and then accept them. If that had been the case, then the Church would have made no headway at all, because these schemata were framed strictly in accord with the status quo, as Hubert Jedin attests. He was a member of a preparatory commission, and in his diary he expresses his concern that the curial party would shape the Council and see to it that the earlier papal and curial regulations were simply gathered together, and all new ideas and initiatives eliminated. Jedin, a historian inclined by his profession to be rather conservative, became a progressive, as he himself admits,[4] as a reaction against this pressure from the Roman Curia. One indication of where the Roman Curia stood theologically at this time is the fact that four months before the Council even began, Karl Rahner, the most striking pioneer of conciliar theology, was placed under preliminary censorship.

—Then came the third phase, that of *implementation through dialogue*, in which the best bishops entered into conversation with the best theologians. At first this led to an out and out rebellion, when the bishops, advised by the theologians, rejected the whole package of schemata—except for the paper on the liturgy, which was composed by genuine experts. Then entirely new texts were worked out and made the Council what it became.

—After this the fourth phase, that of the *euphoric new departure*, positively exploded. There were the first post-conciliar years with the changeover to the new liturgy, the strong interest in theological questions, and the increased pastoral involvement of lay people, in whom the flame of freedom burned bright. This, of course, did not mean just the old "freedom of the children of God": many things got out of hand, and tens of thousands of priests and religious left their way of life. One no longer felt quite right in religion, but one felt that the waves would subside.

—The fifth phase, that of *restoration and stabilization*, followed more quickly, purposefully, and successfully than anyone could have expected. With the inevitable swing of the psychological and historical pendulum it "had" to come, but it didn't have to come in the way it actually did—with the exaggerated centralization, standardization, and legalism. At this moment we are still in this phase, and it has already been sufficiently described.

—But this cannot be the end of the Council. The Council has not yet spoken its last word, not yet discharged its last burst of energy, not yet realized its actual intentions. It has on many points been narrowly and legalistically interpreted. But we may entertain a stubborn hope that the sixth phase will come, namely the definitive *implementation of the conciliar impulses*. For these impulses will continually rise anew, continually assert themselves, and finally prevail—like spring. Furthermore, the local churches too will grow stronger in their self-consciousness, simply go their own way, and thus realize unity in authentic pluralism.

My confidence here cannot be based on human evidence, only—but this is a great deal, a faith that moves mountains—on the power of the Holy Spirit, who keeps surprising us with his creative inspirations and who has strength to change, in one way or another, even case-hardened systems.

e) Never has the split between the Church and the "Church" come so glaringly to light as in the argument over Latin American liberation theology. A good twenty years ago numbers of priests and lay people got together in pastoral conferences and reflected on the situation of the Church in that continent. They came to see that the centuries-old, petrified situation of the few greater landed proprietors and the mass of the people who depend on them, can in no possible way correspond to God's will and shames the Church, which always tolerated it. As a second step the solution was proposed that the people had to liberate themselves by developing a consciousness based on the Gospel itself. These views were spread through lectures and articles. In time some influential bishops joined in the drive and encouraged the group to compose working papers along the lines of these ideas for the approaching congress of the Latin American Episcopal Council (CELAM) in Medellin, Colombia in 1968. Surprisingly, the assembly of bishops accepted them and issued two main watchwords: Option for the Poor, and Base Communities. It was one of the most beautiful things in recent church history to see how in a short time something great grew out of such small beginnings, how quickly a clericalist, sacramentalist, capitalist church could become a renewed church that now challenges the Church as a whole.

Alongside the traditional scholastic theology, which had remained cold and abstract, a new theology now came into being from below, a theology of the people, of life, of the poor. The Latin Americans studied their own situation, asked themselves what the Gospel had to say about it, and tried to change things through concrete steps. Since then, in fact, many changes have taken place. Above all, the people have acquired a new self-consciousness and an Easter hope. This new kind of theology was dubbed "liberation theology."

The rich observed this transformation with increasing restlessness and launched a persistent campaign of defamation, its main burden being that the whole thing was subversive and Marxist. As a matter of fact, the liberation theologians often did use Marxist terminology for their analyses of society. They also spoke more about the Exodus and the social-political liberation from Egypt than about the resurrection of Jesus. Catholicism had hitherto consoled the poor so much with hopes of heaven that the liberationists now put the accent more on this-worldly salvation, without, however, denying the afterlife.

Within the Church too, unfortunately, an extreme right-wing opposition group was organized, chiefly under the leadership of

Cardinal Alfonso Lopez-Trujillo and suffragan bishop Bonaventura Kloppenburg, who for years had been charging, first, that the liberation theologians were Marxists; second, that the base communities were building a people's church in opposition to the hierarchical Church; and, third, that religious were laying claim to their own magisterium alongside the Church's magisterium. Rome paid particular attention to these reports, because they matched its own line. Thus in the fall of 1984 a document was issued by Cardinal Joseph Ratzinger on liberation theology, and in coordination with this Cardinal Joseph Hoffner delivered an inaugural address on the same subject at the West German Bishops' Conference. Both prelates took liberation theology very sharply to task.

For me the personal factors here carry a lot of weight. The liberation theologians and the two most prominent cardinals allied with them, men who are also held in the highest esteem in the Roman synod of bishops and who were elected to the commission on synods, Paulo Evaristo Arns and Aloisio Lorscheider, have millions of poor people behind them, something that can in no way be said of the directors of the anti-liberation theology campaign. Under the leadership of A. Lopez-Trujillo even the Latin American Bishops Council (CELAM), which in the first years sponsored genuine pastoral initiatives, has become more and more a control apparatus for the Vatican, increasingly attempting to blunt the thrust of Medellin, to sweeten the bitter pill of Medellin, as Rome has done with the Council.[5]

The whole matter was brought to the boiling point by the "penance of silence" that Rome laid on Leonardo Boff in May, 1985. For a year this liberation theologian, who was widely read in Europe, was not allowed to give lectures, write articles, or make any public statements. There was a notable escalation here, in comparison with the case of Hans Kung, who was simply removed from his teaching post within the faculty of Catholic theology—something Rome admittedly had the intrinsic right to do. But to impose total public silence on a man clearly violates human rights.

A member of religious order can accept that only "in obedience," meaning he drops the question of justice and injustice in hopes that history will have the last word, as it often has. One thinks of Henri de Lubac, who lost his teaching job in the fifties and received the dignity of the cardinalate in 1983, when he was 87.

The occasion for the reprimand Boff received was his book, *The Church—Charisma and Power*,[6] where among other things, he strongly criticizes the Church and reproaches Rome for talking a lot about human rights but disregarding them on many points. In the official answer to Boff his accusers were careful not to discuss that reproach, trying instead to drive him into a corner with certain dogmatic statements. But by imposing silence on Boff they conceded all the more the justice of his complaint.

We are living at present in a new phase of world and church history. Up until the Second World War and the Second Vatican Council people in the world and the Church, with some exceptions (the resistance to Nazism, say, on the part of a few brave individuals), practiced blind obedience. Orders were orders. Authority still enjoyed undisputed prestige. Since then people have become increasingly aware of freedom and responsibility of conscience, they have acquired some critical distance vis-a-vis authority. Under certain circumstances they feel bound in conscience to become dissenters and protestors, even in the Church.

After "Humanae vitae" for the first time a wind of dissent blew through the Catholic Church; but at the time it took the form of a silent revolution. Still shyly, hand in front of mouth, the rebels posed their questions among laypeople, priests, and bishops' conferences and took their stand. Now in the Boff case we find for the first time, and on a very broad base, an out-and-out revolution has come to the Catholic Church. A shudder of indignation shook the Catholic world. Someone should have done a poll in those months. It would most likely have shown that the larger part of the Church (I would add, the better part) stood on the side of Leonardo Boff and his poor people, and not on the side of Rome.

Groups of theologians from all continents, organizations like "Pax Christi," "Justitia et Pax," priests and lay people voiced their displeasure with Rome and their sympathy for "Brother Leonardo." The position taken by the two most immediately affected bishops' conferences, those of Peru and Brazil, with the tortuous text they released, make all their suffering and embarrassment transparent. They "had" to accept Rome's decree, however grudgingly, so as not to risk the public scandal of a schism. They professed their intention of "continuing the loyal and persistent dialogue with the Holy Father and the Roman Curia"—just as, in the final analysis, the U.S.A. cannot break off its dialogue with the U.S.S.R. But it is a laborious, painful dialogue, of a sort that really should not be taking place in the Church. Ten Brazilian bishops, six of them archbishops, spoke more frankly. They called the silencing of Boff a violation of human rights and Christian love. The Italian nuncio, Carlo Furno, promptly labeled them as "rebels." The General Chapter of the Franciscans, which was held soon afterwards, sent their condemned brother Leonardo an open letter of solidarity, signed by the Minister General, the whole General Council, and over 100 capitulars. The dissent could not have been expressed more clearly.

For God's sake this situation must not go on. Rome, however, seems to remain unshaken amidst these jolts to the members of the Church. It knows that it has the stronger position, that it has already triumphantly endured many storms in the course of history. It also ought to know, of course, that it has paid for such victories with a heavy share of responsibility for the schisms with Eastern Orthodoxy and the Reformation churches. And it ought to know that, unlike other systems, it has no divisions at its disposal to crush any revolts that may arise and to "normalize" the situation. It ought to know that today's men and women, including Christians, including Catholics, in part because of the Council, take freedom of conscience very seriously. Unity can no longer be compelled, but only—and thank God for this—bargained for, through intelligent preparation and follow up, and through genuine dialogue with respect for the other side. Hence Rome should no longer aim at forcing through its model of uniformity, but rather aim for unity in authentic collegiality and pluralism, in deference to the relative autonomy of the local churches, as the Council saw and demanded. Rome, no doubt, always talks about this, but doesn't translate it into practice.

Somehow, though, Rome was shocked and embarrassed by the worldwide reaction to the Boff case. The authorities played down the matter, declaring that they had meant well with him and only wanted to help him retire for a certain amount of time, to think things over in peace and quiet. For their part the Brazilian bishops reacted prudently. They did not lash back, but sent a group of leading bishops to Rome for several weeks, to spend time with the various Roman Congregations, plus eight hours with Cardinal Ratzinger and two hours with the Pope, providing more comprehensive information and postulating for the future a new mode of negotiation between Rome and Brazil. In addition the Brazilians delivered the supporting materials for a promised document on liberation theology; they were convinced that this one would make out better and be treated more fairly than the first one. Thus Rome seems to be going through a certain learning process after all.

As a matter of fact, the new document, which was presented in Rome on April 5, 1986 with the title, *Christian Freedom and Liberation*, was given a generally good reception. It plots the boundaries within which the Christian and the whole Church are to stand up for justice and liberation, boundaries drawn wide enough to make room for "rebellion" in the form of civil disobedience or passive resistance, of the kind announced by the Church of the Philippines against the Marcos regime. It recalls the statement in Paul VI's encyclical, *Populorum progressio* (1967), which the hierarchy was otherwise glad to let drop out of sight, that in extreme emergencies the use of violence might be legitimate. The high quality of the document is due to the fact that 35 bishops' conferences and 40 experts contributed their ideas to it, whereas the first document had admittedly been a small-scale affair, based on rather one-sided information. This should serve as an example for all future Roman decrees.

This document also brought an end to an era in the Church: for the first time a non-European church, Latin America, produced an original contribution to theological reflection and church practice. It had already influenced the episcopal synods in 1971 and 1974, but now it has been officially received, with certain corrections, by the Church as a whole, because it has been recognized that the issue of liberation concerns the entire world. Thanks to this document and to the early lifting of Boff's compulsory silence the troubled communication and the tensions that had burdened relations between Rome and Brazil for years were finally settled. We have, in other words, a model of conflict resolution before us. If the first brief from Rome had been met with silent obedience, no progress would have been made. Due to the worldwide, protest a serious discussion took place that has now led to a good final result.

In any event the course of liberation theology and its particular concerns cannot be stopped. Since December 1985 issue after issue of *Mysterium Liberationis* ("The Mystery of Liberation) has been appearing in Latin America, thinking through and formulating all of theology from the standpoint of the poor. Fifty-three volumes are planned, which will offer not an opposing view to, but a very useful completion of, *Mysterium Salutis* ("The Mystery of Salvation"), the standard theological text, written a good ten years ago by western theologians.

But how did it ever happen that the Roman Curia, despite the Council, again became—or remained—so narrow, so powerful, so disagreeable?

3. Who Is Behind the Roman Curia?

Who is actually behind this mystery-enshrouded power that we call the Roman Curia, that survives all the popes ("Popes come and go, the Curia remains"), that was humbled by the Council and driven into a corner, but afterwards grew still more powerful than before?

Memories are still fresh of how this Curia was outwitted by Pope John XIII with his idea of the Council. By the nature of things Council and Curia don't get along well. The Roman Curia stands as the highest authority, uniting in a single hand the legislative and the executive function. It thus allows for no body to stand over it, to check and inspire its operations—a sort of parliament. Now the Council was suddenly shoved in its face, and a Council (it had been taken as dogma in every age) represents the highest authority in the Church.

Then the Curia tried to manipulate the Council by forcing on it the old-fashioned schemata. This calculation, however, did not work out, as we have already seen. Thus the Curia stood during the Council, ready for action but not moving. No one could say that it was an important inspiration for any of the Council's documents. On the contrary, it occasionally tried to block the works, to go over the pope's head and introduce security clauses at certain moments, as well as take certain topics out of the Council's hands.

With all the tensions, the Council went off surprisingly well. At its conclusion the bishops were left with the unsettled question, "What will become of the Curia?" A good deal of criticism had been leveled at it, and there were many cries for reforming it. To cite only two examples there was the speech Cardinal Joseph Frings gave on the "Santo Officio," to thundering applause from the great hall; and there were many people who said they looked forward to dynamic inspiration and more competent, open-minded leadership from the "Propaganda Fide." Should these wishes remain no more than that? Should their thunder die away like a retreating storm, to be followed once more by mild sunshine, as if nothing had happened? Who will see to it that this part of the Council will be implemented? Will a pope, himself a "Prisoner of the Vatican," ever have the power to change such a system?

Paul VI took up these questions, wishes, reproaches, and proposals in a homily he gave shortly before the end of the Council. Although he defended the Curia against the severe charges that it was "superannuated, incapable, egotistical, and corrupt," he did admit that a genuine renovation was imperative. He made a formal promise to take over the responsibility for this renovation. He said it would proceed slowly—Papa Montini, himself a man of the Curia, naturally could not bring it upon himself to carry out a sort of palace revolution—but it would come.[7]

What came was, as the Italians say, a "dry fig," i.e., worthless. A few names, it is true, were changed, and jurisdictions were redistributed, and a number of high-ranking foreign officials were called to serve in Rome, but only in a trickle, one after the other. But a single individual can never turn a system around. He has to adapt or he'll be gotten rid of. Besides most of the newly qualified appointees prove to be more "Roman" than the Italian cardinals. The orders and religious institutes followed a more radical path of renovation. After the Council they held special chapters where for several months the Council texts were studied and new constitutions framed in their spirit. Then came the electoral chapter. In most cases a whole crew was elected, Superior General and all the Assistants, chosen from the best elements of the rank and file. This sort of new group could provide the community with leadership in keeping with the Council.

Neither of these things happened in the Vatican. Neither did the personnel study and assimilate the theology of the Council (as opposed to its mere juridical viewpoints) systematically and in common, nor were the best elements from the local churches called to Rome as group. In too many cases people were appointed on the principle, "Promoveatur ut amoveatur" (Promote him to get him out of the way). This explains why in many general curias of religious orders and institutes the winds that blow are agreeably different from the spirit of the Roman Curia.

A typical characteristic of the Roman mentality is its ignorance of, and distance from both the impulses issuing from the Council and developments in the Church since the Council. Rome is no longer willing to have experts work up the new problems and give it information about them. Rome always thinks it knows better and doesn't need the experts, who only "cast uncertainty" onto everything. The feeling is that in the immediate post-conciliar period there was enough, indeed too much, movement, experimentation, and aggiornamento going on; that now with the new Code, peace, law, and order have returned. Or so I conjecture. But there is manifest proof that such is indeed the case: The Council had laid down three retrospective criteria for the renewal of religious institutes: the spirit of the Gospel, the spirituality of the founders, and healthy tradition, as well as one prospective criterion: adaptation to the signs of the time, which must be understood as the expression of God's will. For years I have suspected that this fourth criterion has been made a dead letter. In any event it was never mentioned in the letters of the Congregation for Religious to the various general chapters. The new Code of Canon Law has now confirmed my suspicion by saying point-blank that the Church authorities have to see to it that the instistutes grow and flourish in accordance with the spirit of the founder and sound traditions (Canon 576). Over and out. Rome thinks the required adaptation has now taken place, whereas it was supposed to be an ongoing process. No wonder that this sort of Church is increasingly distancing itself from life and thereby isolating itself. The theological background of this attitude lies in the anxious quest for the "eternal verities," which, the old theology manuals taught, had been called into question by the findings of psychological studies and new theological interpretations. Rome preferred to withdraw to the bunker, instead of confronting the new age.

32 **Dreaming About the Church**

With this defensive attitude the Roman bureaucracy has managed systematically to tighten the reins on the Church again. A concrete example of this is the way the experts were handled in the matter of liturgical renewal. Under the leadership of Annibale Bugnini the finest specialists had prepared the schema on the liturgy so carefully that it was the first document accepted by the Council. There followed a series of five "liturgical instructions," a kind of implementing statutes. The first, in 1967, was once again submitted to the experts and was in line with their work. They never got to see the second one, and were all the more surprised and incensed by its deviations from the path hitherto taken. Thus from one case to the next the situation worsened until the fifth instruction, in 1980, which had an altogether pre-conciliar look to it. In the meantime Archbishop Bugnini, Secretary of the Congregation for the liturgy, was unceremoniously ousted, because as a scholar he had always spoken out in favor of legitimate pluralism and genuine inculturation of the liturgy. By thus getting rid of the real expert, the man who admonished them in the sense of the Council, the Roman bureaucrats were free to forbid the "Indian liturgy" around 1975 and to hold up approval of the "Zairean liturgy" to this date. The ritualists and rubricists, for whom the ideal liturgy consists in reading off a printed text, Sunday after Sunday, from the first sign of the cross to the final blessing, have once again gotten the upper hand.

The same pattern occurred on many other issues, regardless of the Council, regardless of the synod of bishops. The Curia is once again successfully fending off the many new ideas and proposals of the local churches, upholding the status quo in case after case, as it did before the Council, with the sole difference that back then the Council blew up this bastion, whereas now the episcopal synods have no power and are helplessly subject to the Curia.

This is how we get the sort of caricatures of the pastoral spirit, such as one finds—to cite a classical example—in canons 960-63 of Church law, on penance and reconciliation. Instead of encouraging people and continually announcing and promising to them God's mercy, "which reaches to the heavens, as far as the skies" (Ps 36), instead of offering and recommending the sacrament of penance as a liberating opportunity, the Code thrusts it on Catholics as a frightening obligation. And so Rome distances itself "toto caelo" from contemporary moral theology, psychology, and pastoral counseling, from the tenor of the bishops' synod of 1983, even from the encyclical "Dives in misericordia," which, without going into all sorts of stipulations and conditions, simply praised God's compassion. The Curia likewise leaves behind any sort of realistic appraisal of the Church's situation, as if mature present-day Christians could be browbeaten with old-fashioned theology and herded back to the confessional in droves. At best only the "good sheep" will still respond to such methods, while the others will retire still further from this untrustworthy Church.

In addition, the new Canon Law and later decrees have been used to build up a centralized system that reserves decisions, for which the bishops in their churches should properly be responsible, to the Roman Curia, as though the pope's authority and the church's unity were hanging in the balance. A recent example sheds light on this situation: From 1974 on the bishops and higher religious superiors in the U.S.A. had the authority to permit alcoholic priests to use unfermented grape juice in celebrating the Eucharist. This permission was revoked by Cardinal Ratzinger in September, 1983, citing as grounds the validity of the sacrament. Then in January, 1985 the possibility was once again conceded, but the bishops and superiors had to make application to the Congregation on the Faith in Rome for each individual case. This was similarly true for many other matters, for which one had to humbly beg permission from Rome, oceans and continents away. Evidently Rome cannot shake the fear that authorities living closer to the members of the Church might let the cold juridical standpoint be outweighed by pastoral—and more human—ways of thinking!

At a time when an unprecedented economic, technological, scientific, and even theological upswing has taken place, when humanity is threatened as never before by the possibility of nuclear annihilation and the reality of imminent ecological catastrophe, when people as never before are foundering as they grapple with the ultimate questions about life and are hungry for understanding, meaning, and hope—at a time like this the Roman Curia is bickering over such questions as, should girls be allowed to serve as "altar boys," should lay people be allowed to preach or not; should India, Zaire, or Brazil be allowed to have a supplementary Eucharistic prayer or not—especially *not*, and with this sort of centralization and legalism sours the last joy one feels in religion. This kind of Church leadership must surely displease not just men and women, but the generous mind of God.

Pope Paul VI was painfully aware of this situation. That is why in Lent of the Holy Year 1975 he held a penitential service for the entire personnel of the Roman Curia, during which he spoke very seriously and openly about the worldwide negative feeling about Rome, which, he said, had to be acknowledged with great humility and reduced through great readiness to serve. Obviously the pope's words had little effect, because anti-Roman sentiment continues to grow, or has changed in many people to indifference and apathy. Paul VI had managed to erect the modern, elegant, functional Nervi Hall for general audiences in the middle of the Vatican, with all its Renaissance and Baroque art and architecture. But he failed to set in motion in the Vatican a new, up-to-date style of leadership that would be accepted by the Church and would diminish the tension between the Church and the "Church."

For seven years now Pope John Paul II has been toiling away at this same task. He evidently shared the conviction that the Curia has not been sufficiently renewed, and that people were expecting precisely of him, the first non-Italian pope in 450 years, to bring this affair to a happy conclusion. That is why a year after his installation he called all the cardinals together in the beginning of November 1979, for a three day seminar in which he discussed as his main theme the renewal of church structures, above all the Roman Curia. At the end of the seminar he encouraged the cardinals to submit to him in writing within three months their concrete wishes and suggestions on this problem. Years have gone by since then, and people waited and hoped, hoped against all hope, or gave up hoping. The appointments of new prefects and secretaries of the Congregations made since that time, however, leave the strong impression that the conservative spirit has been further strengthened. To take only one example, we may recall Cardinal Silvio Oddi, who was never active in the pastoral ministry, never served as a diocesan bishop, never dealt with the clergy, but from the outset had a diplomatic career. But in 1979, he was nonetheless named Prefect of the Congregation of the Clergy. His only "recommendation" was his reputation as arch-conservative.

Thirteen years ago I wrote in my book, *Where Faith Lives*: "The Vatican Curia has not yet been reformed, but it will be. The only question is whether a stroke by the Holy Spirit will suffice, or whether a Chinese cultural revolution will be needed."[8] Perhaps this book too could help to increase the pressure on the Roman Curia. I am convinced in any case that if the effort to reform it thoroughly and radically does not succeed, it will become increasingly isolated and exhausted. Perhaps good Pope John would see that too as a "hidden plan of divine Providence."

I got to know the mentality of the Roman Curia from personal experience, when I lived in Rome from 1970 to 1982 and served as secretary general for the missions run by the Capuchin Order. In a mood of utopian hopefulness I had dreamed at first of loyal and fruitful cooperation with the Congregation for Evangelizing the Peoples. On the strength of my theoretical knowledge as a lecturer in missiology for many years at the University of Freiburg (Switzerland) and of my activity as one of the promoters of the Swiss missionary organization in Rome, I thought I could provide some fresh impetus.

But I was forced to realize that the prerequisites for this sort of cooperation were just not there. The Congregation of the Missions found it unnecessary to seek inspiration from either the rank-and-file or from experts. On the contrary, it reacted to my book, *Where Faith Lives* (which Karl Rahner called the best Catholic book of the year) not with genuine dialogue, but only dictatorial measures and punishment. So instead of the collaboration I had dreamed of—which did continue on the administrative level—there was, on the personal level, a direct collision.

I also introduced myself to other congregations, in person or in writing, and made myself the spokesman of the young churches and their concerns. I argued that they ought to take seriously the statistical shift of the Christian world's center of gravity, have the courage to accept the consequences of this and stop imposing on those churches their invariable, western, Roman form of Christianity.

After all this had gotten little or no results and after I had already written this new book, in shorthand, as my private reaction to the indefensible state of the Roman Curia, the extraordinary synod of bishops from November 25 to December 8, 1985 gave me some unexpected and welcome backing. It was now clear to me that in doing my analysis I was not a lone wolf, an uncomfortable rebel, or a cowardly sniper at the Church, but that I had correctly diagnosed and formulated the conviction not only of a large part of the Church's membership but also of a great many bishops. Now it became apparent that the split between the Church and the "Church" extended into the episcopacy, since the bishops of the most varied countries were expressing quite clearly their discontent.

Before the synod, observers entertained some well-founded misgivings. Of course, one could only hail the decision to take stock of the Council's impact twenty years afterwards. But then Rome made a few blunders that heated up the atmosphere and caused discussion of objective matters to break down in advance and degenerate into a polemic. As early as his visit to the Netherlands and Belgium the pope had suggested that some things had gone awry since the Council, and that was why the synod was necessary. But it was Cardinal Ratzinger above all, with his book *On the State of the Faith*, whose French and German translations came out a few months before the synod, that startled people's minds. The balance sheet he draws up in it presents a very negative picture. He speaks of decadence, disintegration, heresies, self-destruction, rifts, breaks, the demon of the Council—and because of all that he calls for a Restoration.

Some of us wondered whether this influential cardinal was aiming to set the tone for the coming synod, was directing the overture, so to speak. Then when D. Seeber and Professor Hans Kung, among others, reacted very sharply to Ratzinger, Hans Urs von Balthasar shot back in an interview and practically excommunicated Professor Kung. Kung, he said, was now outside the Church and so had nothing more to say to the bishops. Von Balthasar backed up Ratzinger's negative assessment and added, as if by way of consolation, that there had been chaos after every Council.

This gave rise to anxious questions whether the synod would try to make the crooked straight. Would a number of curial cardinals declare how *they* understood the Council and how, therefore, it was supposed to be understood? Would there be a reversal of the opening to the world or of the dialogue with Christians and non-Christians? Would the synod be, at best, a "celebration" of the Council, along with a confirmation of the status quo?

But as soon as several bishops' conferences began to publish their answers to the questions sent out by Rome in preparation for the synod, this nightmare instantly faded. Suddenly a fresh spring breeze was blowing. For example, in a fourteen page document the bishops from the U.S.A. invoked Vatican II to speak out for a modernization of the Church. Specifically, they called for considering the problem of clerical celibacy, for giving women access to positions of leadership in the Church, and for a more authentic collegiality and sharing of responsibility, to avoid in the future tensions harmful to the Church. The bishops of England and Wales likewise maintained that the key problem was the lack of episcopal collegiality: "Contrary to the teachings of the Council we observe in the consultations of the Holy See a lessening of the actual responsibility of the members of the bishops' conferences." They also did not shrink from locating the main cause of this deficiency in the Roman Curia, that is, "in the continued existence of typical features of the pre-conciliar Church, as, for example, the exercise of power by some Roman congregations against bishops, orders, and individuals." As a cure for this they cite more democracy and pluralism in the Church. A similar position by the Dutch bishops has already been mentioned.

When such voices rang out, the Vatican gave the order not to publish these responses from the bishops' conferences. Rome was unwilling to be shown up in public and tried as usual to shut out the membership of the Church not only, as the Americans said, from "decision taking" but even from "opinion making," one of those "typical features of the pre-conciliar Church."

On account of this decree from Rome the Swiss Bishops Conference, to take one example, no longer published its entire document, but made known the most important points in a press conference, stating, among other things, that they wanted an upgrading, and better preparation for, the synod of bishops and if possible with the authority to pass resolutions. In addition the spokesman, Bishop Schwery, criticized the efficiency of the Roman administrative offices. One got the impression, he said, that some of them were operating in accordance with completely obsolete methods.

Three weeks before the beginning of the synod this rumble from the bishops' conferences was followed by a proper thunderbolt, hurled from (where else?) *La Civilta Cattolica*, the Roman journal run by the Jesuits and closely associated with the Vatican. The article denounced the erroneous notions of the papacy that sought to stamp "infallible" on every papal statement ("infallibilism"), the degenerate forms of reverence for the pope ("papolatry"), and the "curial Centralism" connected with it. So long as the "necessity of the Petrine service for the Church" was not called into question, the widespread posture of resistance to centralism, triumphalism, and legalism could be considered a "healthy objection" to a policy that had also been rejected by the Council. For that reason even the often "sharp and unrelenting criticism" of the Pope and Curia was not to be rated as purely negative, since it served to reduce certain exaggerated forms of respect that Jesus did want for Peter's successors and to give greater prominence to Christ as the actual center of the Church. This very pointed article, the editor-in-chief explained, had been "worked out with the approval of the Holy See."

After this quite different sort of prelude we now waited anxiously to see the actual course of the synod. As a final evaluation, we may take as an established fact that:

—There was no manipulation. The curial cardinals did not crowd into the foreground, they remained rather silent and let the bishops of the world say their piece—an opportunity they made the most of. It was too bad, of course, that the journalists could not get the original texts of the speeches, which lasted from six to eight minutes. They had to be content with a twenty-line summary from the press agency. Such summaries naturally lose the whole aroma, the pointed language, the emotion that resonated in the speeches—just as an album of pressed flowers can't reproduce the fresh odors and gaiety of a meadow in springtime. The actual sensation caused by the speeches reached the public as if through a muffler. Nevertheless, the bishops could speak freely, which was a victory in itself. I recall a time ten years earlier when I expressed to a high-ranking official of the Roman Curia the complaints of many Third World bishops about the Curia's narrow stress on centralization and uniformity. I added that the individual bishops were simply powerless, and these grievances would just have to be laid openly on the table before a synod. His answer: "But the synod isn't free either. It's controlled from above." This time that control was not in operation.

—There was also no real confrontation, as might have been expected on account of the two "preludes." Nothing was heard of the "open resistance" of Paul to Peter (Gal 2:11), as offered by the world episcopate to the Roman Curia. There were no startling speeches like the ones delivered at the Council by Cardinal Frings on the practices of the Holy Office or of Bishop De Smedt on the triumphalism and legalism of Roman theology. One can agree with T. Schellenbaum who wrote in the Zurich *Tages-Anzeiger* (December 3, 1985) that the reform-minded moderates set the tone. The issue was "not the undisputed executive power of the papacy but with whom the Pope should govern the Church. The choice is between the Curia, still a powerful decision maker, and the national bishops' conferences, which are still powerless." Extreme conservative or progressive positions, such as the demand for silent submission to the Pope and the Curia or the open request to deprive the Curia of its power, were seldom voiced.

—The synod unreservedly backed the Council. There was nothing like a silent retreat from it. Its good consequences were recognized, while the negative phenomena in the Church, which no one could overlook, were laid at the door not of the Council but of the Zeitgeist, and were to be understood as challenges. Meanwhile it became clear that the clergy and laity were just beginning to react to the Council and that as a result there was still a long way to go in raising their consciousness. The "repressed awakening" had to be given a second chance: an unobstructed path and new impetus.[9]

—Many specific issues also came up for discussion, for example, admitting divorced and remarried people to the sacraments; the generous use of the "third form of penance," namely the penitential ceremony with sacramental absolution; and the method of appointing bishops.

One could not expect the synod to deliberate thoroughly these many questions without more prior study or to say something new about them, particularly since it cannot pass resolutions but has merely an advisory role. On that score this synod too, like its predecessors, was a disappointment. Nothing concrete or palpable came of it, nothing that made one sit up and take notice.

Then the German cardinals Joseph Hoffner, Augustin Mayer, and Friedrich Wetter, under the leadership of Cardinal Ratzinger, tried to demand that first, more reflection was to be made on the Church as a mystery and as a supernatural entity, while structural and institutional problems were to take a back seat; secondly, this Church was not to be characterized by the Old Testament and democratic-political image of "the people of God," but by the more correct New Testament image of "the mystical Body of Christ"; thirdly, the devil and his pernicious influence on the Church and the world had to be taken seriously. These may be partly valid aspects that help to fill out the picture, but the sore point lay precisely in the fact that during the Council and afterwards Catholic leaders simply theologized and did not change concrete structures in accordance with the Council. That is why people were so vehemently pressing these issues and would no longer allow them to be "spiritualized away" by theology.

—The fact is, that from the beginning to the end of the first week the theme of structural problems took priority and became one of the recurrent and increasingly powerful refrains. Observers noted a general dissatisfaction on the part of the bishops with the situation as it had developed since the Council and contrary to the Council. They wanted to shake off the fetters of excessive centralism and rigid standardization. They wanted more genuine collegiality, more of a say, more decision-making authority for themselves and the bishops' conferences. Too many decisions were still being reached in Rome instead of on the diocesan level, where better justice could be done to the concrete circumstances. They wanted more confidence put in the relative autonomy of the local churches and in the bishops, who were to be regarded as the directors responsible for these churches, not simply as functionaries carrying out orders from the Vatican. In short, the principle of subsidiarity should be applied to the Church. The bishops from the Third World (representing 103 of the 165 bishops entitled to vote) demanded above all much greater leeway for inculturation, not only in documents but in practice, in order to accept Christianity not merely as propagators of its European form, but to give it the chance to take shape and body from the local cultures.

This clear language, this sharp accent, which characterized both the synod and the replies previously submitted by the bishops' conferences, was, of course, downplayed somewhat in the concluding report by Cardinal Godfried Danneels; and in the seventeen column final document of the synod one finds only the following lines: "Since the bishops' conferences are so useful, indeed so necessary to the Church's pastoral activity today, their place in theology should be scrutinized, and in particular the question of their teaching authority should be worked out more clearly and profoundly. —A study is recommended to clarify the question of whether the principle of subsidiarity, which obtains in the realm of human society, can also be applied in the realm of the Church and, if so, to what degree and in sense its application may be possible or necessary." Everything now depends on what consequences these two postulates will have.

Thus we can be relatively satisfied with the synod. It set forth the most crucial—and painful—point, namely the anti-conciliar handling of the Council by the Roman Curia, in a genteel but clear-cut fashion. What will come of it? Will it glance off the bastion, fixed for all time, of Canon Law, and fade away like the cries of the Jews at the Wailing Wall? Does "scrutinizing" the boundaries of authority, does "studying" the principle of subsidiarity mean, in Roman terms, putting off the matter till the Greek calends, i.e., shelving it? If the Council could not manage to give the Curia a conciliar orientation over the course of twenty years, what should one expect from a synod? Once again (and with reason) the pessimists are coming forward, the people who despair of cutting this Gordian knot. We should have, in any event, to take stock once more of the synod's assessment of the Council five years from now. Then we would see what if anything had happened as a result of this synod.

This demonstrates the weakness of the whole synodal system, which was already evident before at the Council. Principles were developed and wishes were expressed, but they were not immediately translated into legislation. That did not take place until afterwards, and then in accord with the narrow viewpoint of the Roman Curia. At this synod the bishops demanded, but only in passing, that the synod be reformed and given legislative capacity. Instead of improving and thus strengthening the central administration, the whole stress was on upgrading the periphery, that is, the powers of the bishops. But both areas needed work. If the synod, as the representative assembly of the world episcopate, does not get the authority to pass resolutions, then one continues to run the Horatian risk of the mountains being in labor, only to give birth to a ridiculous mouse. There will never be concrete, sweeping reforms so long as the Roman Curia is allowed to go on making law as it currently does. All the accumulated issues, e.g., rethinking of the law of celibacy, the ordination of women, and concrete steps to advance ecumenism, will be kept on hold so long as the world episcopate, with its mainly pastoral approach, can only talk about them, while the Roman Curia, with its mainly legal approach, rules on them. The Curia, as we have learned the hard way in these post-conciliar years, is not only a "scandalum," a stumbling block, an offence, and a burden for the Catholic Church, but also a specter for the other Christian churches and a major obstacle on the way to the goal of ecumenical unity.

So whatever may become of this past synod, those who argue and work against Roman centralism and legalism, and for genuine collegiality and legitimate pluralism have justice—and the bishops—on their side.

The public paid almost no attention to the three day seminar that the pope held immediately before the synod (as he had twice before, in 1979 and 1982) with all the cardinals and that dealt primarily—apart from the burning financial issue—with curial reform. There were expectations that enough progress had been made for the reform taken up in 1979 to be promulgated at last, twenty years now after the Council. But once again opinions were obviously so widely divergent that the resolutions were postponed, and the session ended without much publicity. According to advance reports, it would deal mostly with new titles and divisions of authority. The Secretariat of State would henceforth be called the Apostolic Secretariat, the Congregation of the Clergy would change its name to the Congregation for Priests and Deacons. The Papal Lay Council would be upgraded to a Congregation, while agreement continued to prove unattainable on the three post-conciliar secretariats, for Christian Unity, for Non-Christians, and for Unbelievers. Should they be raised to autonomous Congregations, or lowered to mere "Councils," without their own decision-making capacity, wholly incorporated into the appropriate Congregations.

Of course, such questions touch upon only the external renovation and not the much more urgent inner renewal of the time-honored cathedral of the Roman Church. And besides, as a matter of principle we should not be content with a mere renovation. We should think on a grander scale and get up the courage for a sort of cleansing of the temple, for a radically new concept of a Curia for the coming third millenium. To cite only one example, back during the Council the missions experts and missionary bishops took offense at the fact that the Propaganda Fide was using all its influence to get its 350 year old historical position confirmed, and to confine the all-embracing mission of God and the Church to the "missions," that is, to certain regions (AG, 6). Now, after twenty years, we realize much more clearly that those former "missions" have become local churches, and that it is high time to place all churches under the same administrative authori-

ty. The Propaganda Fide would thereby lose its territorial respon-
sibilities, but would receive instead the much more important and
more dynamic function of being the missionary conscience of the
entire Church, a center of pastoral research and direction for the
missionary task on all six continents, since in the meantime both
Europe and North America have again become "mission continents." And to that end the Propaganda Fide would naturally
have to be thought of in an entirely new light and equipped with
experts rather than administrators.

The crucial factors are not new titles or new jurisdictions, but
new men and women with a new mentality, with a more pastoral
and less bureaucratic approach, with more competence and less
authority. During these seven years, then, while people were
deliberating over curial reform, they ought to have already mobi-
lized a group of individuals embodying this new spirit and started
working vigorously away within the reformed structures. Yet one
scarcely has the impression that this is what happened. It seems
rather that in the past few years the conservative trend in the
Curia has grown even stronger. To that extent it was very good
that the resolutions concerning curial reform were tabled once
again, so that the whole moral weight of the 1985 synod can still
make itself felt in the discussion. One's imagination cannot be
too bold in conceiving the reform it would take to bring the Curia
truly in line with the Council and the times. Can Pope John Paul
II, who puts so much stress on the Church's continuity and prestige, afford to undertake this sort of "palace revolution"?[10]

The publication of my book comes in this interim period
between new hope and as yet unsurmounted anxiety. After
long hesitation I have decided—and the synod has now further
removed the last obstacles and actually encouraged me to make
this concrete contribution to the debate currently going on—to
publish my private correspondence and conversations with the
Roman Curia. When I wrote these letters, I had no idea at all of
publishing them. I simply wanted to exert my influence through
direct channels and contacts, without calling for help from the

press. But now the pressure has gotten so high that the safety-valve exploded.

In this correspondence all the dubiousness of the groups I dealt with is clearly displayed. I believe I may say that my relations with the Holy Father and the post-conciliar secretariats for the Unity of Christians, for Non-Christians, and for Unbelievers, in which one meets genuine experts and can at once get down to a useful dialogue, were good to very good. But with the powerful Congregations I had sharp, very sharp clashes, which pained me, not for my sake but for the Church's. I now declare, with the passion of disappointed love that in the Roman Curia—for all the personal amiability of individual officials—there persists a way of thinking and acting that suits neither the Gospel nor the Council. I am not arguing that these documents justify the conclusion that the Roman Curia as a whole today is incompetent, incapable of dialogue, dictatorial, and pre-conciliar in the way it thinks and acts. But the materials I am publishing here clearly show that during ten important post-conciliar years this was alarmingly true of an all too large part of the Curia. In the final analysis every reader has the right to judge for himself on the basis of my book and his own personal experiences.

I might have handed these documents over to the archives. Perhaps they might have been published at some point as a historical study. They would still have their interest then, but they would leave history unchanged. But the history that lies gathering dust in the archives is less important than the history that passes through our hands day after day, shaped by our actions. For that kind of history, the one still to be formed, I would like this book to be a helpful stimulus.

Of course, I have the Catholic Church primarily in mind. But it should also be interesting for other Christians to see how Catholics today are protesting against their Church, how they have become perhaps "more Protestant"—in any case more evangelical—than many Protestants. On the other hand, the Protestant and Orthodox churches certainly have their share of case-hardened structures, so that my protest can serve as a model and inspiration for other Christians as well. And that would make this book ecumenical in the broadest sense.

Perhaps, too, publication of this material may encourage lay people not simply to accept things but to do on the parish and diocesan level what I did at Rome, namely to stop simply suffering from the Church and to react, to protest, and to stimulate others. Then the pastors and bishops will be bombarded with letters not just from conservative elements but from the progressives as well, so that they will get the nerve to speak out in Rome in greater numbers and more emphatically for church government in the spirit of the Council.

The delicate question still remains, to what extent the Curia's conservative attitude can be blamed on the pope. With Pope John Paul II one has to distinguish between two spheres of influence. In his "external politics," when he speaks for the world, for man ("Redemptor Hominis" : "Man's Redeemer"), and for humanity, he is tremendous. Humanity was toiling down. . .the path to unity. It needed a spokesman, but had none. Then this pope spontaneously filled that gap. There is no other voice in today's world that speaks with such commitment and competence for human dignity, for human rights, for peace, and against injustice, hunger, and war, as his does. This gives him great prestige in the world.

But in his "internal politics," when he acts for the Church, he obviously cannot escape his Polish origins. The Polish Church, however, is understandably enough a very hierarchical, conservative church. Poland had to fight for centuries for its Catholic faith, against the Turks, against the Prussians, against the Russians, and now against the Marxists. When you have to fight this way for religion, you cling to it, you don't undermine it—or discuss it, otherwise you risk losing everything. It was the faith of our fathers, it is our faith, and it shall be the faith of our children

too. Furthermore, this nation, whose enemies constantly sought
to split it up, needed a strong bond of unity under the Church's
authority. Something of that unshakable, unchangeable faith and
that strong authority lives too in this man Wojtyla. He is convinced that he must restore that faith to the rest of the world as
it goes down the road to secularism. On issues such as the law
of celibacy, the ordination of women, and intercommunion, John
Paul II will never let even an iota be struck from the traditional
position. One has to respect his convictions, but history will one
day judge whether this model, which may be right for a church
under oppression, should also be imposed on the Church in free
countries, and whether the attempt to do this was successful or
estranged still more people from the Church.

4. A Question for My Conscience

To begin with, I would like to stress that the concentration on
reforming the Roman Curia entails a sharp narrowing of perspective. One would have to direct similar postulates to every diocese, every parish, and every community of religious. When we see
how reform often has hard going there, we may take a less harsh
view of Rome. At any rate, Rome plays such an important role
in the service of the Church that it is to her above all that we look
for renewal.

Thus I confronted my conscience and decided to publish my
experiences with the Roman Curia, as the physician has to expose
the wound if it is to be healed. Needless to say, I was familiar
then, when I wrote those letters, as I am now when I am publishing them, with obstacles, as were the prophets Isaiah and Jeremi-
ah, who complained about the call from God: "Woe is me! For
I am a man of unclean lips. . .But the Lord said to me. . .'To
whom I send you, you shall go, and whatever I command you,
you shall speak. Be not afraid of them, for I am with you to
deliver you. . . . See, I have set you this day over nations and
over kingdoms, to pluck up and to break down, to destroy and to

overthrow, to build and to plant.' " (Is 6:5; Jer 1:7-10).

And so I have followed my inner voice and have spoken and written, not "in childlike submission to the Church, but in child-like trust in God. I felt that this has something to do with the New Testament's "parrhesia," with the frankness Jesus shows when he delivered his vehement speeches against the Pharisees, who oppressed and humiliated people by means of the Law, and with the candor of the Apostles in proclaiming the message of Jesus and waiting for the Kingdom of God. In return both Jesus and the Apostles had to endure the "fate of the prophets". They died for their words. But their cause went on.

I think that when I wrote those letters I was acting out of love for the Church, as I am doing now, in publishing the letters. Who can help loving the Church once he has come to know her? This mystery of God's presence among men, this herald of the Good News of Jesus, this People of God on pilgrimage, full of faith, hope, and love. I love the Church, warts and all, the Church of the saints and the sinners, meaning not that part of the Church's members are saints and the other part sinners, but that in every person, in every Christian, there is a portion of holiness and sinfulness, now more of one, now more of the other. I also fully and completely acknowledge the function of the hierarchy in the service of the people of God. All this is the teaching of Vatican II, which I fully and gladly accept as an important complement of Vatican I, to which I likewise declare my allegiance.

I also think that Rome, as a sign of unity and dynamic coor-dination and leadership has a vital role to play, all the more so nowadays as the Church has become more international, and as the Protestant churches too feel a greater sense of longing for unity. But all this doesn't mean that one must greet with respect the sort of behavior we shall see in the following letters. Here we can only chime in with Karl Rahner, when he speaks of "ghastly bosses."[11] One says such things out of love for the Church and for the long-desired union with Rome.

I have repeatedly wondered, then and now, how can I reconcile my "rebellious" attitude with Franciscan loyalty to the Church? Francis of Assisi is praised for being a "wholly Catholic man," for never speaking a critical word about the Church. Of course, in many matters he went his own way, which was not necessarily the Church's way. That means, then, that he criticized the Church in a manner that was pre-eminently vital and not verbal. Still we must point out that time and again he had the courage to resist cardinals of the holy Roman Church to their face.

During his first visit to Rome, when he was planning to ask the pope to approve his way of life for himself and his brothers, the curial cardinal John of St. Paul advised him "to decide for the monastic or eremitic life." But Francis "rejected this demand as humbly as he could, not because he had a low opinion of the advice, but because he was piously striving for something different; he was filled with a higher longing."[12] Later, when he sent his brothers into the northern regions, whence they returned hungry and sick, Cardinal Ugolino, his special friend, tried to persuade him from then on to keep the brothers at home in Italy. Here too Francis dared openly to contradict: "Lord Cardinal, do you think that the Lord has called the brothers only on account of these provinces? Truly I tell you that the Lord has chosen and sent out the brothers for the betterment and salvation of the souls of all people in this entire world; and they will be received and win many souls not only in the lands of believers but in the lands of unbelievers as well."[13] When he finally succeeded in getting to Egypt on a crusader ship, and he observed the wretched war and the atrocities committed by the crusaders before the city of Damietta, he spoke imploringly with the soldiers and condemned the war. In addition he presented the papal delegate, Cardinal Pelagius Galvan, with his plan to visit the Sultan and hold peace negotiations with him. The Cardinal harshly rejected the idea: The Council had decreed the Crusade, which was the will of God. And so they had to see it through to victory. But Francis did not give up, he kept coming back with the same request until the cardinal finally granted it, but at his own risk and providing Christian interests were not compromised. Thus Francis went to the Sultan's camp, stayed there a week, made friends with him; and so was the first Christian who met him not as an enemy but as a friend and brother.[14]

All this shows with perfect clarity that Francis did not practice "blind obedience" to the Church and her prelates, but "responsible obedience," that he viewed his own inner impulses as divinely inspired (one of favorite ideas), and so felt obliged to obey them rather than external commands, and that for the good of the Church. He thought that in this way he could "restore the house of the Lord," after he had first taken this order literally and restored the chapel of San Damiano.

Let me honestly confess that I too thought I was acting in the Franciscan spirit when I wrote these letters and now that I am publishing them. I am convinced that by doing this I am struggling not against the Church but with the Church, and that it is fairer and righter to criticize the Curia than simply to ignore it, as all too many Catholics do today. Through all these debates and confrontations the twentieth century Acts of the Apostles are being played out, a story that, like the first century version, will have a happy ending.

I took, and take, my differences with the Church entirely on my own conscience. I did not want, nor do I now want, my superiors to have to take the blame for me. I wrote my letters and had them taken to the Vatican; only after that would I hand over a copy to my Minister General, Pascal Rywalski, who usually said, "You were right," because it was clear to him that I was acting out of love for the Church, and that at bottom he and many other ministers general silently felt what I was saying out loud. And this time too I informed my superiors of this book only after I had delivered the manuscript to the publisher and signed the contract.

I admit that back then and even now my style often became vehemently polemical, that I was not sufficiently successful in finding a "third way" between well-behaved submissiveness and rebellious insubordination that says the things which must be said in a way that improves their chances of being accepted. In excusing myself I can only point out that in his polemical speeches against the Pharisees and scribes Jesus too did not use a purring, flattering, diplomatic language, but one that was energetic, committed, and prophetic. What was right for Jesus is a reasonable option for me as well.

Still, I don't feel quite comfortable when I accuse and condemn men from the Roman Curia, some of whom are still alive. I do not want to condemn them personally but the system that they represent. Basically every one has the right to act according to his conscience. There must be room, in the Church especially, for all kinds of God's creatures. But when people with objectively false views exercise power over others one may and must oppose them, in the hope that even after harsh words general reconciliation will take place.

One last question concerns me: What effect will this publication have on the laity?

One group of fanatical Catholics will be angered and condemn me, proclaiming all the more firmly their unswerving loyalty and devotion to "Rome." But don't they have a false image of the Church, just as Peter had a false image of the messiah, and for that reason was very sternly rebuked by Jesus: "Get behind me, Satin! For you are not on the side of God, but of men" (Mk 8:33)? God in his plan, for salvation is obviously not to be identified with churchly triumphalism.

A second group of good, loyal Catholics will be confused and saddened. Despite all, they have great respect for "Rome." I am sorry for their sorrow. They should be advised not to get too depressed, but to live all the more intensively in their local church, in their parish, where they should turn their faith into deeds in the liturgy and in selfless love.

Other Catholics, who have long been groaning under the weight of the Roman Curia, will see that their objections are more than justified. They will be all the more attentive to the Spirit, and working together build up a Church that matches the intentions of the Gospel and the Council. Rome ought to be setting a good example for this process. Since in many ways it fails to do that, the responsibility of the rank and file becomes all the greater, as has often been the case in church history.

Needless to say, there is one more group one must think of here and that is the Church's enemies. They will rejoice in this book. But their joy will not be perfect because this report is by no means the beginning of the end of the Church but rather a sign that things are looking up with it.

What will the reaction of the Roman Curia be? Embarrassed silence? Sanctions against the author? Will it take a nitpicking approach and so reject the whole thing, that is, refute a handful of statements that are not precisely formulated, and in this way dodge the main issue? If so, it would only be exposing new weak spots, leaving itself wide open to attack. It has only one credible option: to take stock and make a fresh start. We are left to hope and pray that this affair will redound to the benefit of the Church.

And so I release this book, like a white dove, fluttering its wings to announce the end of the Flood and the dawn of a new age, in which we will no longer need to fight with the Church, when peace will prevail among all men and women blessed with God's grace (Lk 2:14), beginning with the members of the Church of Christ.

Part Two

Suffering from the Church:
A Personal Account

I. SHARING RESPONSIBLE CONCERN

FOR THE PATH OF THE CHURCH

(Suggestions for the Pope)

In the year of the three popes, 1978, I had to make five appearances as the Roman correspondent for Swiss television—the first time after the death of Paul VI, to assess his pontificate; then once before each of the two conclaves, to report on the leading candidates and the general situation; and finally after each election, to attempt a first commentary on the new popes. So I was concerned with contacting first hand certain sources in Rome. Before the second conclave a highly respected cardinal told me: "I'm going into this conclave with misgivings. It's not that three or four names keep coming up, and you'll have to choose one of them. The bad thing is, there's no leading candidate at all. Benelli would be very efficient, but not many people like him. Lorscheider would be excellent, but his health will surely forbid it; Ursi would be a pastoral man, he's somewhat like Pope Luciani, but we know that he doesn't read any more, he just talks. . ."

54

And so there was the great surprise election. After Benelli had foundered on the stiff resistance of his opponents on the first day, the star of Karol Wojtyla rose unexpectedly to the zenith on the second. For the first time in 450 years a non-Italian was pope. There was great jubilation, but still greater were the expectations placed in him.

1. A Book For the Pope's Consideration

In past years I had already had various fights with the Roman Curia, but I never would have thought of turning directly to the pope—although people repeatedly asked me, "You work in Rome? Do you see the pope every now and then?" But it's not so simple to get to see the pope.

Then, one month after the election, Fr. Cyrill Krasinski, a Polish Benedictine from the abbey of Maria Laach, an elderly, intelligent man, who had already contacted me on account of my books, wrote to me that I absolutely had to present his friend, the new pope, with my book, *Where Faith Lives*, on the Church in the Third World.

So I got up my nerve and wrote the following letter, on November 30, 1978, and brought it, along with the German and Italian edition of my book, to the pope's private secretary, Stanislaw Dziwisz, to be sure that my gift actually reached its goal.

Holy Father,

If I venture to present you with one of my books, this is in response to the wish of Fr. Cyrill Krasinski, who wrote me on November:

"I am confident that the new Holy Father really knows your book, *Where Faith Lives*. If not, you *must* somehow get a copy to him. If you should find it uncomfortable to speak 'pro domo sua,' you can simply tell him that his countryman, Fr. Cyrill Krasinski, whom he visited in Maria Laach from Mainz in June,

1977, assured you that the Holy Father *must* carefully consider this book. Even if he were not to agree with everything in it, it will help him to get a truly universal view of the globe."

Let me add that this book has now been translated into seven languages, and has thus far gone into four editions in Italian, six in English, and seven in German. Karl Rahner said it was the best Catholic book of the year, and the American magazine *Priests* wrote, "If you have time and money this year for only one serious book, *The Coming of the Third Church* [the English language title] is the one to purchase and study with an open mind and sincere heart."

Since in your previous activities, except in the episcopal synods, you have had few direct contacts with the churches of the Third World, this book might help you quickly to envision the problems and prosepcts of those churches. Should it happen to do you this service, I would be delighted.

I also enclose a reprint of the epilogue that I had the honor to write as the conclusion to the five volume history of the Propaganda Fide.

Respectfully in the Lord,

Fr. Walbert Bühlmann

The letter was answered on December 30, 1978 as follows:

Reverend Father,

In your letter of November 30 of this year you sent His Holiness Pope John Paul II two editions of your book, *Where Faith Lives*.

On behalf of the Holy Father let me thank you most kindly for this amiable sign of your regard and the loyal solidarity it proclaims with the successor of St. Peter. With sincere good wishes for rich Christmas graces implores for you God's special protection and help for a fruitful and satisfying new year in 1979.

Yours truly in the Lord, G. Caprio, Substitute

2. "Révision de vie" with the Pope

As the first year of John Paul II's pontificate was coming to an end, I was inspired on October 12, 1979 to write the pope a rather long letter, diagnosing quite a number of situations that still occupy us today. Today, of course, I should scarcely cherish the naive hope of changing the mind of such a strong personality with this sort of letter.

Holy Father,

Perhaps you still remember me: In the fall of 1978 I sent you, through your private secretary, Msgr. Dziwisz, at the request of Fr. Cyrill Krasinski, a copy of my book, *Where Faith Lives—La Chiesa alle porte* in Italian.

This time, as a little brother of St. Francis and as one of your fellow men, all of whom you take so seriously because of their unique, irreplaceable dignity, I would like to let you know what I think about you and your pontificate. On the occasion of the first anniversary of your election you will no doubt hold a "maneuver criticism" or "*révision de vie*," probably at Castel Gandolfo. I would like then simply to throw in my opinion, and I hope my remarks will not be as clumsy as Peter's, which earned him the reply, "Get behind me, Satan! You are not on the side of God, but of men."

1. There is no need for me to affirm to you something you experience every day in Rome and on your travels, namely what an enormous amount of sympathy and allegiance you have managed to win for yourself. I believe that if a popularity contest were held today in Italy, Europe, and the world, you would take first place by a wide margin. This is a very good starting point for your work.

2. I acknowledge and admire your "politics," as you try to speak to humanity past the barriers of all systems, to be on good terms with people everywhere, to gain influence on them in this way, and through them to improve the system from within. If

my reading is correct, you are realistic enough to see the various systems (capitalism, communism, national security) as parts of today's world, which cannot be overturned or which can be only at the cost of enormous bloodshed and chaos. Thus the sole meaningful Christian way that remains is to try to change them from the inside, hoping that all systems gradually learn something from history and from their own mistakes. I pray with you and for you that this prophetic effort may bear fruit in the course of your pontificate.

3. With regard to your theological and pastoral positions I have the following reflections to offer. I admire your very open, dynamic, person-oriented philosophy and theology, as convincingly expressed, for example, in the talk you gave at Mainz in 1978 about faith in the post-conciliar period, and above all in your summa, "*Redemptor hominis.*" You start off from a base in phenomenology and existentialism. Your sources were Husserl, Heidegger, and Scheler. I now take the liberty of putting forth the following (hypo) thesis: This dynamic theology seems to exist in a state of tension with the rather static solidity of your Polish experience. Poland has, after all, its own special history. For centuries it has had to defend its faith against the Turks, the Russians, the Prussians, and now against Marxism. A faith that one has to fight for in this way is clung to and not laid out for discussion. Otherwise one would run the risk of losing everything. The more the faith is attacked, the more one affirms it, just as it is. I would like to illustrate this statement a little:

a) In your letter on Latin (*Osservatore Romano*, November 27-28, 1978) you give a very realistic analysis of the situation: The present time is less favorably disposed toward Latin. We are living in a world of technological thought and we prefer to learn the modern languages. Latin can no longer be viewed as the unifying language it once was. At this point one expects this analysis to conclude with a leap forward, e.g., that the members of the Church would be encouraged to work at learning English (which as a matter of fact is already spoken around the world), so that in ten or twenty years English would become what Latin was in the past. Instead, you are unwilling to depart from the line followed by your predecessors in their documents, and so the young people are supposed joyfully to dedicate themselves to the study of Latin. Do they? In any case, we are back at the point of departure, and the whole analysis was actually for nothing.

b) In an address to the nuns and clergy of Rome (OR November 10, 1978) you spoke very clearly on the function of priestly dress and the religious habit. In the letter to the priests on Holy Thursday, by contrast, you emphasized the personal magnetism of the priest, who should stand before men in the complete fullness of his priesthood, with strong faith and selfless love, etc. The only mention of a special kind of clothes occurs "in obliquo," in a footnote. In Ireland and the U.S.A., on the other hand, you stressed special clothing in straightforward language. But can one really establish norms on this issue? At our general chapter in 1968, where the new constitutions were passed, the representatives from Poland said with regard to the Capuchin habit: "We wish to wear this habit all the time. In this way we, together with the people, are a sign of protest against the regime." But the representatives from Latin America said: "We can no longer wear this habit. That would identify us *with* the regime and with that church that stood by the regime in the old days. We, however, wish to stand among the people." And so freedom of choice was left to the different regions, that is, to the respective superiors.

I think that when everybody wore the habit, there were both good religious and some not so good; and now that not everyone wears the traditional habit, the same thing is true. Actually I wonder whether we are not making too much of a fuss over internal church—I would almost say sacristy—problems, such as the Italian bishops' difficulties with placing the hosts in communicants' hands. I wonder whether this sort of problem deserves to be taken seriously.

c) In *Redemptor hominis* (#20) you develop very ably the meaning of the Eucharist as the center and high point of the sacramental life of both the individual and the community. In the letter to the priests (#10) you describe in dramatic fashion the situation of communities that are gathered on Sunday to say all the prayers of the liturgy, but that at the moment of the transubstantiation fall silent, because there is no priest there. Again one expects after this analysis that a new way will be opened to remedy this situation as quickly as possible, that alongside the historical priestly type, with fifteen years of study and celibacy, a second type of priest, the idea of the *viri probati* might be possible. I know about the problems raised by this issue, and that the majority of African priests and bishops are against such a solution. But I wonder whether they think this way on pastoral or political grounds, because they don't want to have their social status challenged by a second kind of priests, who would live much closer to the people. Aren't we making the priest into an absolute value? This is how he is and how he must remain. As opposed to that approach, the priest is entirely at the service of the community. Communities have an intrinsic right to produce enough servants for the needs of their ecclesiastical life. If tens of thousands of communities cannot celebrate the Eucharist, because the only way to the priesthood can't meet the need (and won't be able to, for a long time), isn't this putting positive church law ahead of a pastoral emergency?

d) I understand your repeated opposition to abortion, divorce, homosexuality, and artificial birth control. In taking these stands you confirm the statements by the Italian and American bishops. Clearly the Church has to make its attitude known. Still, in my opinion it has done this enough now. The pastoral question is more important than the dogmatic-disciplinary one. The continually repeated rejection of those modern ideas and practices does nothing to help the millions of people who live in such situations and suffer from them. Mustn't the Church move beyond the assertion of its standpoint by trying to show some human understanding and offering pastoral help to these men and women in their need? "The sick need the physician, not the healthy." It is of little use to keep on telling the patient that his health is bad.

4.   You greatly stress the authority of the bishops and call upon the theologians and religious to obey them. The bishops, to be sure, have a special responsibility and leadership role in the Church. But I would consider it just as important to recommend to the bishops that they continue their theological education and learn the basic principles of management. Otherwise an ever broader chasm will yawn between their authority on one side and the competence and charism of the theologians and religious on the other. Religious have a complementary and critical role to play vis-a-vis the bishops. This leads to a necessary, healthy tension in the Church, which must be accepted and lived with. It can be bridged only in a genuine dialogue. Too many bishops are wholly occupied in administering their diocese and have neither the time nor the desire to continue their theological education. When faced by concrete problems they take refuge all too quickly in their authority, which is not good for the Church. Likewise harmful is the mistrust many bishops feel toward the base communities and the many national and international Christian movements. This drives such people, who want to be authentic Christians, out of the Church; and when things have finally gotten to that point, the bishops say: "We always said they were dangerous." If the bishops showed more trust and entered into more contact and dialogue with such groups, it would be easier to keep them *in* the Church as the fermenting agent of genuine reform.

5.   One word more on the Roman Curia. Great administrative centers, be they political or ecclesiastical, always have a tendency to reaction and self-aggrandizement. People in such centers always know better than the ordinary citizen and the ordinary Christian. History teaches us that Rome at the time of the Protestant Reformation, instead of addressing the genuine concerns of the Protestants, grew all the more rigid in its traditional, hierarchical thinking; and around the time that modernism arose, instead

of critically scrutinizing and essentially approving the efforts necessary to harmonize faith and science, Rome nipped them in the bud. And so the problems piled up and didn't find their theological and pastoral solution until the Second Vatican Council. But the Curia seems never to have had much sympathy for the Council. You know that the schemata prepared for the Council by Roman theologians and the Curia were of little value and had to be totally reworked by the bishops and theologians. I have the impression that the Curia subsequently tried to push its schemata through anyway and to reestablish its control over everything. From my own personal experience as well as knowledge gathered from six continents, I could tell many stories of how individual offices of the Roman Curia, while meeting the letter of the Council, violated its spirit (e.g., several commissions of experts were appointed, but they have no function at all and are not taken seriously); and how in various agencies affairs are still conducted in an ignorant, unchristian, and inhuman manner, with authority but not competence (although I would not deny the amiability of most curial officials). I have also observed, for example, that all serious pastoral and theological research takes place outside of Rome, neither coordinated nor inspired, but rather suspected and persecuted, by the Roman Curia. On this score the World Council of Churches in Geneva, much more than the Curia, is showing real leadership. I get the impression that you and your three predecessors in the papacy have firmly committed yourselves, in the "external" political sphere, to the cause of human rights, the poor, etc., but that under the influence of the Curia the postconciliar Church, so far as "internal" politics goes, is once again behaving like a conservative society. At stake here are not matters of faith but of discipline and historical tradition—but that is by definition a living process and is supposed to surround the permanent corpus of faith in ever new situations with ever new theological interpretations and new disciplinary forms.

Holy Father, I expect a great deal from you. I am very anxious about the November assembly with all the cardinals. Will you after a year of prudent waiting and planning, submit your "governance program" and give concrete expression to the "much needed new structures of collegiality" (your address to the cardinals in conclave) and to the "regional autonomy" of the bishops' conferences (your address to the council of the European Bishops' Conference on December 20, 1978)?

I await with close attention the steps you will take, and beg you to interpret my statements in a favorable light, as the remarks of a Christian who is well-disposed to you and to the Church.

Respectfully in the Lord,

P. Walbert Bühlmann

(No salutation)

The State Secretariat certifies to Fr. Walter [my name is Walbert] Bühlmann, OFMCap that his committed letter of Oct. 12, 1979 has been received, and is pleased to inform him that the Holy Father heartily thanks him for the expression of responsible concern for the path of the Church and prays God for continual help and protection for his life and work.

The considerations presented in the letter have been taken under careful advisement.

Mons. G. Coppa, Assessore

3. Key Ideas Concerning the Missions on the Way to the Third Millenium

Pope Karol Wojtyla got through not just his first hundred days in office but his whole first year without being criticized. But then there was a sudden turn of events. The Küng affair exploded, and it became apparent that the "new order" with respect to dispensations for men who had left the priesthood consisted in greater, but not very comprehensible strictness. This man, who before had spontaneously embraced and kissed children and the sick, who as a former actor had enthralled the masses, who spoke all languages and who had won in a flash the sympathy of the world, now had to learn that a "politician," a figure in public life, is also exposed to the winds of public opinion and criticism.

One highpoint of his first year was the publication of the encyclical *Redemptor hominis* (The Redeemer of Mankind) on March 4, 1979, which generally won great recognition, even though readers were quick to notice a certain tension between his open "world politics" and his rather narrow "church politics." At that time I wrote down some reflections on *Redemptor hominis* under the above title in the *Neue Zeitschrift fur Missionswissenschaft* (Immensee 1981, 1-7), which I quote here:

> The importance of *Redemptor hominis* (RH), Pope John Paul II's first encyclical, cannot be overvalued. It deals with his altogether personal message to humanity, with his conception of the world, as it has matured through his earlier studies and activities. It is also a personal text with regard to style. Many things are said only implicitly and in biblical, not theological, language. There are also many gaps and repetitions.

Among the various aspects of the pope's work that could be elaborated on I shall limit myself here to those affecting the missions. A first glance at RH reveals disappointingly few explicit references to missionary activity. Only incidentally does the pope speak of the "missionary aspect," of the Church in a "state of mission," of "missionary activity and the attitude of the missionary." People had already noticed that in his first homily, given in St. Peter's Square on the day of his installation, which was World Mission Sunday, the pope had made only a brief, though meaty, statement on the subject of the missions: "Today the whole Church celebrates World Mission Sunday, that is, she prays, meditates, and acts so that Christ's words of life may reach all men and be accepted by them as a message of hope, of salvation, and of comprehensive liberation." On the same occasion Pope Luciani had spoken at greater length about missionaries and their work.

We know that on his trips to other lands and continents Cardinal Wojtyla was primarily visiting Poles domiciled in foreign parts, and that only in Australia did he go on an excursion to Papua-New Guinea, where he had his one direct contact with missionary reality. Consequently in his speeches, writings, and pastoral letters, we find scarcely a single reference to the missions in the traditional sense.

But this gap may now be turning into a providential advantage. Pope Wojtyla has not had much experience with the "missions," and so he speaks all the more of the Church's universal mission. He doesn't see the Church here and the missions there; and so his view is definitely more accurate, since the "missions" have become local churches. Hence if we find no explicit references to the missions in RH, we can discover in it many implications for the missions, along with initiatives and directives that could be of the greatest importance for the future of the missions.

In the well known Instruction from the Propaganda Fide issued in 1659, a number of really timely admonitions were given that were repeated in many other documents: The missionaries should steer clear of political activity, they should not introduce European customs and habits, forcing them upon non-European Christians. They should take pains to promote education and the development of a native clergy. For centuries these recommendations served as key ideas. Now, however, they can be looked upon as self-evident and as goals already met. It's time for something new.

For the present, wholly different political and ecclesiastical situation we need new key ideas, new projectors to shed light on the Church's path into the future. If we read RH rightly, we can see such key ideas in it. Essentially, the pope wanted just to describe the path to be taken by the Church as a whole toward the year 2000. But at the same time he staked out the framework within which the missionary church was to see and perform its task in the future. Four leading ideas emerge in the encyclical:

1. The Church as a Sign of Unity for All People

Down through history the Church has, unfortunately, all too long been rather a sign of division. It once cultivated an un-evangelical spirit of exclusion. It divided the world into "Christendom" and the others, the heathen, the idolaters, the savages.

a) From the very first word of his encyclical, Pope Wojtyla speaks simply of "humanity," without any sort of discrimination, "The redeemer of man. . ." He takes as his starting point neither principles nor structures, but human beings. He does not speak, in esoteric fashion, merely of Catholics or Christians, but of people pure and simple. He does not wait for the geographical and quantitative extension of the Church before showing an interest in the new Christians. Instead, he embraces in advance all those who call themselves human. He adopts as his own the text from *Lumen gentium* that says that the Church is "*the* sacrament, that is, a sign and instrument for the most intimate union with God as well as for the unity of the whole human race." He says and repeats that humanity is the way of the Church. We recall that he exclaimed in his very first homily, "How reverently must the Apostle of Christ pronounce this word, 'humanity'!" And man is the leitmotiv of many other addresses given by the pope.

b) When the pope makes himself the spokesman for humanity, one may wonder what right he has to do this. It is understandable that he should speak for Catholic countries. But what about humanity, a majority of which is non-Christian?

Is he simply stepping into the gap caused by the fact that a multifarious human race has no other recognized spokesman? Actually he has far deeper reasons for acting as he does. He draws his legitimacy from the truth of the belief that every person, that all of humanity, is already "in Christ Jesus," the center of the cosmos and of history. Thanks to the Incarnation, "God has entered into the history of mankind. . .and given human life the dimension that he intended for it from the beginning." That is why one can say that Christ "fully reveals the person to himself and opens up to him his highest vocation." "Through his Incarnation the Son of God has, as it were, united himself with all men and women." This statement from *Gaudium et spes* is cited three times, with emphasis.

If that is the case, it becomes clear that the "deputy of Christ" has the right to speak about mankind and for mankind. It also becomes clear that every person already belongs to God, in a certain sense, and so too is part of the people of God. This conclusion is not so clearly drawn in RH, but it follows from the whole context and could be further elaborated, for example, in the well known Christian anthropology of Karl Rahner.

c) The mission of the Church therefore consists in "directing and orienting the vision of mankind, the consciousness and experience of the whole human race toward the mystery of Christ, in helping all men and women to become familiar with the deep mystery of the redemption that takes place in Jesus Christ." "Hence the Church sees it as her basic task to bring every one to find Christ."

This sort of mission does not depend on specific geographical frontiers, but has to be carried out wherever there are people who do not yet know Christ or know him no longer. One can perhaps make the pope's thoughts more explicit and say that the Church is no longer so much the ark of salvation for the privileged few who find themselves in it, but a sign of salvation for all, because all men and women have already been grasped by Christ. The Church, then, has the task of announcing and proclaiming this salvific situation to all people and also, so far as this is possible, of fully incorporating these men and women of Christ into the mystical body of Christ and the Church.

2. The Dialogue with Other Religions

In the meantime, however, and surely for a long time to come the great majority of the human race cannot declare itself for Christ. So we can no longer accept the alternative, "Either baptized or damned." We must look instead to dialogue with the representatives of other religions, which is, all the necessary distinctions having been made, like an extended form of ecumenism.

The pope does not develop a long and comprehensive presentation of the subject. His ideas can be summarized in the following points:

a) He alludes to Paul VI, who spoke in *Ecclesiam suam* of religion and the churches as concentric circles, all of which radiate out from the center, Christ. John Paul II, by contrast, speaks of a "map with different religions." No doubt this is merely a comparison; the pope certainly doesn't mean that religions, like countries, lie autonomous and unconnected alongside each other.

b) An obvious prerequisite for dialogue is the mutual respect of the partners. Hence the pope no longer repeats old-time expressions such as "infidelity" or "godlessness." He speaks instead of the "strong religious convictions of the followers of non-Christian religions." He does call them a "human spirituality," but he adds a few lines later that "these convictions have already been touched by the Spirit of truth" (the Italian text says it better, "effetto anche essa dello Spirito di verita"), "which reaches out effectively beyond the visible boundaries of the Mystical Body."

In another passage the pope repeats the same double statement: He speaks of the tremendous legacy of the human mind that has revealed itself in all religions, but he then adds that this has been achieved by the Spirit, who "blows where he wills."

With this presupposition, one can understand that the pope is recommending that we convey Christ's words to non-Christians as well as to Christians. "The life of Christ speaks at the same time to a great many people who are not able to repeat with Peter: You are the Messiah, the Son of the living God."

c) As a matter of practical policy we should approach those religions "with that appreciation, respect, and spirit of discrimination which has distinguished the missionary activity and the attitude of the missionary since Apostolic times." That is, of course, an idealized picture of the history of the missions which will not bear critical scrutiny. Only a few lines further on the pope admits that "in practice this high ideal has not always been fully met." Paul VI was more honest: in 1964, when he inaugurated the new Secretariat for Non-Christians, he spoke of the prejudices and the more or less conscious bad faith which for so long a time made each side view the other as its adversary."

d) Religious dialogue requires a certain space for religious freedom. The pope appeals to the corresponding declaration of the Council and recommends that while missionaries should "employ all the intellectual arts of persuasion," at the same time they should "maintain a deep appreciation for the person, for his understanding, his will, his conscience and his freedom." Even though he claims freedom of religion in the first instance for the Church, he also says that it "holds as a principle, "independently of the religion that the individual professes."

3. Dedication to Justice and Development

Schools and hospitals have long been a part of missionary activity, but such works were viewed mainly as acts of love and means of proselytizing. It took the Council, the social encyclicals of John XXIII and Paul VI, and the 1971 Bishops' Synod on justice, before we realized that dedication to justice and development constitutes an essential component of the evangelization process itself.

In RH the pope expresses himself this way: "If the Church looks to Christ and to the mystery that makes up her life, then she cannot remain insensitive to anything that serves the true welfare of humanity, just as she cannot be indifferent when that welfare is threatened." If every person is already one with Christ, so to speak, then he is thereby also entrusted to the Church. That is why the Church "views this concern of man for his humanity, for the future of man on earth and so for the direction taken by development and progress as an essential element of her mission."

This development, needless to say, should be not just technically unobjectionable, but also humane and worthy of man. Similarly, the Church regards the question of human rights as very closely "bound up with her vocation in today's world."

The famous north-south differential seems "like a gigantic enlargement of the biblical parable of carousing Dives and poor Lazarus." These structures "cause the regions of misery, with their burden of fear, disappointment, and bitterness, to go on endlessly spreading." To change "this dramatic situation" calls for "a true conversion of mentality, of the will and the heart. . ." The enormous sums invested in armaments could quickly transform the zones of misery or hunger into productive land. One thinks of the pope's urgent appeal in Ougadougou, Upper Volta, to undertake some bold action against the ongoing desertification of Africa.

It is clear from all this that missionaries can no longer be content with converting and attending to individual Christians. They must help bring about the "social conversion" that changes the world. Together with their orders and institutes, they must call out and work for more justice in the world as well as bring home to their Christians the idea that dedication to justice and development is a genuine expression of Christian life.

4. In the Structure of Collegiality

John Paul II likewise addresses the *principle of collegiality*, without, of course, supplying any new or strong emphases. In several other texts from the beginning of his pontificate the pope spoke more forcefully on the subject. For example, at the end of the conclave he promised the cardinals that he would be concerned for the appropriate development of collegial organisms, creating new ones or reforming existing ones. And appearing before the Council of the European Bishops' Conference he came right out and spoke of "episcopal collegiality and regional autonomies," a genuinely sensational phrase for the *Osservatore Romano*.

Do those remain empty words, or can we expect further surprises with respect to this principle, which is so important for the young churches, if they wish to develop an authentic identity? Up till now the collegiality and legitimate pluralism that the Council wanted have remained all too much in the realm of ideas; they have not yet *effectively* entered the structures of the Church. As always, the Church on her way to the year 2000, now no longer merely a Church of the West, but a Church of the six continents, will have to understand and make real her unity in diversity. The leap from *Romanitas* to *Catholicitas* must be boldly ventured.

We have thus derived from RH four key ideas, that are altogether timely, that could be developed from other documents, and that above all ought to prove effective for practical use. These four new ideas could be for the Church on its way to the next millenium what the four directives of 1659 meant for the centuries that followed.

It's true that these four key ideas all derive from the Council—which only heightens their importance. We are grateful to the pope, however, for making them a part, fifteen years after the Council, of his personal message to the world, for giving them, in some cases, a sharper focus, and for recommending them so urgently to the Church as she journeys toward the next millenium.

In conclusion we can still point out a peculiar tension between a certain personalism and traditionalism that the reader of RH cannot miss. In the first part of the encyclical we meet with an open, dynamic, person-oriented theology, as can be seen in the four points already mentioned and as might be shown from other points. Not laws and structures but humanity—and the Spirit—stands at the center here. The pope acknowledges that he is guided "by boundless trust in, and obedience to, the Spirit." Elsewhere he attests to his "stout confidence in the Spirit of truth. The strong expression of John 16:13, "When the Spirit of truth comes, he will guide you into all the truth," is cited three times.

On the other hand, in the second part of the encyclical, which is concerned with internal churchly issues, one observes a marked traditionalism. In the very beautiful chapter on the Eucharist the author abruptly stresses "the duty of conscientiously observing the liturgical norms." On the other hand, there are no new possibilities envisioned for the countless communities without priests, and consequently without the Eucharist. At the same time the pope commends the new practices that aim at highlighting the communal nature of confession, but then he immediately lays a heavy stress on "the age-old practice of the sacrament of penance, the practice of individual confession." On priestly celibacy he strongly encourages fidelity and perseverance, just as married people are called upon to be faithful and persevere. But one ought to note that in the latter case a divine law is at stake, as well as the interests of third parties (the children), whereas in the first case we are dealing with a law of the Church.

This tension no doubt grows out of the two components in the personality of Pope Karol Wojtyla. On the one hand he has roots in phenomenological and existential philosophy and ethics. Husserl, Heidegger, and Scheler are his sources. This explains his commitment to persons and his interest in concrete analysis. On the other hand, he has been stamped by the experience of the Polish Church, which for various historical reasons is very devout but also rather static and traditionalistic.

The future will show whether Pope Wojtyla will try to impose the Polish perspective on the entire Church, or whether the contact he has now with the situations and attitudes of the other churches, and his openness to the Spirit will force him to understand the new realities as a sign of the times, and to act accordingly, even when it comes to internal church matters.

The second encyclopedia of this pope, *Dives in misericordia* ("Rich in mercy"), which appeared a year later, was also a very good text, an agreeable proclamation of God's compassion, minus any stipulations from Canon Law, a Gospel sermon that still speaks to us today.

4. An End to Talk About the "Missions"

In the summer of 1979 I gave three lectures in the course of my participation in the National Missions Congress of Ireland at Knock. The Congress worked mornings and evenings in groups while at midday it celebrated a beautiful liturgy in the large new Marian basilica with many people from all over the country joining in. On this occasion a five minute video-address by the pope was shown each day, using a large number of TV sets. I had an objection to a small feature—but more than just a trifle—of these talks. And so wrote to the pope with an eye to the upcoming missionary feast of the Epiphany and to his planned summer trip to Africa. The date of the letter was December 13, 1979:

Holy Father,

Through Msgr. G. Coppa, who was Assessor at the time, you let me know that my letter to you dated October 12, which I had entrusted to Don Dziwisz, was a welcome one. And so I hope I am not acting improperly if I once again pass along some brief considerations.

The occasion for this comes from your video-message to the National Missions Congress of Ireland (to which I was invited as an expert) and your homily on the eve of World Mission Sunday. Both times you said, "Let us pray for the missions. . .The hour of the missions is not yet past. . .Mary, Queen of the Missions. . ." Perhaps I am not mistaken in assuming that someone in the Congregation of the Propaganda Fide wrote these texts. I am aware that several members of this Congregation are still trying to uphold the status quo in the missions.

But it seems to me that we have here a lack of coherence between theological reflection and the sociological facts of religion on the one side and the sort of language I advert to on the other. Since we are approaching a new feast of the missions, namely the Epiphany, I would like to urge you, if possible, not to repeat this terminology.

In the past we had the Church, in the western world, and over there, in Africa and Asia, were the missions, that is, regions sub-

ject to the Propaganda Fide and entrusted by this Congregation
to the foreign missionary institutes through the "ius commissionis." But in 1969 the "ius commissionis" was revoked for the dio-
ceses. It subsists only in the few apostolic prefectures and vicari-
ates. Today we have local churches on all six continents, though
of course the Church is at the same time in a missionary situation on all those continents. Thus it has become anachronistic to
say: "There are the missions, here are the churches," quite apart
from the fact that the representatives of the young churches no
longer like to hear talk about the "missions," and that the term
had likewise practically disappeared from the vocabulary of the
missionary institutes.

The official Church too has in fact already changed this expression. The draft of the conciliar schema still bore the title "On
the Missions," but the Council itself called it "On the Missionary
Activity of the Church." In *Evangelii nuntiandi* Paul VI completely dropped the word, and left off dividing world into church
regions and mission regions. Instead he distinguished between
religious-sociological groups, namely people who were not yet
Christians, the Christians, and those who were no longer Christians. These three groups may be found on all six continents.
You yourself have said to the executive board of the European
Bishops' Conference that Europe is on the point of becoming a
missionary continent once again (OR December 21, 1978).

We can infer from this that expressions such as "missionaries,
missionary activity, missionary institutes," etc. can still be used to
refer to the first efforts at evangelizing men and women who are
far from Christ (but not necessarily far from Europe). This activity, moreover, has the highest priority in the Church (*Evangelii
nuntiandi*—the Gospel must be proclaimed). Hence one can say,
"Let us pray for the missionary Church; we still need missionary
dedication, work for the evangelization of the peoples. . ." But
we should no longer speak of the "missions," since this expression recalls bygone ideas and realities and seeks unreasonably to
prolong their life.

Holy Father, will all my heart I wish you a happy Christmas, with the radiant love of St. Francis at Greccio.

Fr. Walbert Bühlmann

This was answered by an official acknowledgment of receipt (unsigned) by the State Secretariat, dated, February 23, 1980.

A few months later the pope spent twelve days in Africa, "in the missions" consequently, as we used to say. But in the 72 speeches he gave he did not speak once of the "missions." Instead he mentioned that the era of evangelization had begun 100 years ago, that the missionaries had built up the local churches, in whose service they were still needed, and that the young churches should take their missionary responsibility seriously. . . .

At that time I not only drew up an analysis of these 72 speeches for the "Union of Superiors General," but in a letter of May 15, 1980 I also voiced to the State Secretariat "my sincere joy, my surprise, my satisfaction over these speeches of the Holy Father. . .which disclose first-rate information, rich inspiration, and great courage to say the right and appropriate things at each place." The receipt of this letter was not acknowledged.

5. Taking a Private Trip to Japan

After John Paul II had manifested his appetite for travel and for contact with the local churches, people soon began to talk about his going to Japan. The then president of the Secretariat for Non-Christians, Cardinal Sergio Pignedoli, would have viewed such a visit to that land, with its ancient culture, in which he had many personal non-Christian friends, as a great success for his Secretariat and for the Church. So the initiative was launched from Rome. But the bishops of Japan expressed their deep misgivings with the plan, since the Catholics there make up less than half of one percent of the population. When this reaction became known, I immediately got in touch with Msgr. Pietro Rossano, the secretary of the Secretariat for the Non-Christians, to suggest to him the possibility of an alternative kind of visit. He encouraged me to forward this idea to the State Secretariat. I did so in a letter dated May 23, 1980 to the "Substitute," who is, practically speaking, the Vatican's Secretary of the Interior, Msgr. Eduardo Martinez Somalo.

Your Excellency,

Today the press reported that the bishops of Japan look upon a visit by the pope to their country as unadvisable, because the overwhelming majority of non-Christians might have negative reactions to such visit if it is carried out in the usual fashion.

For this reason I wonder whether for this sort of case an alternative sort of trip could not be planned. Every head of state can pay a visit to another country either officially or privately. Couldn't the pope then also travel privately in certain cases? In this hypothesis, the government would be informed, it would take the necessary security measures, but it ought not put in an appearance to receive him at the airport, nor would there be a military parade. That would mean smaller crowds and less publicity, but the pope could still meet the Catholic community as well as certain groups of non-Christians seeking dialogue.

Thus, to be specific, he could go to the Philippines, with its strong Catholic majority, on an official basis, but privately to the other countries of Asia. In this way no country would feel offended.

I presented these thoughts yesterday in a telephone conversation with Msgr. P. Rossano; I now propose them to you.

With kind regards, fraternally yours

Fr. Walbert Bühlmann

This letter too remained without acknowledgment. Ten months later, however, in February, 1981, the pope went on his first visit to Japan—as a private citizen. It also turned out to be a great success, all the more so because the pope managed to read his speeches rather well in Japanese.

II. Proclaiming the Good News to Those Far From Christ

Discussions with the Congregation for the Evangelization of the Peoples or "De Propaganda Fide"

It was a great moment in the history of the Church, when Pope Gregory XV, "impelled by God," founded the Congregation for Spreading the Faith (*De Propaganda Fide*) to spur, coordinate, and direct both the reunion of divided Christians and the evangelization of the newly discovered western world. The move evoked an enthusiastic echo on all sides. Father Joseph de Tremblay, Richelieu's "éminence grise" in Paris, wrote that the news was received in France with incredible joy, and he himself viewed this founding as the most significant initiative by the Holy See since the pontificate of St. Peter. The first hundred years of this new Congregation brought, in fact, an explosion of new ideas and impulses. People labored tirelessly to disconnect the missions from their links with Spain and Portugal, to promote a native clergy and to get educated and devout missionaries.

Even though the Congregation had its historical highs and lows, and in no way distinguished itself for brilliant inspiration during the Council (the contrary was true), I was sincerely willing, at first, to engage in loyal cooperation with it as secretary general for the missions from the Capuchin Order. I had arranged with our curia general to invite the cardinal prefect, Agnelo Rossi, to a lunch that been a very cordial affair. Furthermore, on the occasion of the 350th anniversary of the founding of the Congregation I had delivered a lecture at the papal University, the Antonianum, in the presence of Cardinal Agnelo Rossi and the two secretaries, Archbishops D. Simon Lourdusamy and Bernardin Gantin, that was very well received.[15] I was even asked to write the epilogue to the five-volume history of the Propaganda Fide, to reflect, after 4600 pages of history, for 40 pages on the future of evangelization.[16] Finally I had also, in 1972, taken upon myself the task of giving three weekly talks on the problem of evangelization (2 hours) and the Church in Africa (1 hour) at the papal university, the Urbaniana. In the spring of 1975 the secretary of the university, Msgr. Jezernik, asked me to set up a program for two years and, if possible, to do four weekly lectures. That would be the minimum for becoming a full professor and not just a lecturer, because he knew, he said, that the students valued my classes.

In February 1974 we professors of the Institute for Missiology held session together with the rector, Luigi Bogliolo. The idea was to raise the Institute to the level of an autonomous school. I voiced the opinion that structure was secondary, that the first thing was inner transformation. I argued for striking out the word "missiology"; it sounded too academic, and had an odor of the European superiority complex about it, as if we still had to be telling the young churches how to go about doing their work. I suggested calling the place the Institute or School "for Evangelization and Dialogue," which would designate the two poles of the Church's activity. But the students should be trained and encouraged to evangelize the entire world and to enter into dialogue with non-Catholics, non-Christians, and ex-Christians. That would also give rise to greater cooperation among the Roman dicasteries, one of which, the Propaganda, spoke only of evangelization, while two others, the secretariats for the Unity of Christians and for Non-Christians spoke only of dialogue. In Rome they had different doors for each of these two tasks. But the missionary was one person, and he ought to recognize and put into practice the synthesis between both activities. The rector asked me to submit these ideas to him in writing, which I did on February 10. So far, so good. Then my book on "the Third Church" appeared; it was supposed to serve as a springboard for reflection, but it turned into the proverbial bull in a china shop.

1. A Book That Caused a Stir

The pre-history of the book went like this: In my first year in Rome I had read the Pearson Report. That Canadian politician had drawn up, with the help of expert consultants, an account of the first official decade of development, 1960-70, noting what had been achieved, how things stood, and what further should be done; in other words a stock-taking and preview. At the next meeting of SEDOS, a research and documentation agency for 50 missionary institutes, I brought up in a general discussion the idea that we ought to get together and do a sort of Pearson Report on the subject of evangelization. We had all sorts of knowledge and experience stored up in our heads and the archives that ought to be put to use. Actually the Propaganda Fide ought to put out this sort of report, but they wouldn't, for lack of competence and courage. If we didn't put our backs into it, nobody would do it.

The idea caused no great sensation, but the next day the secretary of SEDOS, B. Tonna, phoned me to say that my suggestion was too important for immediate action and had to be pursued further. I told him that if he could just call in ten capable SEDOS co-workers from ten different curias general, I would give the idea some further development. That afternoon I explained the idea of the book once again and how I envisaged the collaborative effort. There followed a three-hour discussion, with the final result that one group said they didn't feel qualified to undertake the job, while a second group said they had no time, and the third group said it was simply impossible to write such a book. It was risky enough to write a book about the Church in Latin America, since that continent was so diverse, from Mexico to Chile. How then could one tackle a book about the whole Church in the Third World? One could only utter generalities that were already common knowledge, but nothing new. So I was left alone with my proposal. But after a few weeks I decided to risk it all by myself.

The book was published, in both German and Italian, during the synod of bishops in Rome in October 1974, which had for its theme evangelization in today's world. It immediately became a best-seller and has since been translated into eight languages. I sent 40 copies to 14 different bureaus of the Vatican, including five copies to the secretariat of state with a personal letter, dated November 5, 1974, to Cardinal Jean Villot, which was not acknowledged. Of all 40 recipients of the book only Cardinal Pignedoli thanked me—he assured me he would read it with interest and added, "If only everybody were as zealous as Father Bˉuhlmann!" I distributed eight copies in the Propaganda Fide, to the cardinal, both archbishop-secretaries, and various monsignori, noting that it was a book that should interest them, and that I would be glad to have an exchange of ideas about it after a few months.

There followed an icy silence of eight months. I never learned whether anyone had read it or not. One exception was Archbishop Gantin, now a cardinal and prefect of the Congregation of Bishops. He affirmed that he had read the book and found it highly interesting as a stimulus and groundwork for discussion. I was and always remained on friendly terms with him. In 1982 when he celebrated his 25th anniversary as a bishop, my minister general, Pascal Rywalski, sent him congratulations. In his letter of thanks the cardinal mentioned his "friendship with dear Fr. Bühlmann, whose intelligence and courage I admire."

Then around the beginning of May 1975 my students asked me, "What's wrong, professor? Aren't you teaching next semester?" "Why not?" "The new lecture schedule came out. Your subject is there, but not your name." At that point I asked to speak with the rector and asked him what it meant. "Nothing special," he said, soothingly, "we simply decided to change the position more often. You've taught for three years, so now we'd like to give an African priest the chance to replace you and work up these subjects." "I'm always ready to hand my job over to an African priest, but I'm not quite convinced this was the real reason for the move. I'd like to know for sure whether it has something to do with my book too." Seeing he couldn't dodge any longer, he laid his cards on the table: "Yes, of course that was part of it. There are things in your book that in conscience we cannot accept. The people in the secretariat of state think so too." "Thanks very much for the information. But I would have appreciated it, first, if I had been informed about all this, and second, if I had had an opportunity to explain my position on these ideas."

Thus, from the outset the procedure was neither honest nor brotherly. With no dialogue or respect for a fellow human being, the decision was reached: "This man spreads dangerous ideas, away with him!" From a source close to me I learned that Cardinal Agnelo Rossi was behind the whole thing, the man who as prefect of the Propaganda Fide was grand chancellor of the university. I was told that he himself had not read the book but had only been given a report about it. He was especially indignant over the criticism of the Propaganda Fide. What did I say? Citing the Council I had noted that there was a consistent trend to integrate the former missions into the Church; that these regions, therefore, ought not to remain unconditionally subordinate to a special Congregation, as if to a "colonial ministry"; that the Propaganda Fide was too absorbed in the task of administration, and lacked time for planning and research. Then I added, on a gentle note, "We observe, however, that there has been a turn for the better on this score."[17] I might have phrased it much more pointedly, and I still wouldn't have been exaggerating. But that little was enough for the cardinal to conclude: "Fr. Bühlmann does not mean well by the Propaganda Fide. So away with him!"

Shortly afterwards, in a letter dated May 23, Fr. Jesus Lopez-

Gay, dean of the Missiology Department of the Gregorian University, where I also lectured once a week, informed me that my course would not be offered any more "for various reasons." "Nevertheless, this does not mean that when a new opportunity arises, which we hope will be soon, you will not be invited back to teach in our department." This forced me to conclude that Cardinal Rossi was at work here too. But the expectation—and hope—was that after being in charge of the Propaganda Fide for five years, he would not be confirmed for another five year term: curial regulations provide for a change or reconfirmation in the highest offices every five years. Thus, if he had been replaced, I could have returned with all flags flying. Unfortunately for the Propaganda Fide itself, however, he remained in office.

Of course, I then told my students at the Urbaniana that they were correct in their suspicion, whereupon they asked to speak with the rector. This discussion took place on May 16. In the course of it he repeated that he could not approve the ideas in my book, that I was lacking in love for the Church, and that we Christians had to pray and obey. The students vigorously contradicted him, said they were no tyros, they had already had experience as missionaries and wanted to see their problems treated by an open-minded and balanced person like Fr. Bühlmann.

In the end the rector, tears in his eyes, had to sum the situation up: "You're all against me." Later, on May 27, 1975, the students sent a letter to the rector and also, for their information, to Cardinal Rossi and all the professors at the university:

Reverend Father Rector,

During the friendly talk we students of missiology had with you on May 16, for the purpose of clearing up the rumors about the removal of Fr. Walbert Bühlmann from his teaching post at the Urbaniana University, we learned

—that the University has the intention of carrying out a job rotation in the teaching staff, in order further to strengthen the Institute for Missiology;

—that the decision was authorized not to renew Fr. Bühlmann's contract as a lecturer for next year;

—that this decision was accounted for by his book, since its contents were supposedly marked by "a philosophy that in conscience is unacceptable" and, according to the judgment of "theological spokesmen," have no scholarly foundation and are ill-advised in their judgment of the contemporary situation and structures of the Church.

But we would also like to make our standpoint clear to you. We consider this decision

—onesided, since it was reached without bringing those affected by it into the negotiations, as correct procedure would have required; also without telling the students about it, since according to the University's calendar Fr. Bühlmann was scheduled to teach from 1974 to 1976;

—pointless, since Fr. Bühlmann was one of the best lecturers. We, especially those of us who have returned from the missions to further our education, prized his up-to-date and lively presentation of the problems of the missions (even if we accepted some of his criticisms and proposals with a certain reserve), along with his wholehearted love for the Church and for the cause of the missions;

—improper, since we believe that this decision will have a negative influence on the future of the Department of Missiology, and since no attention is being paid to the sympathies of the students and the expectations of the missionary institutes.

We therefore strongly urge that this decision be revoked.

The Students of Missiology
(19 signatures)

In the meantime, on June 13, the rector had let me have a two page document, whose authors were anonymous, but evidently the "theological spokesmen," about whom he had spoken to the students. He added: "These are ideas that cannot be presented in our University without doing harm." Anyone reading these two pages would really have to conclude how right they were to remove someone like me from teaching.

The author proceeds from the basic assumption that after the Eastern Church it is now the turn of the Western or Roman Church to go under, while a new Church, that of South America, Asia, and Africa will enter upon its legacy. His certainty on this point has deeply influenced the book, which aims to shed light from above, from a "satellite viewpoint," on the whole Church, about which he believes that things go from good to bad to utterly bad, as one moves from its periphery to its center. Thus all our hopes lie in the "Third Church," while in the Western Church the evils are increasing, ruin is on the way, as can be seen if one comes to Italy; and there is something rotten in Rome, especially in the Vatican Curia (it's hard to see why the contagion should stop just short of the pope). In fact Rome has supposedly crushed Africa underfoot *(I omit here the page references given in the original: W.B.)* The author cannot understand why the Catholic-Coptic students of theology are forced to attend the Roman universities, since Haile Selassie University in Addis Ababa has had an excellent reputation for years now. English should replace Latin as the language of the Church. The most important task of the missions consists in de-Latinization. The Congregation de Propaganda Fide has hitherto not been engaged in missionary work but in colonialism and conquest, and has been primarily concerned with Latinizing the world. The nuncios have been intent on advancing their own careers, and on tale-bearing in Rome. They are not familiar with local languages and customs. People forget that the reasons for the Eastern Church's split with the West were not dogmatic, but legal, brought about by the centralism of the Curia, the Latinizing bias of the missionaries from the Propaganda Fide, and by the steady insistence on western philosophical terminology.

But the basic evil of the western Roman Curia was dogmatic too, in that its officials spoke only of *one* correct revelation, whereas the God of humanity had, on the contrary, given as many revelations as there were historical religions of the various peoples. Christ, Buddha, and Muhammad had basically not founded any new religion, but reformed the existing one. Besides, there is only one true religion, the "holy," which constitutes the universal content of all historical religions and all rites, which are to that extent relativized. Paganism, Judaism, and Christianity are all ways to salvation, they are all good, and they go from perfection to perfection. Only the degree of perfection is different.

Conscience alone is the source of salvation. There is one universal religion, and the historical religions are so many unfoldings of it. Nowadays syncretism must be in part affirmed. Not only in Asia but in the western countries as well we find after the thesis (Christianity) and the antithesis (the non-Christian religions) a synthesis taking shape, a mutual enrichment (syncretism). Consequently missionaries ought to give up trying to convert men and women, to "save their souls," but simply labor to found the Church as "sign" for non-Christians.

Once this one religion has been declared universal, it follows as a matter of course that priesthood too is universal. In the early Church it was still very flexible, one functioned alongside the others, without any sort of preferential status. It was identical with the role of head of the eucharistic celebration. Only after the time of Constantine did it become a social class, with bourgeois privileges and cultic and administrative monopolies, a caste, against the wishes of Christ, who wanted a priesthood of all believers. Everyone should be a priest, including married people and women. Accordingly, the seminaries should be closed too; in any case they serve only to coddle the seminarians and give them the notion of their privileged state. Hence celibacy, which threatens to become simply an external convention marking a ghetto group, has lost its major justification. It is maintained only thanks to artificial means, on ideological grounds and for its financial advantages. But many clerics have supposedly come to terms with it, made an Italian-style "arrangement."

In conclusion, Bühlmann's book claims to be a prophetic book, preaching the syncretistic religion of the year 2000, in which Christ, Buddha, and Muhammad have equal rights and proclaim a common message, that of the one universal religion. Thus the pretension of the western Church to be the one true Church, the one, holy, Catholic, and apostolic Church, proves to be an act of pride, of domineering on the part of Rome, which aims to link everything to itself and to Latinize everything. And this contrary to the will of Christ, who never founded a Church but only— like Muhammad and Buddha— reformed the existing religion.

Against this sort of avalanche of accusations I had to defend myself for the sake of the truth:

Rome, June 25, 1975

To Fr. P. L. Bogliolo, Rector, Urbaniana University

copies to His Excellency, G. Benelli, Secretariat of State
His Excellency, Cardinal A. Rossi, Propaganda Fide
His Excellency, G. M. Garrone, Prefect of the
  Congregation for Catholic Education,
His Excellency, S. L. Lourdusamy, Propaganda Fide
The Deans of the Urbaniana University

Reverend Fr. Rector,

On June 13 you sent me a two page list of ideas from my book on the Third Church, with the observation that these were "ideas that cannot be presented in our University without doing harm." So I view the matter of my dismissal from teaching at the Urbaniana University as settled.

I thank you for letting me know the concrete motives for this measure, so that at least after the fact (since you did not accept my suggestion of a prior dialogue) I can make this response to the situation. Obviously this list of "theological spokesmen," which you mentioned to the students, was put together to justify my dismissal.

First of all, I would like to tell you that I accept this measure and have no intention of appealing it. I shall also, so far as it is up to me, do everything to avoid a media campaign, which might unleash a new "case," like those of Küng and Pfürtner. I don't know whether I shall succeed or not: I have already been approached by a representative of an important press agency and asked to provide him with the necessary data, which he would then forward to the world press. I firmly resisted this proposal out of love for the Church, because, as will emerge from this letter, it would be too humiliating for the Church, and I have absolutely no intention of making myself a name at her expense. On the contrary, I claim for myself the fullest degree of freedom and frankness, of the *parrhesia* that I repeatedly speak of in the book, so as to tell the proper authorities in this letter what I think about such procedures, as they are still practiced in the Church of Rome. I hope that in this way I can do something to prevent such cases from repeating themselves.

1. I in no way maintain that my book is unassailable, and I am always ready to subject my ideas to scrutiny, to try and deepen them. I am also prepared to accept objections and reservations, since I am aware that the official Church, at least for the moment, cannot approve all my ideas. But presuppose, as ever, that there is a serious, objective, and brotherly dialogue going on here.

It now appears to me, however, that this presupposition is precisely what is lacking to the two pages you sent me. From beginning to end you reveal a tendency to exaggeration, to onesided and false interpretation. Here are only a few examples: On page 193 of the Italian edition I refer to an author who says that Christianity had crushed the African religions; but the "theological spokesmen" claim *I* said Rome crushes Africa. On p. 214 I mention that at the time of the Second Vatican Council people wondered whether the young churches might not feel discriminated against, because, in contrast to the other churches, they were subject to a special Congregation (like a sort of colonial ministry). But the "theological spokesmen" have me asserting that the Congregation De Propaganda Fide has hitherto carried on not missionary work but colonialism. On p. 219 I say that the nuncios represent the Roman standpoint among the local churches, but they don't represent the standpoint of the local churches in Rome quite as vigorously because everyone is thinking about his career. The "theological spokesmen" twist this into the statement that the nuncios are intent only on their own careers and on talebearing in Rome. I could cite many examples like these.

If readers aiming to summarize all my ideas say that in my view "things go from good to bad to utterly bad, in proportion as one moves from the Church's periphery to its center,. . .that in the Western Church the evils are increasing, ruin is on the way, as can be seen if one comes to Italy; and there is something rotten in Rome, especially in the Vatican Curia (it's hard to see why the contagion should stop just short of the pope). . . . The most important task of the missions consists in de-Latinization. . . . Missionaries ought to give up trying to convert men and women. . . ." etc., then I can say only that I really don't recognize myself in that summary, which tactlessly falsifies and betrays my ideas. I protest energetically against this sort of interpretation.

I cannot avoid the impression that the "theological spokesmen" read only a few pages on the hot topics but not my whole book. They ripped my ideas out of their context and criticized them on the basis of an oldfashioned handbook style theology, without an adequate knowledge of post-conciliar theology and the new realities of the world. And all this combined with an uncritical fixation on the Church's central authority and an almost psychopathic fear of the new arguments from those who want to establish a balance, not only theoretically but practically, between Vatican I and Vatican II. In short, these two pages would belong in some cheap tabloid, but they are not worthy of a university and still less of the authority of the Church. Thank God I am intelligent enough not to identify those "theological spokesmen" with the Church, not even with the Roman Curia, in which I know several persons who have an altogether different opinion of my book.

2. This judgment of mine is strengthened by a thick dossier of letters and published reviews, which in general speak very positively of my book and of the hopes it raises, as well as by the fact that in six months it went through three Italian and two German editions, while contracts for a French and a Dutch edition are in the offing. I may add that when my dismissal from teaching at your university became known abroad I was offered a professorship of missiology at two universities, an offer I naturally refused, since I am in the first instance secretary general for the missions of the Capuchin order.

3. All this pains me so much because "theological spokesmen" of the sort I am dealing with drive the Church into a state of sterile isolation, which undoubtedly contradicts the spirit of *Gaudium et*

spes and many other church documents.

I love the Church, the missionary Church, which now finds itself confronting a historic challenge, at the beginning of a new and extraordinary era. That is the thesis of my book. But with a mentality of fear, conservatism, centralism, authoritarianism, and triumphalism (gladly accepting flattery but not tolerating the truth, though it makes one free), we shall inevitably miss our chance. Fine words about the signs of the times are not enough, if those who take upon themselves the risk of interpreting those signs are punished for it. The procedure followed in my case shows quite precisely the continued operation, in content, method, and style, of a system that I continually denounced in my book and that, from every point of view, brings shame upon the Church. There is no cause for wonder that the authority behind such a system is undergoing a crisis.

But as I have already said, I identify neither the Urbaniana University nor the anonymous authorities who were at the bottom of my dismissal with the Church. That is why I continue to work for the Church, full of hope.

Respectfully and fraternally yours,

Fr. Walbert Bühlmann

I also sent a copy of this letter to Bishop Anton Hanggi, the president of the Swiss Bishops Conference, to inform the bishops of my homeland about what was happening to their charges in Rome. The bishop answered me on Sept. 10, 1975: "I am sincerely happy to find in your remarks, among other things, a great love for our Church. Together with you I hope that this "honest way of thinking and speaking—proves to be a real service to the Church's leadership."

None of the Roman clergy to whom I sent the letter of June 23 reacted to it except Rector Luigi Bogliolo, who begged me in a six page handwritten letter (undated, but around the beginning of July) to take the matter in good part, not to dramatize the situation, and to think of the holy Capuchin missionaries...We may well assume that he had in the meantime received a reprimand from the then "strong man in the Vatican," Archbishop Benelli, whom I had also told about my case. His letter went as follows:

You have not been dismissed, your course is simply suspended. The University is ready to invite you back again to teach as soon as this becomes possible. [This confirmed once more my surmise that my "suspension" had taken place under pressure from Cardinal A. Rossi, but not actually on account of my "ideas that cannot be presented at our University without doing damage." W.B.] Please believe me that there were no evil intentions on anyone's part, and I am sure that you too do not presume that I or others harbor any malice. Nemo malus nisi probetur. (No one is bad unless he is so proved.) That holds for everyone. Only on this basis is a dialogue possible. . . .

With that as a presupposition, I should like to tell you that the observations of the theologians, if not "trustworthy," are nevertheless competent, and have something to them. I personally spoke of impressions, of spontaneous feelings that I had when I read the book. I am in agreement with you on many points, but not with the way you make them. How can you possibly believe that so many Capuchin missionaries, who have devoted their lives usque ad sanguinem (to the point of bloodshed) to proclaim Jesus to the world—I'm thinking especially of St. Fidelis of Sigmaringen and Cardinal Massaia—were simply promoting colonialism or were stupid tools of some colonial power?"[18] Merely thinking of this sort of thing insults them. I believe that the Church and her missionaries have, in general, always acted in this spirit. There may have been exceptions, people with bad intentions, but that was no longer the Church.

I am in agreement with you that many things must be reformed, and must be presented in a manner acceptable to the modern-day mentality, as I am trying to do in my field of philosophy. . . . From beginning to end you use the expression "theological spokesmen" ironically. But when irony comes into play, is there still room for dialogue? Doesn't the ironist a priori have the right on his side? I can well believe that there are theologians (or at least those who call themselves theologians) who see everything in black or white. The truth lies no doubt in the middle, because the extremities touch.

Dear Father, I would never dare to impute "fear, conservatism, centralism, authoritarianism, and triumphalism" to my neighbor and still less to the Church (i.e., Christians, and the pope and the bishops are Christians too). Why presume such malice from one's neighbor? Are we to believe that only today, with you, has the Church awakened from her conservative and authoritarian slumber? Do we have to wipe off the board everything that holy missionaries, primarily Franciscans and Capuchins, have done?

[He then admonishes me, for one whole page, to accept the criticisms, which were meant for the best.]

Dear Father, let this letter attest how seriously I have taken your last letter. I can assure you of one further point: I am not fronting for anyone, and I had only the best of intentions. I am prepared at any moment to withdraw from this post, which I never sought. I am trying to do right and thereby prepare myself for the account that I shall one day have to render to God for my words and deeds.

May the Lord help you and me to find salvation. May he give us ever more and better light to know what we ought to do, say, and write, and how we ought to do, say, and write it.

With brotherly love I remain, yours truly,

D. L. Bogliolo, Rector

I was convinced of the honesty of this letter and for my part showed that I was ready to make peace once more, after the feud we had been through, in my answer dated July 10, 1975.

Dear Father Rector,

The day before yesterday I received your letter (undated), for which I sincerely thank you. I deeply appreciate your effort to explain your thinking about my case in such a brotherly tone. By the way, I have never presupposed any "malice" toward me on either your part or others'.

I would rather not address the details of your letter, which at any rate shows clearly that we are operating on two different planes, are speaking from two different perspectives. I don't mean by that yours is the false perspective and mine the correct one, nor vice versa. . . . We must therefore accept this fact of plural approaches both in language and modes of thought. For my part I nonetheless hope that I have not completely removed myself from the realm of evangelical and Franciscan spirituality.

The thing that has impressed me about this whole affair is a certain ambiguity, what I would call a lack of fairness in the entire procedure. Not only was I left in the dark, so that I first had to get my information from the students and then from the missionary institutes, but even in the dialogue that I carried on openly, something was wrong:

—You maintain that this is not a matter of "dismissal" since no contract was signed. But I *was* asked as late as March to submit my course schedule for the next two years. So if there was no legal contract, there were words spoken and good relations established, in Christian and human terms, that ought not to be have been broken off so brusquely.

—You maintain that the University was aiming at a more frequent rotation of professors and that I should have been prepared to resign my place to a representative of the Third Church, but at the same time you said in the presence of the students that the decision was brought about by my book, which was based on a philosophy that could not in conscience be accepted. Furthermore you sent me those famous pages, which I still do not consider as scholarly criticism that should be heeded but as a superficial and largely unfounded accusation that I simply had to reject.

—You maintain in your last letter: "I can assure you of one further point: I am not fronting for anyone." But various well-informed people dropped me hints that you *were* serving as a front for another authority, especially since, at the same time, the Gregorian University also let me know that, contrary to an agreement reached a few weeks before, my course was no longer scheduled for the coming year. Hence I was justified in my assumption that there was a higher authority behind all this. Which one? It was precisely this anonymity that troubled me.

In any event, I consider the issue settled. I hold no grudge against you; on the contrary, I regret to have caused you all this unpleasantness. I shall therefore not give my course in the 1975-76 academic year, because, among other reasons, I already have planned a heavy schedule of lectures and seminars in various countries of Europe and Africa. Personally I feel no animosity, I am only sorry for the sake of the Church, which had none but this negative reaction to the book that Karl Rahner called "the best Catholic book of the year."

I wish you a good vacation and, despite all this, something of the Christian joy about which Pope Paul VI has recently spoken with such eloquence.

Fraternally yours,

Fr. Walbert Bühlmann

After the vacation, on September 19, 1975, the rector answered me and assured me, in concluding: "Please believe my sincere and brotherly affection for you. I hope to have the opportunity to give concrete proof of this."

So I felt good about this newly made peace. For myself personally I looked upon the whole thing as a providential stroke. I was now free to lecture in all the continents of the world, an activity that began in 1975 on account of my controversial book and has gone on without interruption till today.

I made peace with Cardinal Agnelo Rossi as well. He himself invited me to have a talk with him on October 11, 1975 and approved my continued serving as the representative of the Capuchin Order for negotiations with the Propaganda Fide. To be sure, I later found out that he had passed on my book to the Congregation of the Faith (the old Holy Office). Cardinal Rossi remained another eight years as the prefect of the Propaganda Fide, although the executive board of the Union of Superiors General, in their private conversations with the pope (once with Paul VI and twice with John Paul II), often asked for a change of leadership, since there was no dealing with this cardinal, who would accept no opinions but his own and harshly snapped at people, even religious superiors. That's how hard it is to change a system.

2. A Congress Full of Ideology and Anxiety

In the first week of October 1975 the Urbaniana had organized a large scale international congress on the subject, "Evangelization and Culture." The idea was to celebrate the tenth anniversary of the decree on the missions "Ad gentes" by selecting this theme, to illuminate and encourage the transition from the western cultural forms of Christianity to other cultures. The dean of the school of theology, Jóse Saraiva Martins, president of the organizational committee, went to great lengths to assure its success.

He had, among other things, invited Karl Rahner, to present his interpretation of the non-Christian religions. When Cardinal Agnelo Rossi later learned of this, he tried to pressure Fr. Martins to cancel this invitation. It took Fr. Saraiva's courage—and his threat to resign as the person in charge of the congress—to dissuade the cardinal from his purpose. Thus Rahner appeared as an unwelcome guest of the authorities, but for that reason he was applauded all the more by the congress participants.

In 1982 the Urbaniana held a colloquium for the twentieth anniversary of the beginning of the Council, solemnly inaugurated by Cardinal Rossi. Of the four speakers three vehemently and explicitly savaged Karl Rahner, describing him as an arch-heretic and his "anthropological turning point" as the ruination of any kind of theology. They would have liked to put this man, who played a leading role in shaping conciliar theology, on the index of forbidden books.

Another professor, by contrast, was really given the heave-ho. This was Carlo Molinari, who had taught dogmatic theology at the Urbaniana for many years, to the enthusiastic response of the students there, and who was also secretary of the Italian Theological Commission. Like me, he had learned in the summer of 1975 that he was being dismissed from his teaching job because of his dangerous ideas. This firing was effective immediately so that he could not put in an appearance at the congress, although his topic had already been accepted.

I was treated more kindly. I had likewise been invited to give a lecture and had chosen the subject, "The New Theology of Religions and Catechetical Practice." To address this question I had sent a questionnaire to five catechetical centers in Africa and five in Asia. The results clearly indicated that nowadays people no longer speak as they used to of paganism, unbelief, and idolatry, but take the existing religions seriously as life-experiences and try to bring them to fulfillment in Christ.

Unlike Carlo Molinari I was allowed to give my talk. Why? I had told the rector that my case might have consequences at the congress. At the beginning of the affair, on May 10, 1975, I had also informed Archbishop Benelli in a personal letter—which was not deemed worthy of an answer. In it I had written, among other things: "Above all I would like to call your attention to the repercussions of my dismissal, should it occur, from the Urbaniana and the Gregorian University. For me personally this constitutes no particular penalty. I did not ask to be allowed to give these courses, and I undertook them despite the many things I was busy with, as a service for others; and I think I am not deceiving myself when I say that the students greatly appreciated my lectures. I may also say that the professors of missiology from four universities outside Italy wrote to me about my book and declared their solidarity with my ideas. One of them, Prof. A. Camps of Nijmegen, is at the moment president of the IAMS (International Association for Mission Studies). Now in October the Urbaniana itself will be the scene of the International Congress of Missiology. I am afraid that because of my dismissal the Urbaniana will forfeit any sort of credibility just at the point when it is trying to strengthen its department of missiology, and that during the congress there might be a lot of discussion, if not a protest movement, created by my case. I would like to spare the Urbaniana, the Propaganda Fide, and the missions this sort of mischief."

Thus it is clear that the authorities let me speak out of sheer anxiety, and acted as if nothing had happened. But the blade of the guillotine was to fall, if not before the Congress, then afterwards. A year later when the Proceedings of the Congress were published in two imposing volumes, my paper just so happened to be missing, even though I had turned it in on time. So I wrote Rector Bogliolo on November 30, 1976:

Dear Father Rector,

After our encounters and conflicts some two years ago I thought you would leave me in peace. But I have just now—quite accidentally—discovered that in the Proceedings of the International Congress of Missiology the lecture I gave has not been printed. In this regard I would like to ask two questions:

1. Back then you struck my name from the curriculum without any prior discussion, without even telling me, so that I learned about the incident only from the students. Now you have once again chosen the same sort of procedure; that is, you have engaged in a onesided exercise of authority without any dialogue, without any communication, hence without any respect for the dignity of a fellow human being. I ask you: What Church do you think you are representing in this kind of operation? Certainly not the post-conciliar Church. You strike me as a typical repre-

sentative of a sort of Church that the rest of us shun, loathe, and struggle against, in the name of the Gospel and the Council. But let's leave it at that. I have complete confidence that the Church of Vatican II will survive, while that other one will not.

2. In contrast to the earlier incident, where I had no "right" to defend, in this case you have violated one of my rights and positively committed an act of public discrimination against me. I was asked by the University to give that lecture. The statement was made that all the texts delivered at the Congress would be published in the Proceedings. But now my lecture is missing. I have the right, and I insist on it, to know the reasons why this happened. Because of the simple fact that I am the author of the book on the Third Church? Or because the lecture did not seem orthodox to you? In this case I await the evidence.

Fraternally yours,

Father Walbert Bühlmann

The laconic reply to this letter came very quickly, on December 6, 1975:

Reverend Father,

In answer to your letter of November 30 let me specify the following:

All lectures and communications of the Congress are scrutinized by experts, and some of them have been judged unsuitable for publication. Your lecture belonged to this group. You are nonetheless free to publish it somewhere else.

Yours very truly,

L. Bogliolo, Rector

This is what we've come to. We are once again living—or we have never left off living—in a Church that without the burden of proof declares people unorthodox and ousts them, as if the Council had never spoken of human dignity, freedom of conscience, and the autonomy of learning. And this sort of thing calls itself a "papal university."

3. An Accusation Full of False Interpretations

In the course of my many lectures and seminars I went, in January 1977, to Angola, where I gave a week-long series of talks in two places. The younger Angolan Capuchins were enthusiastic; some older missionaries, however, from the province of Venice raised questions about certain new ideas or reacted rather violently to them. I also did a program for the Catholic broadcasting station in Luanda, speaking about the Church in Marxist countries. I encouraged Christians to take a realistic view of the situation as it was, and instead of sterile opposition to strive for positive cooperation in all things. The next day I received a phone call from the president of the state, Dr. A. Neto, thanking me for this spirit of reconciliation.

I also visited the city of Malanje, where a Venetian Capuchin, P. Emidio, directed a catechetical center. He introduced me to three Basque priests in that city who were trying to work in the direction of the African socialism of President Julius Nyerere and to urge the people to collaborate in building up the country as an expression of Christian faith amidst everyday life. But the bishops' conference was on rather tense terms with the regime and not well disposed toward these priests.

A year and a half later the then bishop of Malanje, now Cardinal A. do Nascimento, came to Rome and complained to the Propaganda Fide that I had spoken ill of the pope in Angola, had said that communism was good for Africa, and encouraged those Basque priests to take a hard line toward the bishops. Cardinal A. Rossi was triumphant, believing that he finally had concrete charges against me in hand. He summoned my minister general, Fr. Pascal Rywalski and presented these complaints to him, expecting him to fire me and send me back to Switzerland. Father Pascal answered that for the moment he couldn't say either yes or no, he would speak with me. But he also asked the cardinal to begin by speaking with the accused and giving him an opportunity to defend himself. The cardinal at first energetically rejected this suggestion, only agreeing to it when he saw that Father Pascal would not give way. He would have much preferred simply to negotiate about me as if I were a commodity.

The next day, July 2, 1978, Father Pascal wrote the cardinal the following letter, in which he garnished what was essentially a harsh confrontation with French charm:

Dear Cardinal,

I sincerely thank you for the invitation to visit you on Saturday, July 2, as well as for the kindness and simplicity with which you spoke to me. Allow me now to comply with my duty of justice and love toward a brother whom God has given me, Fr. Walbert Bühlmann. I would like to supply information that yesterday, in my extreme surprise I was unable to.

First of all, however, accept my heartfelt thanks for having granted, at my request, that it would be in accordance with justice to give Fr. Walbert Bühlmann the possibility to defend himself before a decision was reached. Thank you, Cardinal, thank you.

Please let me now lay before you some factors to be considered in judging my confrere. Fr. Walbert Bühlmann has my full confidence, as well as that of the governing council of the Order and our confreres in the Curia. [There follows a long song of praise for my religious spirit, my deep faith, my brotherly comportment, my love for the Church, my openness to dialogue.]

Believe me, my dear cardinal, that I keep an especially sharp eye on Fr. Bühlmann's position in matters of faith, so that I can have a proper assessment of the situation in granting or denying him permission to publish his books as well as permission to give his lectures. Fr. Bühlmann is constantly being invited to speak before bishops, at general chapters of religious orders and communities of men and women, in the presence of confreres and superiors. [There follows a longish account of my activity with laudatory judgments of myself.]

And so you will now understand my extreme surprise yesterday. Fr. Bühlmann was in fact in Angola from the 2nd to the 21st of January, 1977. Encouraged by Fr. Alfonso Nteka, the superior there, he contacted the Basque priests, whom he was previously unacquainted with and who at the time had not yet been placed under sanctions by the Church. . . . His attitude toward these priests was characterized by the words he later wrote to them: "I wish you good cheer and hope you will let yourselves be led by the Spirit of God. In this way the matter will finally end well." Now, eighteen months later, he is under accusation.

Truly I find it impossible to condemn him after all the letters of thanks and praise about him that I get from all over. I would simply like to add to this the fact that the missionaries of our Order as well as its superiors have expressed their deep gratitude for the spiritual guidance and support they have received from our secretary general for the missions.

Your Eminence, I have put your patience to the test with this long letter. In your kindness, which is recognized by everyone, please forgive me. And permit me to ask you, with humble and forceful urgency, to take into account my confidence in our secretary general, who will be happy to speak his mind to you in person.

Father, would you give us all your blessing.

Father Pascal Rywalski
Minister General of the Capuchins

The fact that a superior general would dare to stand up to a cardinal in this way for one of his brothers is a sign that some things have changed since the Council. It gives grounds for hope.

Months went by before a conversation finally took place between Cardinal Agnelo Rossi and myself, on December 11, 1978. Across from me sat the cardinal and Archbishop Lourdusamy. I thanked the cardinal for the opportunity of speaking to him, which, I said, was the only way to break down prejudices. It was a brotherly talk, and we parted company in peace. That afternoon I composed the following "memorial," which I sent to the cardinal.

Your Eminence,

On July 2, 1978 you summoned our minister general, Father Pascal Rywalski and presented to him charges against me. In his reply Father General demanded for me the right to speak for myself, in accordance with the old maxim, "audiatur et altera pars" (let the other side be heard too).

And so this morning I had an open, fraternal fifty-minute dialogue with you and with Archbishop Lourdusamy. I hope this exchange of views was good for both parties. As I promised you, I am now drawing up a sort of "pro memoria," with the aim, above all, of putting my answer in the archives alongside the accusations against me.

I. The Charges From Angola

1. I am supposed to have encouraged the Basque priests (who at the time had not yet been suspended) to take a hard line.—In fact they were just then awaiting the measures to be taken by the bishops' conference against them, and they asked me what they should do afterwards. I replied: "Nobody can answer that sort of question for you. In such questions of conscience you yourselves must reach your decision by listening to the Holy Spirit and to your conscience. And once you do, you must also, of course, be ready to take the consequences." I think this kind of answer is the right one for such a delicate case, and that it would also be approved by every church authority that takes seriously Vatican II's decree, "Humanae dignitatis."

2. I am supposed to have spent ten days with those Basque priests without even greeting the bishop of the city.—The fact is that I did not arrive that day until darkness set in, and I then ate supper with a Venetian Capuchin, Father Emidio. Afterwards he

called the three Basque priests, and we spoke with one another for an hour. The next morning before I traveled on, I placed a phone call to the episcopal curia to greet the bishop, but he unfortunately was not at home.

3. I am supposed to have said that communism was good for Africa.—I do not speak in such a primitive fashion. I did, of course, give a lecture to the Capuchins about the attitude of the Church in Marxist countries. I also spoke on the same subject from the Catholic broadcasting station in Luanda. This radio talk was later printed in the pastoral magazine, *O Apostolado*. I gave a copy of it, along with an account of my trip, to the Propadanda Fide. If you can use this printed talk to prove false statements about me, I would be glad to discuss this. But I categorically reject the charge that I made that generalization.

4. I am supposed to have spoken ill of the Pope.—I have never yet spoken ill of the pope, neither in my book nor in my lectures. One piece of evidence for this can be found in the Swiss newspaper, *Vaterland*, which I gave you this morning. There you will find letters to the editor, reactions of the people after the TV discussion about the dead Pope Paul VI. The readers were angered by the very critical judgments voiced by two theologians, and added, Thank God there was a third theologian present, Fr. Bühlmann, who put the historical greatness of this pope into the proper perspective. If I spoke favorably about the pope in Switzerland, where he had little popular sympathy, it is hardly likely that I would have spoken ill of the pope in Angola, where he had a great deal of it.

Thus all those accusations are either simply false or wildly exaggerated. Fortunately I have now had the opportunity of setting the record straight.

II. The Larger Context

Since the appearance of my book on the Third Church there have been many charges or at least suspicions leveled against me, all of which were guilty of a lack of dialogue:

8

104   **Dreaming About the Church**

1.   When the book came out, I brought eight copies to the Propaganda Fide and expressed the wish to discuss it at some time. But there was no dialogue of any sort, only an authoritarian decision to strike my name from the course offerings.

2.   When the students from the Urbaniana University sent a letter of protest to the rector and all the professors, the Propaganda Fide at once suspected me of being behind this. But it was, in fact, a completely spontaneous reaction by the students, and I only urged them not to take the story to the press.

3.   When Professor Friedli from the University of Freiburg sent a letter to Rome about my case, the Propaganda Fide again accused me of instigating trouble. But I knew nothing about the existence of such a letter until I heard of it from the Propaganda Fide. So I couldn't have been responsible for it.

4. In 1975 when the International Congress of Missiology met, I delivered a lecture there that was not included in the Proceedings of the Congress—though no one informed me of this. . . .

Your Eminence, if every now and then I raise something of a protest not against the pope, but rather against certain methods of operating by people in the Roman Curia, against a glaring lack of dialogue, against the gulf between the Church's authority and its competence, I do this out of conviction, out of love for the Church. I think that the Church of Vatican II does well not to eliminate such elements of opposition, because otherwise the salt that Jesus tells us to have in ourselves (Mk 10:50) would be lacking.

Thanking you once more, and with best wishes for Christmas,

Fr. Walbert Bühlmann

In the letter dated December 21, 1975, acknowledging the receipt of mine, the cardinal closes "con sensi di distinta stima, della Paternita Vostra Reverendissima devotissimo" (with feelings of the highest esteem, the devoted servant of your most reverend paternity. . .) I would have preferred him to use fewer unctuous words and to have, instead, somewhat more honesty in his heart. Because only a few weeks later I learned that at a visit to a Latin American bishops' conference he had inveighed violently against the "dangerous ideas of Fr. Bühlmann, who was destroying the missions." Two year later the cardinal launched against me an attack so brutal that I had recourse to the highest authority in the Church, the secretariat of state, and now for my part brought charges against the cardinal. I shall have more to report on this later.

There is still more that might be said about the Propaganda Fide, which would only confirm the reader's earlier impressions. The Council had wanted this Congregation to be not simply a center of administration but also an "organ of dynamic leadership, making use of scientific methods and up-to-date tools, and taking into account the findings of contemporary theological, methodological, and missionary-pastoral research. . . . The Congregation should have at its disposition a permanent group of expert advisors of proven knowledge and experience. . . ." (AG 29). Thus the goal was an altogether exemplary modernization of this historic institution—a sort of blueprint of a dream. If the Council Fathers were to come back today to judge the course of developments since then, they would be rather disappointed. Expert commissions were appointed—I myself served for six years as a member of the pastoral and the catechetical commission. But we had almost nothing to do, we were presented with insignificant problems. Nobody dared touch on the real problems—or nobody saw any problems, since the answers to all questions have already been given in Canon Law. In this way the letter of the Council was fulfilled but not its spirit. The commissions and their members are solemnly listed in the *Annuario Pontificio,* but nothing happens. The whole business is only a facade.

Immediately after the Council, it is true, things had begun well. The experienced missionary bishop Cauwelaert and the specialist P. Brunner, SJ, along with a nun as secretary, were named as the catechetical commission. It went bravely to work, contacted all catechetical centers in the Third World, and after a year drew up a very good report on the situation, which included future perspectives. Instead of being able to take this report and build on it, the commission was informed that it had only a provisional status, and the real commission was now about to have its say. The three pioneer members were dismissed, evidently because they were operating too independently, which is not compatible with the system. Then eight new members were named, who were supposed to have worked under the eye of the Propaganda Fide. But from that point on nothing happened. One may doubt that the situation has improved in the last few years since I left Rome.

At the time that I left my position as secretary general for the missions of the Capuchins, I wrote the following farewell letter, on February 15, 1983 to Archbishop Lourdusamy, the secretary of the Propaganda Fide, now a cardinal and prefect of the Congregation for the Eastern churches, a man with whom I was on basically good terms:

Dear Archbishop,

Tomorrow I am leaving the Curia General of the Capuchins and the office I have held for twelve years with joy and enthusiasm. I would like to take this opportunity to thank you. All things considered, we have got along well, I think. I have repeatedly told you that you cannot condemn my ideas and my books, because they correspond quite exactly to the ideas and endeavors of your brother Amalorpavadass. . . .[19]

I am reminded of an analogous case from the 1920's. At that time there lived in China the well-known Fr. Lebbe, a critical man with ideas like mine. He criticized the mission system, the missionaries, and the bishops who were too much the toplofty Europeans and treated the Chinese priests as second-class clergy. This sort of criticism made Fr. Lebbe unpopular, and he was actually expelled from China by command of the apostolic delegate. But Fr. Lebbe was also in contact with the Propaganda Fide, where the farsighted Cardinal Van Rossum was then the prefect. Van Rossum listened to Fr. Lebbe, and it is Fr. Lebbe and through him Cardinal Van Rossum that we chiefly have to thank for Pius XI's consecration of six Chinese bishops in 1926 and for his saying in a startling letter to all missionary superiors in China that a new age had begun and the Chinese clergy had to be taken seriously. That was a stroke of luck then: a far-sighted cardinal. Unfortnately in the last twelve years we have not had a repetition of it. That is why there have been so many lost opportunities, so much clinging to the status quo, leaving missionary experts and mission institutes now just to smile at the Propaganda Fide—lest they have to lose their temper. What a shame for the young churches. "Jerusalem, si tu cognovisses" (Jerusalem, if you had only known. . .).

Despite everything I go on, because I believe in the Spirit of God who is alive in his Church, above all in the people of God and among those bishops who are close to God's people.

With best wishes, I remain

Yours,

Fr. Walbert Bühlmann

Part Three

Proclaiming the Power of Christian Doctrine, Rather Than Issuing Condemnation

(Negotations with the Congregation of the Faith)

1. Don't Feed the Children Too Much Theology

In December 1975 I indirectly had a little preliminary skirmish in Rome with the Congregation of the Faith. I found myself on a three month lecture tour through East Africa: Mozambique, Tanzania, Madagascar, and Kenya. In Dar-es-Salaam I was invited to give a three day seminar on "Evangelization and Culture" to the bishops' conference. I also paid a visit to pro nuncio Archbishop F. Brambilla. I passed on to him the latest reports on the Church in Mozambique. Then he abruptly raised the subject of my book on the Third Church: "I completely agree with what you say about the congregations of African nuns—there are too many of them and so far they've had too little education." "I hope that's not the only point we agree on." "But what you say about the nunciatures, that they're lodged in palaces, that their staffs lack knowledge of the country, often don't even speak the language, are ignorant of recent theology, and haven't had any sort of preparation in missiology; that the nuncios live isolated in their residences with their equally solitary secretaries and a few sisters to serve them—all that is false and unfair." (Though an employee of that nunciature, who had likewise read the book, said that if I had lived ten years in a nunciature I could not have described the situation better.)

I had arranged my trip so that I could spend a day in Nairobi at the general meeting of the World Council of Churches. The pro-nuncio there, Archbishop P. Sartorelli, whom I knew from the nunciature in Bern, was so kind as to offer me his hospitality. Shortly before this Fr. Jeremie Bonnelame had sent me a letter from the Seychelles Islands in the Indian Ocean, filling me in about his catechism incident. Swiss Capuchins work on these "paradise islands," and in 1959 they had sent two seminarians to Switzerland, where they made their novitiate, studied theology, and then were ordained in 1964. Fr. Jeremie was, in addition, sent to the Institut Supérieur Catéchetique in Paris where he received a diploma. Upon returning to his homeland he was put in charge of catechesis in the diocese of Victoria. As part of this job he wrote a catechism entitled *With Jesus*, following the criteria that had just then become accepted. To some of his confreres the work seemed insufficiently traditional, and they sent a copy to the pro-nuncio in Nairobi. On May 9, 1975 the bishop received from that city a list with ten points that were to be borne in mind for the next edition. That meant, among other things:

—The concept of God, as expounded in Vatican I, had to be reflected in the catechism.

—In connection with the Trinity the concept of nature was missing.

—In the connection with Creation there was no statement that Creation had been "ex nihilo."

—The section on moral training failed to discuss the theological and moral virtues (above all the virtue of purity), vice, and natural law.

—In connection with the Eucharist the real presence of Jesus was dealt with, but no mention was made of transubstantiation.

—In connection with the Last Things nothing was said about the personal and general judgment, Purgatory, and the resurrection of the body. There was likewise no mention made of the fact that heaven and hell are places, etc.

I took the opportunity to tell the nuncio how concerned the author and I were by these remarks. He had taken honest pains to present the faith to children that they could understand it and make progress toward it. And now the nuncio was making demands that made a mockery of all the criteria espoused by modern catechetics. The nuncio was insisting on a complete presentation of doctrine from the very beginning, disregarding the principle of graduality, i.e., that in organic growth such completeness can be achieved only step by step, as is recognized in the *General Directorate for Catechesis*, which was published by the Congregation of the Clergy. The observations were shaped primarily by the notion that scholastic theology, with all its formulae, was also at the same time catechesis. *Kerygma*, on the other hand, does not pursue scientific aims, but is rather a training in the faith, with its own dynamic. Children should not, for God's sake, be fed too much theology. People are disappointed, provoked, and discouraged when the Church throws such stumbling blocks in front of them.

Archbishop Sartorelli then observed, as if to excuse himself, that the observations hadn't come from him, but from the Congregation of the Faith, to which he had passed on the catechism. "So much the worse," I answered, "if the Church's highest authority is still expressing such old-fashioned views and continues to try to impose an anti-reformation, apologetical brand of religious instruction. I would really like to put those gentlemen in a schoolroom some time and see how they would do with the children."

2. A Heresy Factory

One of the saddest and most tragic things in the Church's whole
history is the way "heretics" were treated. Down through the ages
there have been uninterrupted condemnations and "anathemas."
Today, if we take an honest, critical view of the situation, we
must admit that in most cases there was a lack of dialogue and
hence mutual misunderstanding.[20]

A typical instance of this can be seen as early as the first great
doctrinal controversy of the patristic period, which led to the
schism of the Nestorian church. In the last few decades this
prototypical heresy has been the object of renewed attention.
Scholars argue today that the doctrine condemned by the Council
of Ephesus in 431 was rightly condemned, but that it did not
correspond to what Nestorius meant. Nestorius, in other words,
was not a Nestorian. People then were not in a position to listen
to one another, to understand one another, to view the other
person's opinion as the other side of the same reality. Instead
each side absolutized its own approach and made its partner its
opponent. Thus that first heresy was created, and not avoided as
it might have been.

Similarly we find ourselves today in a position to do better justice to the many medieval heretics who were persecuted by the
Inquisition with the greatest severity. For some years now a community of scholars has been at work to trace the history of heresy
to its roots, systematically and without bias. Hitherto there was
only polemical literature for or against heretics. Their own writings were practically unknown. Now those heretics are allowed
to speak for themselves; and we notice that most of them wanted
with their whole hearts to be Christian, indeed they claimed to be
the good and true Christians. Heresies, therefore, arose in general through the complicity of the Church, that is, from a lack of
dialogue and from neglect of what were in each case quite specific
values and concerns. Heretics function as alarm bells. From the
self-criticism of the Church that they generate reforming energies
can and should arise. Often enough the defeated heretics were

vindicated. They became the pioneers of new ideas.

The period of the Reformation reveals, alas, the same picture. There was too much of one side talking against the other instead of with it. To be sure, Martin Luther did launch a tremendously fierce (and largely justified) attack against Rome and the pope. But the Catholics also misunderstood the Reformers, heaped abuse on them, did not take their genuine concerns seriously, and condemned them in a burst of premature self-confidence. We had to wait until the second half of this century until finally men like J. Lortz and H. Jedin could write an objective history of the Reformation and sketch out an objective portrait of Luther.

Around the time of anti-modernism a new wave of overhasty charges of heresy swept over the land, as the best representatives of the Catholic Church tried as best they could to harmonize theology with modern science. I am not denying that some of the "modernists" caused confusion by failing to make distinctions or that some actually landed in error. They were all discovered through a well-camouflaged network of spies directed by Rome, issued warnings, and, in many cases, condemned without further ado and removed from their posts. Even the young priest Angelo Roncalli, later to be Pope John XXIII, was in danger of ruining his career. He taught church history at the seminary of Bergamo and was highly prized by the students and the bishop. But Don G. Mazzoleni who—as Roncalli noted in his diary—"belonged to those zealots who were never lacking in any diocese back then," reported this professor's apparently dangerous ideas back to Rome. Thus Don Angelo was given a warning, "which became the occasion of a deep mortification, but did not trouble my inner peace." As pope he had his file brought out of the archives of the Holy Office for his inspection. The file bore the note "Suspected of modernism." That was consoling for many people then—and now.

That was how they treated not just heretics, but Jews, pagans, and Muslims: for centuries there were polemical and even warlike clashes. One of the finest things about the contemporary era is that since John XXIII and the Council we now have dialogue and prayers in common with all these groups.

In Rome, however, they still seem not to have learned enough of history's lessons. I have myself seen how they try to get rid of anyone who dares to formulate any specific kind of criticism of the Church, by piling up the dogmatic difficulties. It began with a letter from Cardinal F. Šeper, the prefect of the Congregation of the Faith, writing on August 12, 1975 to my superior general, Fr. Pascal Rywalski:

Most Reverend Father,

The attention of our dicastery has been called to the book, *The Third Church At Our Gates* [German title, *Where Faith Lives*] by Fr. Walbert Bühlmann, OFMCap, which was published by Edizioni Paoline in 1974.

The contents of this book seem to have stirred up a certain amount of opposition. Given that fact, I would be very grateful to you if you would be so kind as to have the book subjected to scrutiny and the appropriate comments sent back to me, together with the measures, if any, that you consider advisable to be taken against the book and the author.

I am glad of the opportunity to assure you, most reverend father, that I am sincerely yours,

Franc. Card. Šeper, Prefect

Thus the original idea was to have the most elegant solution: get the minister general himself to play executioner to his confrere. But Cardinal Šeper and Co. miscalculated. After Fr. Pascal had spoken to me and likewise dealt with the case in the General Council, he unequivocally stood up for me, as he once had against Cardinal Rossi, against the highest authority in the Church after the pope. In his response on September 14, 1975, he stressed that he had wished at the time to submit the manuscript to three recognized experts, Professor B. Haring (Rome), Prof. K. Kriech

(Solothurn), and Prof A. Camps (Nijmegen). The judgments of all three were independently from one another extremely positive (copies were enclosed). Prof. Haring had stressed, among other things, the "boundless love for the Church" that characterized the book. And so he, Fr. Pascal, had been glad to give the imprimatur. He further included letters from three university professors, K. Rahner, Innsbruck; K. Piscaty, Vienna; R. Friedli, Freiburg (Switzerland), and from experienced missionaries who were downright enthusiastic about the book. Finally he repeated the judgments in praise of me and emphasized that I might have easily made a media event out of it. "He early rejected such publicity. What he wants are competent and honest dialogue partners who are ready openly to discuss the disputed points so as to get as close as possible to the objective truth."

His final verdict: "In my humble opinion the book is really valuable. It appeared just at the right time. The work contains no erroneous teaching contrary to faith and morals. It is undergirded by a genuine love for the Church, by a faith and love that from time to time express themselves in critical judgments and in formulations that will provoke debate. The author would be happy to be able to speak candidly and openly about these matters with a qualified member of your Congregation. Forgive me, your Eminence, if I request such a conversation on his behalf."

This cloud of witnesses in my favor did not have the desired effect. The Curia had more faith in its own "experts." On May 6, 1976, that is after seven months of silence, there was another letter to my superior general from Cardinal Šeper:

Dear Father,

In reply to your esteemed letter of September 14, I must affirm to you the solid reasons for the opposition stirred by the book *The Third Church at the Gates* [German title, *Where Faith Lives*].

After a first examination of it our dicastery has been strengthened in its conviction that this book contains assertions which seem to be incompatible with the teaching of the Church. Apart from the polemical tone and from certain statements that are doctrinally ambiguous or pastorally unacceptable, I would particularly like to draw your attention to what the author writes in the chapters on ecumenical ties with non-Catholics and non-Christians, as well as about the problem of the official ordained priesthood.

He seems, in fact, to underestimate the special mission of the Church with regard to salvation and evangelization. Indeed he misjudges that mission when he speaks of the kenotic attitude, which the various churches must accept with a view to the self-realization of the Church. But he understands this sort of self-realization not with an eye to the Catholic Church, nor even to another, non-Catholic church, but to a third church reality.

Furthermore, his "prophetic interpretation of religions" seems to deny the uniqueness and transcendence of Christianity, and he falls into a certain religious relativism, when he speaks of a universal, transcendent religion lying at the root of all religions and taking on concrete form in the many religions.

Finally, what he says about the ordained priesthood seems unacceptable, namely that it is merely one function among others that belong to the category of services. The author appears to confuse the sociological vision of the priesthood with the theological.

I would be grateful to you if you would convey to Father Bühlmann the wish of this Congregation that he shed further light on these ideas.

You suggested, in addition, a conversation between Father Bühlmann and a qualified member of this dicastery. We would be inclined to organize something along these lines at some point, but only at a later point, after a more thorough investigation into this book. In the meantime we await an explanation on the part of Fr. Bühlmann.

Respectfully yours,

Franc. Card. Šeper, Prefect

Owing to the fact that I was on a lecture tour in various African countries and because I wished to request expert reports from two consultants, my answer was postponed until June 15, 1976. As far as the general reproaches went, I could give only a general answer. But on the subject of the kenotic attitude of all churches I referred to the decree on ecumenism from Vatican II, which states that the Church must realize and reveal its identity in accordance with Christ's example precisely in the attitude of kenosis, so that through its own reform it can launch a "movement toward unity." I thought a "certain" religious relativism was surely called for after centuries of absolutist thinking, in which all other people were labeled barbarians, savages, pagans, and idolaters. Besides, I explicitly stressed in the book "the sublimity of the Old Testament's revelation, the uniqueness of the New Testament's." I in no way denied the ordained priesthood. My purpose was not, however, to develop a theology of the priesthood, but to put it in the context of the contemporary pastoral situation, which naturally led me to cite sociological data.

I continued: "I can't resist the impression that the difficulties raised against the book were based on individual sentences torn out of context and, in addition, viewed from a narrow perspective. In a book with so broad a subject, written from the 'vantage point of a satellite,' as I say in the Foreword, certain things are necessarily presented in abbreviated fashion, so that any specialist can readily find points that are not expressed with precision. Other statements are deliberately formulated with an argumentative edge in order to stimulate pastoral research based on the new realities. This is framed not in the form of dogmas, not even of theological tractates, so that again anyone who wants to look for them can make out ambiguities with respect to Catholic doctrine. But if one adheres to the fundamental hermeneutical principle that every text is explained by its context, things should be clear, and there should by no doubts about my loyalty to the Gospel and to the authentic teaching of the Church."

Since the main objections were raised concerning ecumenical

relations with non-Catholics and non-Christians, I wanted to consult two real experts on these subjects, Fr. M. Zago, then a consultant to the Secretariat for Non-Christians, and Fr. P. Duprey, undersecretary to the Secretariat for the Unity of Christians. I explained to them that I was having difficulties with the Congregation of the Faith, and asked them not to write a defense for me, but to give me their expert opinion on the chapters in question from my book. Both did me this favor and reached the clear conclusion that my remarks were definitely modern Catholic theology and that there was nothing in them contrary to Catholic faith.

I enclosed these two documents in my answer to Cardinal Šeper, which ended as follows: "In your letter you made a casual allusion to the 'often polemical tone' of the book. If this tone and the criticism of certain structures of the Church contributed to the opposition of which you speak, I would be happy to give an oral presentation of this argument. I am thus available at any time for a dialogue—which I would, of course, not view as a theological disputation or a polemical debate, but as a brotherly conversation on topics relating to our Church, which we love so much."

Both at the time of my conflict with the Urbaniana University and now, one of the major stumbling blocks was my interpretation of the non-Christian religions. In point of fact there may be no aspect of theology where such radical changes in thinking have taken place since Vatican II as this one. As late as thirty years ago people in the Church commonly spoke of heathens, idolaters, and unbelievers. Nowadays the better theologians say that from ancient times God gave his grace and love to men and women of all religions, and that he awakened prophets and mystics among them. It has to be understood that people who have not kept in step with this are now getting confused and are quick to cry "heresy." I am glad to submit here the assessment of my "controversial" book, sent to me, undated, by Fr. M. Zago. Fr. Zago took his doctorate in missiology, and then served as a missionary in Laos and as the director of an institute for the study of Buddhism. Later he became assistant general of the Oblates of the Immaculate Virgin Mary, worked continually as an advisor to the bishops of Asia, and in 1983 was appointed secretary to the Vatican Secretariat for non-Christians. He was, in other words a man whose competence could not be doubted.

I would like to make just a few observations about that part of the book that deals with the non-Christian religions or about ecumenical relations with non-Christians. Let me say in advance that the book strikes me as a valuable contribution to missiological reflection and to missionary activity in the present-day situation.

1. This chapter takes as its starting point a series of immediate pressing problems. . . . The discovery of [the non-Christian] religions; the quest for religious experience and meditation, the challenge to our Christian originality; the impossibility of continuing to live in a religious ghetto, whether in Venice or London, Bangalore or Bangkok; the lack of conversions in the regions that have been shaped by the great historical religions, etc.—these are genuine problems for missionaries and for Christians from both East and West.

Unless one faces these questions, which are experiential rather than abstract, no theoretical or practical solution is possible. Discovering them and just seeking the signs of the times are an effort to know God's will and already a necessary beginning of a solution. Fr. Bühlmann has the special merit of seeing these problems, ordering them, and directing our attention to them.

2. The elements suggested by Fr. Bühlmann as a foundation for missionary work are valid. Those who ask themselves these questions and live with them will find these elements a help in remaining faithful to the missions in today's world. . . . The reflections he offers will be a much greater inspiration for missionary activity than the repetition of the usual arguments. The author does not deny the value of the traditional motives, but he adduces new ones that respond to the actual problems.

If Bühlmann speaks of the value of the non-Christian religions as ways of salvation, as channels of human, religious, and salvific values, equivalent remarks can be found in the statements made about evangelization at the episcopal synod by Bishops Parecattil, Picachy, and Fernandes (all three from India), and in the final declaration of the first meeting of the federation of Asian bishops' conferences, which was held in Taipei in 1974. These remarks do not call the missions into question as such, but they do challenge a certain way of ecclesiastical life, above all in the countries that bear the imprint of those great religions.

3. The pastoral method advanced by Fr. Bühlmann is dynamic and Christian: the future of the Church in Asia and the Muslim countries will largely depend upon it. The point is not to renounce the missions but to be loyal to them by taking seriously not only the individuals and their cultures, but also God's whole plan of salvation. The pastoral recommendations given could make the churches in these countries a truly missionary Church and help them out of the ghetto, to bear authentic witness.

There is no lack of pastoral prudence, for the author recommends translating these alternatives into reality in a progressive and complementary fashion. He does not postulate a radical change in all forms. The problem of degrees of membership in the Church was addressed both by the bishops of Asia during their conference in Taipei as well as by the synod of bishops in Rome. This step-by-step approach is a real pastoral necessity, whether to open a progressive path for those seeking the truth or to make it possible for the Church to adapt, inculturate, and acquire a local character.

The concrete forms must always be tested on the spot, but B̈uhlmann has the virtue of pointing out the ways leading to them; he has the imagination to suggest possible solutions.

The reference to the pastoral problems that result from the interest in non-Christian religions, both in Europe and in Asia, is of the highest importance. One need think only of the fact that in Thailand there are more foreign bonzes than foreign missionaries. The only legitimate reaction to this is for the Church to reform itself and to give a practical Christian answer to this quest.

From the practical standpoint, Bühlmann's theological and pastoral principles are not only not harmful, but they provide a stimulus for renewing Christian life, for adapting to present circumstances, for testifying to Jesus Christ. I can say this on the strength of my own experience in Laos, Cambodia, and Thailand. Naturally Bühlmann's ideas need to be prudently implemented, in order to be properly understood and realized, without demoralizing breaks with the past or facile and superficial applications.

4. There is also, no doubt, some language in this book that might shock readers, if taken out of context, and that might perhaps have been smoothed and focused somewhat more than it has been. There are also some over-simplifications. But this affects only the style and manner not the substance of the content. Finally, everything here must also be understood from the altogether personal standpoint of Fr. Bühlmann, a man who has a sincere love for the Church and her mission, which aims not at destruction but at progress. Each one of us must be prepared to undergo questioning, even if that demands humility and openness to conversion. . . .

In conclusion, I can say with a clear conscience that not only are there no errors contrary to the faith in this presentation, not only are there no positions taken that would harm the missions, but that, on the contrary, this book is a positive contribution to missionary theology and practice. Needless to say, it may be a kind of fare that certain people find hard to digest and assimilate the way it was meant to be.

Marcello Zago, OMI

Fr. P. Duprey's equally long expert's report on ecumenical relations with non-Catholics expresses a desire for some more precise phrasing, but he likewise unequivocally attests that there are no doctrinal errors in my book. Would the experts from the Congregation of the Faith back down in the face of so much authority and let the matter rest? Some still more pointed words would be needed to get them to do that. But in the meantime the Roman summer vacation had begun, a time when the Vatican too works at a more leisurely pace. Cardinal Šeper wrote me on July 10, 1976 a preliminary note acknowledging receipt of my letter, asking me to inform him when I would be in Rome that fall for the planned discussion. And he added a pregnant sentence: "Meanwhile we ask you to suspend any new publications or translations of the book in question." What was brewing? I obediently cancelled several articles, but I neither would nor could do that to my various publishers. I could not suspend the sale or production of my book for an indefinite period, since everything had been settled by contract.

One day, in the meantime, there was a delightful entr'acte. I was walking, in a pensive, dreamy mood, along the beach at Ostia, where the diocese of Rome has a large tract of land reserved for priests. There is also a restaurant where you can take your meals and a hotel with 40 private rooms, where you can take a vacation. One would also meet Vatican prelates there, from minor monsignori all the way up to cardinals. Well, I was enjoying the sun, sand, and water, when a gentleman, wearing a bathing suit just as I was, suddenly stood in front of me and said hello, "Ah, you're here too, Father Bühlmann?" It was Archbishop J. Hamer, secretary to the Congregation of the Faith. Naturally we fell to talking about my case. He told me that he himself had not read the book, so I knew that he was not the man behind the whole affair. I mentioned that I had delivered the answer requested of me and that now the ball was in the Congregation's court. He wanted to change the subject. "Let's not talk about your book, but about the sea."

The same Archbishop Hamer informed me on September 21, 1976 that my response had unfortunately been viewed as unsatisfactory. To the general objections that had been raised I had, of course, been able to give only general replies. Now he enclosed in his letter four reports by anonymous experts from the Congregation of the Faith, from which I could now finally gather what

I was concretely being reproved for. The first two reports were rather broad in nature, and raised the general objections that we have already heard. The other two went into particulars.

Very quickly, on September 29, 1976, I answered in a long letter. I demonstrated, above all, the way those experts continually presented the opinions of authors I quoted as if they were statements by me; the way they took utopian sketches and questions that I offered to get the reader thinking and presented them as outright assertions; the way they pulled texts out of context, and then radically abbreviated them, so as to produce heresy; the way they considered truths I didn't stress as already denied. I will not go into details now, because I will repeat certain points in the following, more sharply defined letter. Let me just quote a few examples here.

Five sentences are noted, "in which one does not see the uniqueness of the Catholic Church." I answered: "My book is not a fundamental theology whose goal is to prove the uniqueness of our Church—I take that for granted. This is enough not to deny it, either directly or indirectly, as I in no sense do. Even the checked off sentence, 'We must shift the emphasis from an extreme and exclusive ecclesiology to Christology' has a positive meaning. For example, the well-known manual of dogmatic theology by A. Tanquerey spends 68 pages proving that the Church is a real society, a hierarchical society, and a monarchical society, and then at the end there are two pages about the Church as the Body of Christ and the Bride of Christ: here we have a typical example of an ecclesiology that ought to put the accent on Christology."

I was further reproached for not distinguishing sufficiently the ordained priesthood from the general priesthood of all believers. My answer: "The fact that I speak about the possibility of ordaining married men, who could celebrate the Sunday Eucharist with their communities in addition to the observation that according to a survey only 20 percent of the work carried out by priests could not also be done by lay people, does show quite clearly, I think, that I accept this distinction." I then explained my basic position: "In the face of a changing world, in the face of the totally new realities of the present, I am trying to touch off a pastoral reaction in my readers through recommendations, reflections, and suggestions, often in the form of questions. Such formulations, needless to say, should not be pressed too far nor placed under the theological microscope, but must be understood in their pastoral intent. Merely repeating answers that have been given over and over again, that are self-evident to the Church, is no way to meet the challenges of the contemporary moment. The Church's magisterium has the task of repeating what has always been believed, but theologians have the task and the duty of pressing forward with their research."

One expert took 13 propositions on the topic of ecumenism and claimed they all "contradicted the teaching of the Church," in other words that they were heretical. I first pointed out several fallacies here and then said: "In my conscience and the presence of the Lord I cannot, with the best will in the world, discover any heresies in these thirteen propositions. I grant, however, that they are presented in a non-traditional schema. Here is the real sore point. What does it mean, after all, "to contradict the Church's teaching?" The actual experts in the secretariats for the Unity of Christians and for Non-Christians find in my argument, which pertains directly to their field, nothing inimical to the faith, quite the contrary. This commentator, on the other hand, sees in my book a long list of heresies. Is the Church divided then? Which part should we believe? I don't know whether I am deceiving myself with the suspicion that this report comes from Father Elders, SDV, who was active until recently in the Congregation of the Faith.[21] I do not, it is true, know him personally, but from his articles, which he has long been writing against the new interpretation of religions. In one of his articles on "Christianity and [non-Christian] Cultures" in the *Neue Zeitschrift fur Christentum* (1962, pp. 1-21), we read, for example,

"We maintain that Christianity in its developed form can subsist only within the framework of a culture with essentially the same features of the civilization that is called the Christian West." I believe that not only the theologians of Africa and Asia, but also the majority of European theologians, along with the texts of Vatican II and *Evangelii nuntiandi*, do not share this opinion of Father Elders."

In conclusion, "For the third time now I ask for the opportunity to have a dialogue, not so much to discuss a handful of propositions from my book (though that too, if you still think it necessary), but to present some of the basic assumptions of my book that will, I hope, make clearer what I had in mind and so contribute to a solution of this affair."

Once again six months passed by until finally I was invited to the dialogue that I had been requesting, which was now set for March 10, 1977. Feeling somewhat tense I walked into the Palace of the Santo Ufficio, the erstwhile residence of the Inquisition, which after Vatican II had been renamed the "Congregation of the Faith." It is a gloomy, fortress-like building whose interior and exterior should have been renovated long since. I was led into a rather large room, where Archbishop J. Hamer, the Secretary, Father Miano, the secretary of the Secretariat for Non-Believers, and a monsignor to record the minutes all took their places across from me. Archbishop Hamer opened the meeting, noting with a smile that most theologians shied away from invitations to come here, but I myself had asked to appear. He would now hand me over to Father Miano for the discussion, since he wished to leave for some other work he had. I at once replied that this was not what I had had in mind, I wanted to present my ideas before the appropriate authority. "Take the situation as it is," he said, and disappeared.

A little embarrassed, Fr. Miano now set about opening the dialogue. He more or less repeated the objections that were contained in the expert reports and that I had already answered in writing. I realized immediately that he himself was the author of one of those reports. So for the third time, twice in writing and now orally we went over the same questions and argued over the same points. Needless to say, we could not agree this time either. After about an hour I stood up and said, "I'm through with this. It makes no sense. We're talking past each other, because we stand for different kinds of theologies." And I took my leave.

Four days later, on March 14, 1977 I sent Cardinal Šeper the following letter:

Your Eminence,

I have decided to write you this letter for two reasons.

First of all, in my letter of September 29, 1976 I asked for the "opportunity to have a dialogue, not so much to discuss a handful of propositions from my book. . .but to present some of the basic assumptions of my book that will, I hope, make clearer what I had in mind . . . ." This dialogue took place on March 10, but it was totally different from the one I had asked for. Thus, the only thing left for me to do is to explain myself in this letter.

Secondly, in your letter of March 6, 1976 you mentioned the "often polemical tone" of my book. As early as my response of June 15, 1976, I said that I would be "happy to be able to express my thoughts on this subject in person." Since I did not have the opportunity to do this at the last "dialogue," I am now doing so in writing.

Some Preliminary Remarks:

It is superfluous to stress that I never had, nor do I have now, the intention of abandoning the framework of Catholic faith, though I have no use for the vision of the so-called "Roman school." The Second Vatican Council took the same stance, when it changed the schema on the Church prepared by the "Roman school" into the splendid constitution *Lumen gentium*.

—If I occasionally criticized certain structures of the Church in a "polemical tone," I did this very cautiously. I could have said far more concretely polemical things, but I did not wish to, really because of my love for the Church. But the same love that led me not to say certain things in the book, that is publicly, now leads me to say them privately to the persons most involved. I consider it false to entrust the right to criticize the Church exclusively to the historians, whose work will come too late to help. The Church that continually preaches conversion must herself practice it in all her members and organizations, and in the here and now.

—You are surely aware of the widespread "anti-Roman feeling." Pope Paul VI spoke of it during the penitential service for the Roman Curia during the Holy Year (OR February 23, 1975). Hans Urs von Balthasar has even written a book about it. I have found this hostility to Rome everywhere on my lecture tours and seminars in Europe, Africa, Latin America, and Asia. The problems I have had over my book at the hands of the Roman bureaucrats have given many people a new occasion for feeling this sort of antipathy for certain attitudes of certain representatives of the Roman church. When I speak of this affair, I do so objectively, but also with the biblical "parrhesia," which is a right of all men and women, namely to speak openly and freely. Only the slave lacked this right. But we, who are all children of the same Father, surely have it. I pass over other experiences that I have had with the Roman Curia, limiting myself to the matter of my book. Basically the Roman Curia, and in particular the Propaganda Fide, ought to have drawn up an "ecclesial Pearson report," i.e., a general overview, an analysis of the situation of the Church in the Third World, with an inventory of the present and perspectives on the future. But the Propaganda Fide had neither the inspiration nor the time for that—perhaps it also lacked the courage and the competence. Thus "I took upon myself the risk of making that sort of try, a risk in terms of both scholarly effort and Christian commitment" (Foreword). The subject was immense, and since taking stock also means criticizing, one runs a genuine risk vis-a-vis the Church's many representatives . . . .

As for the affair with the Congregation of the Faith, my grievances are as follows:

1. The long duration: this business has been going on now for a year and a half, and it is still not done with. In your letter of July 10, 1976 you asked me to "suspend meanwhile any new publications or translations of the book in question." But how can I order six publishing houses to put everything on hold for an indefinite period of time? They sell out two or three editions in the first years. Who will compensate them for their losses? I have signed contracts with them and am caught between two obligations.

2. The anonymity, which is widely known and widely deplored: why this anonymity in the Church of all places, which should promote human relations more than the world does, and should show that the faith is something living and personal, not abstract, not concentrated on a proposition? Why shouldn't your experts be identified? Perhaps because (one cannot help suspecting) they in fact have no reputation in the field of theology. Why is Mother Church becoming an anonymous corporation?

3. In my case two anonymous experts (although I had no trouble guessing, from internal and external evidence, who they were) wrote two reports, to which I reacted with restraint in my last letter. But now I am writing the way I think. Now I say that I find these two reports unscholarly and untheological. I do not mean to question the right of your dicastery to have the last word. But in this preparatory phase I regard those two experts as private persons. Anyhow it is distressing to see negotiations with your dicastery beginning in such a disgraceful manner.

So the reports are:

—unscholarly: almost every accusation consists of a proposition from my book, often taken out of context and abbreviated, thereby radicalizing and downright falsifying what I said. Thus, for example, I am chided for proposing: "Today sin is no longer looked upon as an individual matter, but is seen as incarnate in

structures and unjust conditions." To which the commentator
adds, "Sapit Marxismum" (this smells of Marxism). But what I
wrote was: "Today sin is *by and large* no longer viewed . . . ."
Further ascribed to me is the sentence, "We should no longer
think of Christ as the supreme teacher of religion." But I speci-
fied, "We should no longer think of Christ *in the first instance* as
the supreme teacher of religion; rather our catechumens should
do as the Apostles did: travel with him, listen to him, gradually
realize who he is." I have cited still other examples of such abbre-
viation and falsification in my earlier letter.

—untheological: one expert finds 13 propositions relating to
ecumenism and the non-Christian religions that are "contrary to
the teaching of the Church." But Fr. Duprey, whose secretariat
has jurisdiction here and whose competence no one can doubt,
has written that, despite some objections to my statements on
ecumenism, "It is clear that we are dealing here with inaccuracies
of expression and by no means with errors of doctrine." With
regard to the other subject Fr. Zago writes that my ideas on the
non-Christian religions are fully in line with sound contemporary
theology and, pastorally speaking, are not only not harmful but
the only realistic access to these religions. You received these two
reports with my last letter of June 15. In addition Professor A.
Camps, who teaches missiology at Nijmegen, has written that he
is ready to come to Rome at any time to defend my theses.

Hence if the real experts can find nothing contrary to the faith
in my book, what must we think of your expert, who declares
13 propositions contrary to the faith, who is thus continuously
fabricating heresies . . .? Your dicastery does indeed have the task
of ferreting out errors. But this has led some of your members to
want to discover errors, and so of course they do.

Many people, of the sort I would call "normal Christians," have
read my book without finding such errors. . . . These Christians
have written to me and thanked me. . . . If they had seen errors
or, worse yet, heresies in my book, they would not keep on

inviting me to give lectures and seminars. On the contrary, they find my book full of hope, something that helps them to love the Church again.

Unfortunately, last Thursday's conversation brought nothing new. It merely repeated the charges taken from the reports, and I could only repeat my answers, which I had already given in writing. It was fundamentally a confrontation between two different theologies.

Hence even now I can in conscience see no heresies in my book. My remarks can be accounted for:

—within the framework of theological pluralism. On this point I might also refer to the book *Unity in Belief and Theological Pluralism* by the International Commission of Theologians;

—on the basis of the hermeneutical principles that every text is to be understood in its context and that one must also pay attention to its literary genre. My book is not about dogmatic theses but an interpretation from the "perspective of a satellite." Thus it is not legitimate to put every word under the theological microscope, as with a technical monograph;

—on the basis of realities in the world and the Church that demand new reactions. It is not enough to talk about the signs of the times. I do not believe that my "sociology" is as contrary to "theology" as the reports claim. It is precisely in the sociological facts that we must recognize God's hidden plans.

4. Going beyond my own case, I would like to say once more how many Christians are suffering from certain kinds of behavior by the Church of Rome. One need think only of the many new books on the pope and the Vatican, written not just by the enemies of the Church, but on the contrary by people who are lovingly dreaming of another Church.

Have we not made of the Gospel a kind of gnosis, a system of truths, instead of an impulse that changes our lives? A classic example of this was provided by the "highly orthodox" Emperor

Haile Selassie, who was a friend of the West and the pope and at the same time an exploiter of his poor nation and a shame on the Christian world.

I am not saying that religious formulae are meaningless, but I am worried less about heretical propositions than by heretical attitudes that are repugnant to human dignity and honesty, to Vatican II and the Gospel, even when they are put into practice with the best of personal intentions.

It is a historical fact that in the 19th century almost all good theologians had problems with the "Roman school," which too often identified itself with the Holy See, and that they were put on the Index or actually excommunicated. They wanted to interpret the faith in the light of modern science and in a way that modern men and women would find credible (as Vatican II later did), but instead of being encouraged and protected by Rome, they were stabbed in the back, only to be honored 50 or 100 years later, even in Rome. One thinks of Newman, Rosmini, etc.

The situation followed the same pattern in this century until the opening of the Second Vatican Council. We need only recall the names of Chenu, Congar, and De Lubac, or what Karl Rahner said at the first meeting of the International Commission of Theologians in 1969.[22]

We find much the same sort of thing in the area of the liturgy. The Indian liturgy, which was celebrated there for several years, was forbidden by Rome last year; and the Zairean rite has not yet been approved, though the country's bishops have asked for it. To many of us this sort of attitude on the part of Rome seems to run contrary to a great many of the Church's own theological documents. The documents stir up hope, then comes the legislation, which stifles that hope once more in the name of unity (understood as uniformity). The same documents that speak of unity also speak of legitimate pluralism, e.g., SC 37, LG 13, 13, AG passim, EN 63: all very fine texts, but empty words.

When it is claimed that the liturgy must everywhere be the

same, because it is the response of the universal Church to God, I find this statement theologically false. The universal Church, per se, does not exist. There are thousands of local churches, which, all the documents agree, have the right to be themselves and not simply a copy of the Roman church. Together in their manifold diversity they form the truly Catholic Church. The genuine foundations of unity lie much deeper than in mere uniformity. Even though in the Zairean liturgy some externals are shaped differently, the same Christ is present there, the same Gospel, the same faith, a community linked with Rome and with all the churches.

The upshot of all is that, unfortunately, there still exists, instead of authentic dialogue, a communications gap between the authority of the Church and theology, both at the Roman level and below. This leads to increasing isolation of the hierarchy and on the part of the people of God a growing antipathy or indifference.

So, not having had the opportunity in our "discussion" to say these things in the proper place, I have taken the liberty of doing this in writing. I do not intend to publish this letter, and I hope I shall never be forced to do that.[23]

Having said all that—I realize that I am an unpleasant man to have in the Church, but not, I hope, a harmful one—I declare my readiness to contribute to the solution of my case in every acceptable manner. . . . I thank God, who has given me such splendid work to do in the service of my order and of the Church.

With cordial greetings and best wishes, I remain, yours fraternally

Fr. Walbert Bühlmann

I addressed the envelope to Archbishop Hamer, the secretary, for relaying the letter to the cardinal, and I added a note to him: "Perhaps it would be useful, if we could meet for ten minutes sometime to find a human and evangelical solution to this case. Don't you think so?" That same week I got a telephone call and an invitation from him. We had an open and brotherly conversation. I told him: "You can do me no harm. I am only sorry for the Church, which has once again made itself look bad with this affair." The archbishop told me that he had been a student in Freiburg (Switzerland) at the time that I was submitting my doctoral dissertation on Christian terminology in the languages of the missions. He urged me to go back to writing that sort of "scholarly," as opposed to "prophetic," books. I replied, "What if Jesus had just written scholarly books?"

One month later, on April 22, 1977, the last letter about this business came from Cardinal Šeper. The Congregation had evidently noticed that it was not easy to deal with me, and that it was time to clear up the case without losing face in the process. Naturally they did not admit that their experts had been made to look foolish, but stuck firmly to their guns. But in any event the thing came to an end.

Reverend Father,

With regard to your letter of March 14, and to the informal conversations that took place with you, this Congregation informs you of its opinion in this matter as follows:

Above all, I am anxious to tell you that no one wished to deny your good intentions or your zeal, no more than we wanted to condemn your book as such, containing as it does much good and useful material. We simply wished to clarify individual points (and not merely sentences taken out of context) that are, after all, debatable, to which we repeatedly tried to direct your attention and which remain ambiguous, even after your oral and written explanations: ecumenism, non-Christian religions, the difference between priests and believers.

On the other hand, you yourself have several times admitted a certain imprecision and ambiguity in a number of statements. This only increases the possibility of their being misunderstood. But you know that in writing a book, one should above all think of the readers and therefore avoid unclear and equivocal passages, even though these may seem clear to the author.

In your judgment the only thing at issue is a difference in basic theological approaches. This dicastery does not share that opinion. Its particular concern is not to defend a "theology" of its own, but rather to take the standpoint of the Church's magisterium, whose vocation is to promote the faith and to defend its purity.

In any case, even if the only thing at issue *were* theological opinions, it does not seem opportune to adopt debatable positions and make questionable recommendations in a book that is widely disseminated and intended mainly for missionaries and other pastoral workers.

That is why this Congregation would ask you to demonstrate concretely the attachment to the Church that you have repeatedly stressed, by making a clear presentation of these controversial points in any new editions of your book or in other future publications.

Yours truly,

Franc. Card. Šeper, Pref.

And so I was still caught between two loyalties, between the competent experts—acknowledged even by the Vatican—who supported me, and the "magisterium," which appealed to "experts" with no credibility, who condemned me. Since my case really was not about questions of faith, I believed in my conscience that I could side with the genuine experts. The Congregation of the Faith, practically speaking, took the position that one was permitted to argue only for "sure doctrine," to tread only the beaten track, but not to venture on winding paths into new territory. Or to borrow an image from the Gospel, one could only continue to carry the old wine in old skins, rather than filling new skins with new wine (cf. Lk 5:37). One might not stimulate readers to think for themselves and expect of them a certain amount of discrimination, so as to know by themselves what to make of new ideas and proposals. With the best will in the world I could not accept such a viewpoint. In my answer of May 5, 1977, however,

I no longer wanted to bother with this controversy.

Your Eminence,

Thank you very much for your letter of April 22, which I—
thank God—consider the conclusion of our negotiations. After
all is said and done, it has been a good experience for me to
see how one can come through an open dialogue to a fraternal
solution.

Needless to say, I recognize the concern of your dicastery for
promoting the faith and protecting its purity. Nevertheless, this
point of view must always be confronted with the reality of rapid
social changes and the unparalleled progress of the sciences, so
that the faith may be credible to men and women even today
and so that the Church can carry out its salvific function even
in the world and not live an isolated existence, barricaded in an
ivory tower and hence ignored by the world. That was the most
important message of my book.

Appropriately enough, as a member of the catechetical commission of the Propaganda Fide I have recently been studying
two reports from two bishops' conferences in Africa, which were
sent to Rome for the next episcopal synod. They both independently agree that a Church which is too traditionalist and back-
ward-looking risks losing touch with the realities of today's world
and thereby further widening the fatal cleft between religion and
concrete life. The Church, they say, should not only teach but
listen. "We must have an examination of conscience: To what
extent have we remained true to God and man with our presentation of the gospel message? To what extent have we put forward
Christ's ideas—or rather imposed our own? Have we obeyed his
one new commandment—or rather multiplied our laws? God's
method is clear: He has made himself one of us, in order to reach
us. He has spoken the language of mankind, not simply to be
heard but also to be understood. Thus we are left with no other
way but that of the Incarnation . . . ." Fundamentally these bishops believe that what we need is not a new catechesis, but a new

Church.

As always, I shall go on, together with so many bishops, priests, and lay people, abiding by my concern for a contemporary answer from the Church to the challenges of the kairos, and at the same time maintaining my loyalty to the authentic message of the Church, as you have amiably and insistently asked me to do.

Best wishes. Fraternally yours,

Father Walbert Bühlmann

Thus my case wound up without doing me much harm. In the end there was no more talk of "heresies," but only of ambiguities, of statements that *might* be misunderstood, of prudent regard for readers, for whose sake any kind of "scandalum pusillorum" (offense to children) had to be avoided. But my book had never been intended anyway for people stuck fast in childish faith, but for mature, responsible Christians. At all events, the whole affair showed that nowadays one can fight and defend oneself honestly, something that was not yet possible in the '50s. But in the final analysis it does leave a bad taste in one's mouth to think that such conservative experts, men so out of touch with real life, are called in to consult for the Church's supreme authority on matters of faith. One extremely respected person in the Vatican said to me five years ago, that from what he had seen, "Unfortunately in the Congregation of the Faith too many people carry a lot of weight without having the faintest idea of modern theology."

Yet in this instance the Congregation could have called on some thoroughly competent experts. I am thinking not only of certain of its consultants, but above all the International Commission of Theologians that was requested by the episcopal synod of 1967 and then set up by Pope Paul VI in 1969, "in order to help the Holy See and especially the Congregation of the Faith in dealing with doctrinal questions of great importance." Since then this commission of around 40 theologians meets yearly. The members assign themselves a subject or receive one proposed by the Congregation of the Faith, but they were quick to notice that their findings had little effect. They were unable to influence the basic attitude of the Congregation, no real dialogue has taken place, both parties have nothing in common. Like the expert commissions of the Propaganda Fide, this commission of theologians remained a facade that was pointed to with pride, but behind which there wasn't a whole lot. Their reports are frequently met with a counter-report by an anonymous "specialist" or simply ignored. It is just not yet part of Rome's style to do business with commissions. What counts in Rome is still, first and foremost, authority, not competence. Rome still pays homage, theologically speaking, to the monarchical principle and believes that any influence by the people of God on the hierarchy is by nature repugnant to the Church. These are the sort of complaints people active in the Commission of Theologians were still making a few years ago. I wonder whether things have improved in the meantime.

3. Taking the Young Churches Seriously

After my last letter of May 5, 1977 I had five years of peace from the Congregation of the Faith until 1982, when a second clash developed. The occasion for it was a longish article on "Marriage and the Family in Africa" that I wrote in connection with the 1980 synod of bishops on marriage and the family, in order to stress the concerns of the young churches.[24] For the reader to understand the conflict I shall first have to summarize some ideas from the article.

Starting out from the fact that on the average fewer than half the marriages of African Christians are contracted in church—and in recent years the numbers have been rapidly declining—and that in many places 70 percent or more of the adults are barred from the sacraments because of irregular marriages, one has to ask whether there might not be something wrong with this sort of church discipline. The Church is not there, after all, to serve an elite group, but for all God's people.

As early as 1978 the bishops of Africa had held a symposium on this topic in Nairobi, without making very much progress. Now the episcopal synod of 1980 was to be an occasion for them to force a breakthrough. The key point at stake was a new pastoral approach to polygamy and "progressive" marriage.

No one will dispute the fact that the future basically belongs to monogamy. Monogamy corresponds better to modern thinking about the equality of man and woman, and especially to the exalted level of unity that the sacrament creates between two people. But that doesn't answer the pastoral question facing the Church during the period of transition, namely what is to be done with polygamous catechumens. We can understand the protest registered by Bishop Michael Ppakula (Liberia) in the name of the bishops' conferences of Gambia, Liberia, and Sierra Leone: "In the text of the Nairobi symposium it says on this subject: 'On the one hand, we are very anxious to uphold the ideal of monogamous Christian marriage and to encourage everyone to live according to this ideal. On the other hand, we sympathize with those men and women who, in keeping with tradition and their religion, live in polygamy but seriously wish to be baptized, in most cases because their children have already been baptized.' The current regulations of canon law do not solve the problem. We hope that the sympathy expressed in Nairobi for the polygamists who would like to be baptized is felt here too, and that the problem can be resolved."

Other bishops too spoke along these same lines, while Bishop Francis A. Arinze of Omitsha (Nigeria), who is now a cardinal and president of the Vatican Secretariat for Non-Christians, categorically argued the opposite position: "Clarity in doctrine is essential. Priests and theologians should make it clear that polygamy runs contrary to the Christian ideal of marriage. They ought not to indulge in ambiguous discussions and tell the Africans that the problem is still being studied. Polygamy should simply be condemned." Here we see a fundamental error, the inability to distinguish between a doctrinal and a pastoral standpoint.

With regard to "progressive" marriage, one must distinguish between patriarchal pastoral culture, where girls always entered marriage as virgins, and matriarchal farming culture, in which the young man, after a suitable agreement had been reached between the two clans, built a hut on the girl's farm and simply started living with the girl. Over the course of a few years he had to show that he could work, that he treated the girl well, honored his parents-in-law, and that he and she could have children together. If all that went off smoothly, and if in the meantime the bride-price had been paid, the marriage would be celebrated in the tribe. For the Church this has up till now counted merely as public concubinage, as a state of mortal sin, and the young Christians who were following their tribal tradition were excluded from the sacraments during the best years of their Christian maturation. It was and is a terrible burden not only for the missionaries, but for those young Christians too. For some years now a new approach has been in the making. The issue was not to decide which was the better way to marriage, but simply to note the fact that the African way was not so bad and that the Church's better judgment might find it compatible with the Gospel. Consequently, the "pastoral solution" was increasingly put into practice, meaning that one did not come right out and announce from the pulpit that such people living together could henceforth take the sacraments, but the individual case was laid before the local church, their specific community. The local church would then say: "These people are fundamentally two good Christians, they live in accord with the customs of our tribe. And so we admit them to the sacraments." What should the bishops say to this practice: They wanted to get a clear view of it in Rome.

Speaking on behalf of the bishops' conferences of the Congo, the Central African Republic, and Chad, Archbishop Barthelemy Batantu (Brazzaville) argued that these steps toward marriage should not be disparagingly characterized as "concubinage, trial marriage, or irregular unions," but should be called "progressive marriage." This, he said, has always been the traditional and good way to marriage. Couldn't the Church recognize this way as legitimate and hence admit the young people involved in it to the sacraments, under certain conditions? What was the role of the local bishops' conferences in this matter? This pointed question was to be presented to the episcopal synod.

Bishop Andre Kaseba (Zaire) gave a still more profound justification for this way: A life process, he argued, goes forward step by step, no stage may be left out. Just as the catechumenate of baptism leads to baptism step by step and in principle already anticipates the grace of baptism in faith, so with this catechumenate of marriage. All this has already been integrated into marriage, which is not effected in a momentary ceremony but in an evolutionary process. Consequently, in the name of his bishops' conference, he asked the Church to recognize this way and to fit it out with the right sort of liturgical solemnities. Three other bishops spoke in a similar vein, each in the name of his bishops' conference.

A year later, in 1981, the final document was issued by Pope John Paul II under the title *Familiaris consortio*. I shall limit myself here to the two questions I have already raised. With respect to polygamy the pope speaks unequivocally: he totally rejects it. But the bishops were, in fact, concerned not so much with the theoretical principle as with the pastoral problem: Can one, while fully acknowledging monogamy as the norm, permit a polygamous catechumen—on an individual basis, by way of exception—to be baptized? One cannot and must not expect a man to get a divorce and leave wives (except for one) together with their children out on the street. Do we really have to condemn polygamy, which was tolerated in the Old Testament and is clearly not unquestionably contrary to natural law? Do we have to judge it as so un-Christian that no path can lead from polygamy to baptism—although of course it would always be assumed that the path cannot go in the opposite direction, i.e., that no baptized Christian can become a polygamist again.

With regard to progressive marriage the pope does not even discuss the special case of Africa, but throws everything together into the same pot under the heading, "trial marriage, irregular situations, free liaisons," which he rejects, unsurprisingly. But in taking this stance the pope has not done justice to the special situation in Africa.

After discussing the questions of the African bishops and the pope's answers, which were basically no answers at all, in the third part of the article I tried to suggest some starting points for reflection and to develop three pastoral principles that might help progress along. The principle of the "sensus fidelium" does not, of course, mean that everything done by the majority is a priori good, but that the magisterium should feel continually challenged by the believing lay people who try to live by their consciences, and that it should not think that, thanks to the "eternal verities" it already possesses the truth in advance, that it has always had the truth in its entirety.

The principle of gradualism can be applied to the process of marriage. It is not a question here of "all or nothing," but of growth, of what is possible here and now. In this case the sacrament of marriage is no longer seen as a single ritual moment but as the conclusion and culmination of a two to three year process of growth. As a matter of fact, in making their confession on the eve of being married in the church, after some years of exclusion from the sacraments, African Christians seldom accuse themselves of cohabitation. They do not look upon this as a sin, much as the foreign missionaries have claimed that it is. But when the young men have had relations with another girl during the same time, they confess that as a sin. Hence it is time to overcome the distance separating a legal morality from a morality that is autonomous in the best sense.

The principle of pastoral solutions, which is also called *epieikeia*, holds that in individual cases and under certain circumstances one may and must dare to make an exception from the acknowledged general norm. This can be justified by the following considerations:

—Laws that are supposed to be valid everywhere in the world are so general that they cannot pay sufficient heed to some individual cases. It is thus not merely permissible but obligatory, in individual cases, to find solutions more sensible and appropriate than those foreseen by the general law. In this way the harshness of the law is mitigated, and the pastoral care of Christ and the Church finds expression.

—On the basis of freedom of religion and conscience, which was officially recognized by the Council, we can distinguish between an orientation toward the law, where one simply asks what the law says and then obeys without question (which used to be the attitude of the majority of Catholics) and an orientation toward conscience or the Gospel, where one asks, what one's honest conscience says, or what Jesus would do in such a case. But Jesus, without calling the law of the Sabbath into question, nevertheless repeatedly transgressed it. The reader of the Gospel actually gets the impression that Jesus sought out opportunities to heal on the Sabbath, in order to provoke the scribes and Pharisees, in order to teach them a nobler lesson, namely that man was not made for the Sabbath, but the Sabbath for man (Mk 2:27). The same is true of all laws. State authority, unfortunately, ignores the conscientious orientation; it judges on the basis of external compliance with the law. But the Church cannot help recognizing this higher, evangelical orientation, which befits the mature Christian, even though those in authority generally do not like to see people following their conscience and the Spirit rather than the law. This tension must be endured on both sides.

On the strength of this principle, we can say something new on the subject of the polygamous catechumens. For all the recognition due to the law of monogamy one may administer baptism to such people, if after conversation with them and with the Christian community one thinks it good—always presupposing that scandal and rifts are avoided. Because for the sake of the greater good of unity, so as not to scandalize our brother, we should not do certain things that we otherwise would be allowed to, as Paul suggested to the Corinthians (1 Cor 8:1-13). Fortunately in Africa one need not worry about scandal if one admits a good polygamist to baptism or if one ceases to bar from the sacraments young Christians involved in "progressive marriage." On the contrary, a sigh of relief will spread through the ranks of African Christians, after having to endure for so long a contrary attitude on the part of the Church. Of course, the transition from the old to the new practice should be prepared in a pastorally intelligent manner. And, of course, it has to be admitted nowadays that the good old tribal order has already been largely destroyed; and even in Africa much freer notions of love and marriage are coming into use, so that with these new solutions, which presuppose that tribal order, we are coming rather late, if not too late, onto the scene.

Those are some of the thoughts that I discussed at much greater length in my article. On the occasion of the pope's second trip to Africa in 1982 I presented some ideas from the article—e.g., the case of the polygamous catechumens, who under certain circumstances could be baptized—in a newspaper article. I was aware that Christians fixated on traditional doctrine could be shocked by such thinking. Nonetheless perhaps one has to raise such questions on account of the pastoral emergency.

In any event a certain Herr O. Gilgin from Zurich was stung by this article, as if it were a tarantula. He immediately wrote me a letter asking me whether I thought polygamists could be baptized. I answered: In principle no, in individual cases, under certain circumstances, yes. A few more letters followed, a kind of theological fisticuffs. Then on May 8, 1982 he sent the following article to my minister general, with a copy to Cardinal J. Ratzinger, of the Congregation for Christian Doctrine:

Dear Reverend Father General,

I am venturing to call your attention to the following publications of Fr. Walbert Bühlmann, of Rome, which I regard as misleading [there follows an exact listing of the objectionable pieces].

In the *Neue Zurcher Nachrichten* and, worse yet, in the *Schweizerische Kirchenzeitung* Fr. Bühlmann maintains that the baptism of polygamists is permissible, and makes the untenable distinction between an outmoded (as he sees it) "doctrinaire" point of view and a "pastoral" one, which should be employed today.

In his book *If God Goes to All Men*, Fr. Walbert Bühlmann defends an untenably optimistic view of salvation.

Fr. Balthasar Huppi, OFMCap has answered, in the *Schweizerische Kirchenzeitung* no. 15, April 15, 1982, the article by Fr. Bühlmann, "Marriage and the Family in Africa." The books of Fr. Walbert Bühlmann are given an extensive critical review by Rev. Dr. Athanasius Kroger, OSB, Benedictine of the Abbey of Gerleve, in the periodical *Theologisches*, a supplement to the *Offerten-Zeitung fur die katholische Geistlichkeit Deutschlands*, no. 140, December, 1981.[25]

The article, "Journey to the African Giant," led me to exchange letters with Fr. Bühlmann. This correspondence, however, failed to bring about satisfactory results. I therefore turn to you, as the superior of the order, because I am of the opinion that Fr. B¨uhlmann is spreading serious errors, which are all the more dangerous in that he is a missionary theologian. Also, the readers of a newspaper such as the *Neue Zurcher Nachrichten* might get the idea that the Capuchin Fr. Bühlmann was protected by superiors in expressing his indefensible notions.

As a layman I am surprised and shocked by the ease with which many contemporary theologians skip over the question of truth or at least risk deviating from the truth with their ideas. And this in full view of the public!

I recommend this matter to your care and send you, Reverend Father General, my cordial and respectful greetings.

Otto Gilgin

In his reply of May 29, 1982, a copy of which was likewise sent to Cardinal Ratzinger, Fr. Pascal Rywalski wrote that he did not wish to get involved in the details of the discussion, but to deliver a broad statement of principle: "First of all, thank you very much for your letter. It attests to your concern for the purity of truth, which in fact is nowadays all too often lightly gambled with. Thank you too for the confidence that you have in me as the minister general of the Capuchin order. I ask you now to maintain this trust in me, even though, drawing upon my better knowledge of the situation, I defend Fr. Bühlmann against your objections. . . . I admit that not all the ideas which Fr. Bühlmann stands for can just be accepted without further ado. Even in our house we tease him now and then about his avant garde attitude. He would be the last person in the world simply to demand blind allegiance. He is ready for dialogue, for clarification, and on individual points he accepts correction. What he wants, though, is not hasty charges of heresy, but respect for another's convictions, and an objective exchange of views. For my part I can assure you that his ideas do not offend against the faith of the Church, provided one understands this faith correctly and in a modern-day sense. . . ."

As might have been expected, Herr Gilgin was not satisfied with this reply, and he showed it. On June 7, 1982 he wrote back, again sending a copy to Cardinal Ratzinger: "My complaints against Fr. Walbert Bühlmann refer specifically to his published opinion that it is permissible to baptize polygamists, and beyond that his blanket optimism about salvation. After raising these two concrete issues I have not gotten an objective answer from Fr. Bühlmann nor now from you either, but only general explanations that leave the issues at stake untouched. What you have written to me amounts to "full support" of Fr. Bühlmann. Your statements refer not to the matter at hand but to the person involved. . . . All the positive things you advance in his behalf are irrelevant to the issue. The decisive point here is what the Church's magisterium says. In your letter you write: I can assure you that his ideas do not offend against the faith of the Church, provided one understands this faith correctly and in a modern-day sense. . . . Should you mean by 'modern-day sense' that the faith could or must signify something different from what it used to, then I would emphatically repudiate this view . . . ."

Now the spark had ignited in the Congregation of the Faith. On June 15, 1982 Cardinal Ratzinger sent his best wishes to the newly appointed minister general Fr. Flavio Carraro and at the same time recommended that he keep an eye on Fr. Walbert B¨uhlmann, since the latter had advanced erroneous opinions in his article on marriage and the family in Africa. In his answer of July 11 the minister general said that he had spoken with Fr. B¨ühlmann about the matter, and that I was prepared to explain the case in person to the Congregation of the Faith.

On September 23, 1982 the reply came from the cardinal: "In thanking you for your kind response, I hasten to inform you that this dicastery gladly accepts the proposal of a conversation with Fr. Bühlmann in this Congregation. However, in view of the importance of the question, I ask you to be present together with me at this discussion."

Thus I had the prospect of a second direct confrontation with the Congregation of the Faith, as well as with its new prefect, Cardinal Ratzinger. I had met him for the first time three years earlier in Munich, when I was giving lectures to the clergy of that city. At the time I handed him a copy of my pointed letter to the Congregation of the Faith and remarked: "As a cardinal-theologian, you will sooner or later surely have dealings yourself with the Congregation of the Faith. I would simply like to bring to your attention how things are still going on over there." How would they go on now, when he himself was the man in charge?

The discussion was provisionally set for the last week in October. When I phoned on Monday, October 22 to ask when it would take place, Cardinal Ratzinger's private secretary informed me that it would very hard to say, since the cardinal's schedule was already filled up. He would call back. On October 29, however, I was informed that it had been decided a discussion was no longer necessary, a letter would be written instead. But then on October 29 the cardinal announced that "After renewed consideration of the case, this dicastery judges it appropriate that the agreed-upon discussion should take place in the agreed-upon form, that is, in your presence, Father."

But at one time the cardinal, then the minister general, then I myself were absent from Rome, the meeting did not take place until March 8, 1983. It began on March 8, 1983, at 9 o'clock in the morning and ended around 10:30. On one side of the table sat the cardinal, flanked by Archbishop J. Hamer and Monsignor Mosl, on the other myself, Fr. Flavio Carraro, the minister general, and Fr. Victrizius Veith, the German-speaking assistant general. After a brief, friendly greeting the cardinal waded right into the controverted questions. Later I drew up a memorandum that I also sent to the cardinal as a record of our conversation. Thus it became an official document, which I reproduce here:

Ratzinger: Your article says that under certain circumstances polygamy could be tolerated, and, second, that in Africa people on the way to Christian marriage could have marital relations. The tradition of the Catholic Church and *Familiaris consortio* say the opposite. You, on the other hand, seem to be undertaking a separation of doctrine and practice. Can you speak to that?

Bühlmann: Thank you for the opportunity to say a few things in my defense. Of course, I can't say in a brief time more than I argued at length in the article. This article, anyhow, has got solid backing. Since I knew that it was a bold treatment of a delicate issue, I wanted it to be read in manuscript by Fr. Pascal Rywalski, the minister general, and Fr. Benedikt Frei, the vicar general, as well as by Prof. B. Haring and Prof. K. Kriech, a Swiss expert on ethics and morality. Nobody had any objections to it. I also have Africa on my side. . . . What I argue for in this article is basically no different from what five African bishops have already proposed, in the name of their bishops' conferences.

But I should now like to discuss not just symptoms but root conditions, and explain the context for writing this article and others like it, namely because the interests of the young churches are not represented in Rome. This was perfectly evident in 1973 when the decree was issued establishing the four Eucharistic prayers in the Missale Romanum as the only permissible ones. At that time I went to Archbishop Bugnini, the secretary of the Congregation of the Liturgy and a recognized expert in the field, and complained that now the Africans and Asians had been cheated and were caught between two loyalties, loyalty to Rome or to their own culture. Monsignor Bugnini said: "Father, you are 100 percent right. I myself argued the same point. But look, we are in a system of congregations here, and the cardinals set the tone." A similar case occurred in 1975, when Bishop G. Dupont of Pala (Chad) wished to speak with the pope about the possibility, for example, of Africans being allowed to use manioc and palm wine for the Eucharist. He was twice denied an audience and told he should speak with the Propaganda Fide. It gave him only the familiar, prefabricated answers. The bishop handed in his resignation, which was promptly accepted.

The Propaganda Fide speaks only for the Roman position vis-a-vis the young churches, but not the position of the young churches vis-a-vis Rome. The inability to respond to other points of view comes from the fact that there are no experts at the Propaganda Fide, only administrators. Not one single person in the whole bureau could be called a missiologist or theologian. In addition, the expert commissions called for by the Council (AG 29) have indeed been set up, but they have no function at all. The letter of the Council has been carried out, but not its spirit. Finally, the cardinal at the head of the Congregation is a man who combines harsh authoritarianism with astonishing incompetence and ignorance. His leadership is marked by an absolutely preconciliar theology, so that for years now missionary institutes have not taken the Propaganda Fide seriously. . . . You now understand that this situation has led me to speak out all the more loudly for the interests of the young churches.

Ratzinger: Thank you for the information, even though I would prefer not to adopt all your views. But let's return to the real subject here. You seem to be making a split between doctrine and practice. You also distinguish between a legal and an evangelical orientation. But that is strongly reminiscent of the Lutheran dialectic of the law vs. freedom.

Bühlmann: Now that we are in the Luther Year [the 500th anniversary of his birth], and the Reformer is being called, even by Catholics, the "common teacher and father of the faith," I believe that we should no longer be afraid of learning something from him—especially since Pope John Paul II quoted Luther's commentary on Romans during his trip to Germany. Today, after all, it is clear that the ultimate norm is the Gospel and not the law of the Church. This conclusion can be drawn, in purely human terms, from *Dignitatis humanae* and, in theological terms as well, from *Dei verbum*. When the Council failed to focus more clearly on the judicial function of Scripture with regard to the Church tradition, many commentators on the Council, among others Joseph Ratzinger, deplored it. He wrote: "We can only describe as a regrettable omission the fact that this has been neglected" (LThK, The Second Vatican Council, II, 524 f.)

Ratzinger: Furthermore, you seem to go too far in seeing the Church's tradition as merely "western," thereby relativizing it. Yet it is the tradition of the Church as such.

Bühlmann: That is the key problem of the contemporary Church. In the documents of Vatican II and in *Evangelii nuntiandi* the right and even the duty of inculturating the Gospel is very clearly expressed. But as soon as we try to translate that into practice, Rome begins to put up a fight. So long as the Church was at home only within the western cultural sphere, it was to some extent tolerable to identify unity with uniformity. Today when the bulk of the Church's numbers live in Latin America, Africa, and Asia, the problem of inculturation becomes a fiercely urgent one. We are standing just on the threshold of the third millenium, when we shall experience what it means to be a Church on six continents.

Ratzinger: We have no interest at all in having a host of independent churches, of sects, with each one doing whatever it likes.

Bühlmann: But I hope we get a host of local churches that, under the supervision of the bishops and the bishops' conferences, go their own way and show forth unity in the variety of their forms. That will only enrich the Catholic Church . . . .

I would like to present two further basic reflections. You, your eminence, were at the time that you belonged to the International Commission of Theologians the main author of the theses on "The Unity of the Faith and Theological Pluralism." Moreover, the right to dissent in the Church has been recognized in *Octagesimo anno* and by the papal commission "Justitia et Pax" . . .I believe, therefore, that I am justified with my ideas within the framework of theological pluralism and the right to dissent in disciplinary matters.

Ratzinger: Evidently we haven't been able fully to convince each other of our different positions. I would like just like to ask everyone to say a final word, should you wish to.

Fr. Flavio Carraro: It may be that Fr. Walbert is somewhat lacking in pastoral prudence when he presents his ideas to the people [Fr. Flavio obviously thought that the *Schweizerische Kirchenzeitung* was a popular weekly, which is not the case]. I have never doubted his love for the Church. My predecessor, Fr. Pascal, who knew him better, had a very high opinion of him. In principle I agree that in individual cases the biblical and juridical viewpoints can diverge from one another.

Fr. Viktrizius Veith: I too think that some of the statements by Fr. Walbert in this exposition were somewhat exaggerated.

But one could perceive in the positions of both sides a great love for the Church. I likewise agree that there can be a dynamic development from certain traditional views to more modern ideas.

Archbishop Hamer: Fr. Bühlmann separates too sharply faith and "western" tradition. And one cannot solve individual cases by violating the general doctrine.

Bühlmann: First of all, thank you very much for this fraternal and sympathetic conversation. It will remain in my memory as a good one. Then, I would like to ask that too much attention should not be paid to extreme right wing elements. Herr Gilgin of Zurich, a reactionary Catholic in touch with the same sort of people in Germany, denounced my article. By listening to such groups, one encourages them to write still more. They do the Church damage. And Rome could compromise its good name and appear to be acting in a preconciliar fashion.

Ratzinger: I had no idea that Herr Gilgin had denounced this article. I read it in complete innocence.

Bühlmann: I would like to say one last thing. I am still working on another book, together with Karl Rahner and J. B. Metz, about church models for the year 2000. In doing this it is naturally unavoidable to criticize certain existing structures. Besides, I am no longer at the general curia and I am also somewhat tired of battling with the Vatican Curia. In the future I would rather turn to other subjects, and so we shall have peace.

Walbert Bühlmann

I was glad that both my confreres had the courage to declare that "in individual cases the biblical and juridical viewpoints can diverge from one another" and "there can be a dynamic development from certain traditional views to more modern ideas." Indirectly they were granting that I was right in my attempt to take a fresh view of certain things and to give them a fresh interpretation.

Looking back on the discussion itself, I had to acknowledge

that for all the amiability there had been no real dialogue, no real exchange of thought, but a onesided question-and-answer game. The cardinal raised four questions, had me answer them, but then let the answer stand until at the end he came right out and said we had not been able fully to convince each other. Thus one position faced off against another, without an attempt to get closer to the other side, if possible in a reciprocal manner.

As for content, there were two main points which Archbishop Hamer nailed down in a negative way, at the end: One was not allowed to separate the faith from "western" tradition, nor solve individual cases against the grain of general doctrine. As always, I could not say yes to this sort of approach. I had the impression that my partners had still not yet seriously taken into account the fact that the western Church has become a world Church. They did not realize that this must and will have consequences, even if the "western" Church doggedly insists on thinking that the historical form it has taken on is the only possible and legitimate one. The logic of history runs in an entirely different direction, namely: If these concrete forms of the Church could arise in western history, then a corresponding variant to it can and should be fashioned on other continents and in other historical epochs. The cardinal was right to worry about getting a host of independent churches, with each one doing what it liked. At this moment there are something like 8,000 such churches in Africa alone. This phenomenon is precisely a result of the official churches' still going about too often dressed in western garb and not paying enough heed to African sensibility. Thus it would be a fatally false conclusion to persist all the more stubbornly in the Roman party line. The only correct response readily suggests itself: boldly to undertake the Africanization of Christianity, under the supervision of the local bishops, of course. We are barely at the starting point of real inculturation. Soon it will no longer be western theologians and authorities, "outsiders," who say what will do in Africa and Asia. Instead, it will be theologians and bishops of the young churches, who are "insiders" and who also have responsibility and a sense of the faith, deciding on what is the best theological, liturgical, and disciplinary way to be followed there. This pressure from history can be resisted for a while longer, but then it will break through with all the greater violence.

When I take the principle of pastoral solutions seriously, then I am not simply appealing to the great number of pastorally minded priests who practice it, but also to the doctrine of *epieikeia*, which down through the whole history of morality has been recognized as self-evident and praised as a "virtue of freedom." This pastoral solution of individual cases thus does not take place simply "in violation of general doctrine," but in accordance with another aspect of accepted teaching, on the strength of the ecclesiological reality that the Church is not only a "magistra" (teacher), but also a "mater" (mother), who sympathetically mitigates the rigor of the law. Even the new Code of Canon Law manages to recall as the last canon, as a sort of principle of interpretation for the whole, the old saying, "Suprema lex animarum salus" (the highest law is the salvation of souls). Hence might not the separate positions move toward a rapprochement? If that was not accomplished at this discussion, it will happen thanks to the power of life, and for a change history will take note of it.

But was my base not closed after all? The fact that "we haven't been able fully to convince each other" led me to expect that the episode would have a sequel. And on April 6, 1983 the cardinal did write to the minister general, first asking him to thank me for the "memorandum" and then handing down his verdict in clear language:

Reverend Father,

. . .I am anxious to take this opportunity to invite you, Father, in your capacity as minister general, to keep an eye on the doctrinal opinions of Fr. Bühlmann.

In the course of the discussion it became increasingly clear that despite all the author's good intentions his thinking is based on a false distinction between the pastoral and doctrinal aspect of theology, as though pastoral proposals or solutions did not have to agree with doctrine and take their inspiration from it. This fundamental notion finds a special application in the area of inculturation, for which the author has offered concrete suggestions (e.g., for the problems of polygamy and so-called African marriage), without taking into account that the certainly justified and necessary demands of pluralism must always be contained within the bounds of the necessary unity of faith.

An opportunity to exercise the above-mentioned vigilance by applying the norms that define the granting of the imprimatur is offered to you, Father, in the book that Fr. Bühlmann is in the process of writing, in collaboration with K. Rahner and J.B. Metz. About this book he himself has said that "it is naturally unavoidable to criticize certain existing structures."

Best wishes. Yours truly,

Joseph Cardinal Ratzinger

Fr. Flavio Carraro, the minister general, sent me on April 30, 1983 a photocopy of the letter from Cardinal Ratzinger. I answered him on May 9.

Dear Fr. Flavio,

Thanking you for passing on to me Cardinal Ratzinger's letter of April 6. I cannot, in fact, take any pleasure from its humiliating command to place me under surveillance, in other words, under a guardian's care. And this on account of an article in which I see no need, even now, to retract a single sentence. Besides, the article, as you know, was read by Fr. Pascal Rywalski and Benedikt Frei, as well as by two experts, Professors B. Haring and Kajetan Kriech, which shows that normal people in the Church nowadays think as I do. I cannot fully accept the content of a letter that reproaches me for making a "false distinction between the pastoral and doctrinal aspect of theology. . . ."

In addition the cardinal tries to hinder my criticism of certain structures in the Church, which is to be expressed in the book I

am writing with K. Rahner and J.B. Metz, a book that will be
cast entirely in the mode of futurology. By that I mean that it
aims not at confirming the status quo, but at sketching alternative
models of the Church based on the signs of the time and always
following the lead of Vatican II. I cannot accept the suppression
of the human right of free speech in the Church . . . . Everything
depends now on the way in which you exercise the "vigilance" the
letter asks for. If you appoint a censor like Fr. Viktrizius Veith
or Fr. Pascal Rywalski to examine my text, I can be confident,
because those men will judge my reflections in the spirit of the
truth that sets us free. In that case I would be ready for dialogue
and cooperation to make the compromise solutions that might
prove necessary. If, on the other hand, the censor should be
someone ruled by the spirit of servile obedience and given to
narrow notions of inculturation as well as to fear of criticism from
the Congregation of the Faith, then I reserve the right, in the light
of my conscience and "in the Lord," to go my way, taking all the
risks and consequences, and saying that we must obey God rather
than man.

At the close of our past general chapter you announced that
you "wished to encourage the prophetic men in the Order." Here
is a concrete opportunity to keep your word. Not that I would
call myself a "prophet," but many others are doing that. In the
very same mail that brought me the cardinal's letter I received a
review of my last book, *If God Goes to All Men*, by a man named
J.J. Hughes, a professor at St. Louis University, a spokesman for
Cardinal Bernardin, who is now the leader of the Church in the
U.S.A. The review begins this way: "The Swiss Capuchin and
missiologist Walbert Bühlmann is one of the prophetic voices in
contemporary Catholicism . . . ." Thus I feel the duty to continue
on my chosen path, despite all the difficulties raised by the Vatican. It seems to me as well that in the light of the example of
St. Francis this is a way of "repairing the Church."

Fraternally yours,   Fr. Walbert Bühlmann

At this point I ought to say a word about the book project I have already made repeated mention of. In January 1982 Prof. Karl Rahner had invited his friend and former student Johann Baptist Metz and myself to Innsbruck. He revealed his intention of writing a book with us on the Church, a sort of ecclesial futurology. The book would have to make it clear that, contrary to many people in the Church, who think that the Council is now over and that serenity and order have now returned to the Church, the Council has not yet said its last word, not yet discharged its last energies, not yet translated its last impulses into reality. We had to show how the Church of the future, based on the Council, could be and should be. We made up our minds to collaborate on this sort of book. One initial notion was for us to get together from time to time, to exchange ideas, and then for one of us to write the book in the name of the three. I observed: "This doesn't strike me as the right way. You, Karl (I was now on a first name basis with both of them, as they had already been with each other), approach the subject from the angle of dogmatics; you, Johann Baptist, from the angle of orthopraxy, while my angle is the new situations faced by the Church. I believe each of us ought to present the same theme from his own standpoint for about 80 pages, put it together, and there's the book." We agreed on that, although no firm schedule was made. The reason Prof. Rahner chose me to collaborate on such an important project went back to his esteem for my earlier books. A propos of my book on the Third Church he had written me on October 21, 1974:

Dear Fr. Bühlmann,

Three days ago I received from you, through the publisher, your new book, *Where Faith Lives: Glimpses of the World Church*. Thank you most cordially for this kind attention, which gave me great pleasure. Since getting the book, I have been reading it, though I have not yet quite finished it. On the back of the book are printed judgments of the highest praise for the book by very competent critics. But I should like to say for myself that I find your book quite outstanding. It is one of those books that makes one wonder why there hasn't been something like this for so long, because it really is a vital subject, and that makes one all the more happy and thankful that one now has it. I admire the vast abundance of information that, so far as I know, can be found in no other single place. I admire the tact, the measured prudence, and at the same time the courage with which you handle the many critical questions that are suggested by your glimpses into the situation of the world Church. I am delighted to see here how a person who is rightly concerned, in the final analysis, with what the Church does in real life, brings up insights and problems of contemporary theology that can otherwise be found only scattered about. In short, I find your book unique, at once critical and hopeful. I am convinced that it will gain a wide readership. It should be made required reading, for example, for German bishops and ordinaries, because they are only too happy to engage in head-in-the-sand policies, to produce a lot of paper and leave everything the way it was before. I shall take pains to recommend the book where-ever I can. Just yesterday I wrote to someone (whom you cite, as it happens, at one point) to call attention to your book. I hope they take up your book in Rome too with the same openness and willingness to learn that it deserves.

With heartfelt thanks and all good wishes, yours truly

Karl Rahner

In response to the other book, *If God Goes to All Men*, on the new interpretation of the non-Christian religion, he had written me on July 10, 1981:

Dear Fr. Bühlmann,

Your new book just arrived today. Naturally I have not yet read it through after only a few hours. But already I would like to thank you and congratulate you. It is wonderful to read a book that strides ahead, but sensibly. A thousand thanks and every compliment. Let us hope they read it in Rome too, learn from it and—leave you in peace. I am old and can, so to speak, put myself out of reach by dying. . . . But you must live and go on writing. In these times a great deal does depend on how quickly the Church learns to become a real world Church in the midst of the one humanity. You were born only in 1916, so you are still a young man. Hence you must go on. I wish you all the courage, all the strength, all the help God can give. How glad I would be to see you again and thank you in person. But I probably won't be able to get to Rome any more.

With all wishes, as ever, your

Karl Rahner

Thus in this letter he suggested that he would like to see me some time. And so in October 1981, between two of my lectures in Stuttgart and Augsburg, we had a visit with a long conversation in Munich, and in January 1982 we had the meeting, already mentioned, in Innsbruck.

By the end of the year I had my 80 pages together. But Rahner and Metz, after agreeing among themselves, let me know that they had not yet gotten so far, that the earliest they could get to work would be June, but then they would like to take care of the job as quickly and as well as they could. So in the meantime I put my section on the shelf to wait.

It then happened that my part of the book had to be subjected to pre-censorship, in keeping with the order from Cardinal Ratzinger. My minister general, Fr. Flavio, asked me to give him the names of possible censors, preferably from outside the Order. In my letter of June 14, 1983, I suggested "Prof. Bernard Haring, CSSR, who enjoys an international reputation and is besides a very spiritual man, a positive saint; or Fr. John Fuellenbach, SVD, who has a doctorate from the Catholic University of America in Washington, D.C. and for six years has been directing continuing education courses for the Steyler missionaries and members of other institutes; or Prof. Karl Rahner, a man of international authority, who combines with all his knowledge a profound faith and a childlike love for the Church. As a co-editor of the book, he has every interest in avoiding any heresy in it or unjustified criticism of the Church."

We agreed on Karl Rahner. On June 30, 1983, I sent him the text with the request, "to read it through for our minister general and to scrutinize it from two points of view:

—Have any heretical ideas crept into it?

—Do the criticisms of the Church, which are admittedly there, go beyond the limit of what is expedient, that is, may they and should they be expressed in such a way? Hence they must not reflect the viewpoint of authority, but the complementary viewpoint of a committed Christian, who believes he has something to say for the Church of tomorrow. If in doubtful cases you suggest alternative formulations, I would certainly be agreeable to them."

Upon returning from the Salzburg University seminars, where I had four lectures to deliver, I visited Prof. Rahner. We looked over the manuscript together and made some minor corrections. On August 6, 1983, he then wrote the following letter to my minister general:

Reverend Father General,

You asked me to draw up a report on the manuscript by Fr. Walbert Bühlmann "Forty Years of the Church." I am, it is true, not convinced that I am the right man for the purpose that you have in mind for this report. Nevertheless I did not want to refuse your and Fr. Bühlmann's request. I have carefully read the manuscript and revised it together with Fr. Bühlmann. I am of the conviction that no compelling objections can be raised against this work from the dogmatic standpoint. I further believe that the critique of the Church presented here is the justified opinion of a man who has the right and perhaps even the duty to voice such ideas and suggestions. Of course, in this matter we are dealing largely with discretionary judgments that others do not share.

But I see in this no reason to forbid their being voiced. How could we make progress in the Church (which is surely the duty of "ecclesia semper reformanda"), if we were allowed to argue only for ideas of which it was certain in advance that they were shared by everyone in the Church? I do not expect, as a matter of fact, that these ideas will be shared by all the leading men in the Church. But that is no grounds for me to think they ought not to be said—especially, since I myself by and large share these opinions and have myself already defended them in print.

Respectfully yours,

Karl Rahner

After Fr. Viktrizius Veith had also read the text, the minister general gave me the green light to print it. But during that visit K. Rahner told me that neither he nor J.B. Metz had begun to work on the book, and that they took a dim view of its future. So they advised me to publish my section by myself. I had to come to terms with this unpleasant surprise. Then on instruction from the Styria publishing house, which wanted the book to have a certain bulk, I put together from various lectures a first part under two headings: geopolitical structures (from the western Church to the world Church, the continental Church of Latin America, Africa, Asia) and kerygmatic accents (justice, peace, hope, universal brotherhood).

Thus the book was published in the spring of 1984 under the title, *New Dimensions of the World Church: A Model for the Year 2001.*

I hope that in it I was aware of the interests of the young churches and won interest for them among a broad spectrum of readers. I felt a quiet satisfaction on December 2, 1984, when on Vatican Radio the director of the German-speaking department, Fr. Eberhard von Gemmingen, reviewed it as follows:

The book, *Dimensions of the World Church,* is exciting because it shows that the Church in its contemporary worldwide reality, is already quite different from the idea of it we usually carry around in the back of our heads. *Dimensions of the World Church* contains bundles of information about the churches in Africa, Asia, and Latin America, about their history, problems, and future prospects. It tells us what "mission" means today, namely a worldwide exchange of faith from continent to continent. Missionary work is done not out of fear for the salvation of souls but out of love for God and for human beings. Bühlmann contrasts the Church's documents on the missions with the present-day reality of the Church, noting successes and shortcomings. He argues for a great deal of pluralism, for regional autonomy, the establishment of continental patriarchates, the holding of regional and local synods—in short, much greater autonomy for the local churches and a certain restraint on the part of the pope. *Dimensions of the World Church* actually belongs only in the hands of people completely loyal to Rome. They will find the book a source of fruitful irritation. Anyone who loves the Church and does not take pleasure in its self-destruction will profit from reading the book and gain all sorts of previously missing information.

4. The Church's Magisterium and the Cry of the Poor

In the early winter of 1984 two synchronized documents on liberation theology by Cardinal Ratzinger and Cardinal J. Höffner appeared, and in the excitement of the broad wave of protest they stirred up I, too, wrote a reply under the title, "Liberation Theology: Heightened Polarization" in the Capuchin magazine *Neues Forum* (Lucerne, 1984). I sent a copy of it to Cardinal Ratzinger. In the accompanying letter, dated November 22, 1984, I declared: "I consider it an obligation of honesty to inform you of my reaction to the two documents by the cardinals on liberation theology . . . ." Needless to say, I expected and received no answer to it.

The Latin American Church has taken the Council seriously as few others have, and has translated it into fact. Formerly a church-as-hierarchy, it became a church-as-the-people-of-God.

Once a church of sacramentalization, it became a church of evangelization; once a church as part of the system and a landed proprietor, it got some critical distance from the system, and exchanged more than a few palaces for ordinary houses. A church of abstract, universal theology became a church of contextual, life-changing liberation theology. The Latin Americans also learned to use the mass media, not just internally to educate the people, but also to make an "image" that is increasingly making people talk.

In Europe people became almost envious of this miracle of fundamental change. It was seen as a sign of hope. There was silent expectation that old Europe might reform itself in a similar fashion. Of course, one had to be careful not to idealize the case of Latin America. Not by a long shot were all bishops there "converted," nor did all the people belong to base communities, perhaps only one to five percent. But compared with the past, that was already a great deal.

This "Hosannah" mood has now abruptly turned into a "Crucify him." Liberation theology, the theological background and expression of the whole reform, has come under heavy fire from two coordinated church documents. What is to be said about this?

The Ratzinger Document

One cannot forbid the Roman central authorities to oversee and in some cases to correct new theologies. But one has misgivings in advance whether the staff in Roman palaces have the empathy necessary to understand sufficiently the local color, the context, and the social background of liberation theology, to do justice to its non-intellectual but wholly praxis-related style. We can freely admit that in the beginning the document does recognize the efforts by liberation theologians. Then it launches two unprecedentedly sharp attacks both against Marxism, with its oppression of millions of people, "this shame of our time" (XI, 10), and against the capitalism "of military dictatorships, of the oligarchy of wealth without social conscience . . .the unchecked practices of foreign capital . . .the new technological, financial, monetary or economic colonialism . . ." (VII, 12). Ever since Pius XI condemned in the same week the leftist system of communism and the rightist system of national socialism, such harsh tones had not been heard coming from Rome. It is too bad that not only has war been declared on two fronts, but also on a third front as well, where people were trying to set up an intermediate model.

The document itself, however, is theologically most unsatisfying. It bristles with unproved assertions. One has to take it on faith that "some" or "certain" or "many" liberation theologians are drifting through Marxist waters and expounding what is only a perversion of the Christian message. We are bidden to "accept with childlike respect" everything the magisterium says, but this desire could be carried to absurd lengths : if the bishops of the Council had done just that, they would have simply accepted the prepared schemata—and there would have been no progress at all.

Furthermore, pedagogically speaking, the document is highly awkward. In dealing with a mere criminal, one immediately comes forward with the charges. Dealing with one's fellows, assuming this is not simply dogmatic oneupmanship, but a matter of honest interest in seeing him better himself, one first creates a basis for trust, and only then are the objections raised. When the Congregation of the Faith holds out the prospect of a later document "that will bring to light—in a positive sense—all the riches (of liberation)" (Foreword), we wonder why they didn't begin with this positive presentation and then announce their reservations at the end. That would have been much more pedagogically adept and sympathetic.

Finally, the document is also politically disastrous. The strong statements on right wing regimes are quickly suppressed by such regimes, which pounce instead on the main message, that the liberation theologians are Marxists, which is what they have been claiming all along. This is the jubilant reaction in the right-wing

Latin American press. Instead of solidarity there is betrayal. One feels sad about the whole thing.

The Höffner Document

The opening address by Cardinal J. Höffner at the German Bishops' Conference on September 24, 1984, was more methodologically satisfying to the extent that concrete evidence for the accusations was cited from the main theologies of liberation. But here too there was no room for gratification. First of all, the text is stamped with professorial European arrogance and assumptions of superiority. One might sarcastically sum up the remarks in this way: "My dear little children, keep on being so good. Just follow the seven guiding principles of the Church's social doctrine, which we have long since compiled for you. Then you will be on the right track, while the seven options of your liberation theologians are all on the wrong track." The speaker overlooks the fact that what is at stake here is not right or wrong, but the question of dynamics. Catholic social teaching as a system was known twenty years ago in Latin America, but it accomplished nothing, while liberation theology has made some changes and given the people a new self-consciousness and hope.

There are, furthermore, two momentous fallacies in the Höffner text. Because the liberation theologians have borrowed elements of Marxism, it is concluded that they are Marxists. By the same "logic" one would have had to say in the Middle Ages—and some of his opponents did say it—that because Thomas Aquinas adopted many elements of the pagan Aristotle, he thereby became a pagan. Anyone who has even a nodding acquaintance with the liberation theologians, knows that they are not Marxists.

Moreover, the text sings the praises of the German economic boom that overcame the poverty of the 19th century and ensured prosperity for the great majority of the nation. Time will therefore work in the same manner in Latin America. One simply has to "hold out through the epoch of pauperization." The fallacy here lies in the fact that the German socialized market economy is in no way to be compared with the brutal capitalism in Latin America, and that prosperity was not capitalism's gift to the work force but a fruit of the pressure and struggle by the workers, using every democratic means. Why should not the same thing be allowed to happen in Latin America as well, and if possible not under pressure from the left but under pressure from Catholic liberation theology?

If we let the personal criterion count for anything, we shall quickly know where to stand, because the best Latin American bishops and cardinals, Arns and Lorscheider among others, who enjoy the full confidence of the Rome bishops' synod and were elected by a large majority to the synodal council, fully support their liberation theologians, while the informers and stage managers of the anti-communism campaign, even if they act with a good conscience, hardly have the poor behind them.

Summary

This contemporary clash can be put in to larger contexts, stressing the following points:

—The tragedy of Nestorianism: Ten years ago A. Grillmeier did a study pointing out that Nestorianism, the first great religious controversy of the Patristic Age, which continues to this day in the form of a "schismatic" church, was based on a misunderstanding. The Council of Ephesus created an erroneous doctrine on the nature of Christ and rightly condemned it. But the condemned teaching did not correspond to what Archbishop Nestorius had in mind. Owing to a lack of dialogue both sides talked at cross purposes, and so engineered the first heresy instead of avoiding it. Nestorius was therefore not a Nestorian. Things like that have been repeated a number of times, and are unfortunately still happening even today. Owing to the lack of dialogue with the liberation theologians, by taking their statements out of context and absolutizing them, their critics have constructed a communist specter and hurled anathemas at it. But the liberation theologians do not identify themselves with that specter.

—The tragedy of *Humanae vitae*: When *Humanae vitae* appeared in 1968, the document did not end the discussion about birth control, but triggered fresh and vehement controversy. The upshot was that a majority of priests and Catholics distanced themselves from the encyclical and followed their own conscience. Thus the document could no longer keep the course of events under control. It will be like that now. These two documents will change nothing but only heighten the polarization and widen the gap between one "Church" and another.

—The tragedy of the liberation of the young churches: The liberation of the poor, which is the chief concern of liberation theology, suddenly enters the broader framework of the liberation of the young churches. Once the center of gravity of the Catholic Church has already swung from the world of Europe into the southern hemisphere, so that by the year 2000 around 70 percent of all Catholics will live there, we will finally have to translate into reality the fundamental thinking of Vatican II on inculturation and legitimate pluralism, and stop forcing the Roman model of unity upon the young churches. Liberation theology is the first non-European outline of a self-contained theology. It sees itself not as contrary but complementary to western theology. We must give such an outline a lot of time and trust and not immediately try to throttle it, quite apart from the fact that in the long run there are no prospects of measuring those mature churches by the standard of the European church.

—A ray of hope: In conclusion let us admit that some liberation theologians give the impression of taking shortcuts and of favoring Marxism. This is a matter of emphasis, which must be understood as deriving from their dramatic situation. If these theologians are really evangelical and "return good for evil," they will not strike back hard now, but avoid that impression by explicitly confessing not only the exodus but also the risen Lord, and otherwise by peaceably going on their way. Then these two documents with their thunder and lightning will have had the effect of a cleansing, fructifying storm, and the church of Latin America will continue to be a source of hope for the materially poor of that continent as well as for the spiritually poor of Europe.

Part Four

The Highest Administrative Office In the Catholic Church

Negotiations with the Secretariat of State

As you approach the Secretariat of State, the highest administrative office of the Catholic Church, in the "Terza Loggia" of the Vatican Palace, you do not hear, say, the busy clicking of many typewriters. Everything is wrapped in a mysterious silence. One enters the waiting rooms, like it or not, reverentially.

I had had good experiences with the Secretariat of State as the pope's chancellery, in that letters which I sent the pope were always answered. But to the degree that the Secretariat is an autonomous authority, which presides over the "internal and external policy" of the Vatican, I have to complain about its peculiar anonymity. I have often sent copies of my grievance letters there "for your information." I never got an answer, which was understandable. But I have already mentioned the three personal letters written directly to this agency, which did not even deign to acknowledge receiving them.[26] And in the following two cases we shall see that I wrote weighty letters to the Secretariat of State, but consistently never got a receipt, much less an answer.

Was this due merely to the work overload? Or is it a system to

keep brooders and borers at arm's length—while gross flatterers
could always count on an answer? One insider thought it was simply embarrassment: They didn't know what to answer, so they just
filed correspondence away. That is certainly not an exemplary
sort of administration, nor can we call it evangelical. Despite his
fatigue, Jesus listened to the concerns even of unpleasant ques-
tioners.

1. A Hierarchistic Church

The term "hierarchy" (=holy rule) has come into general
use, even if it doesn't sound very agreeable for a function that
is entirely given over to serve the people of God, as Vatican
II emphasized in "Lumen gentium." But when the hierarchy
monopolizes all offices and identifies itself with the Church, so
that the laity is degraded to a Church that listens, obeys, and
pays, that is supposed to care about the salvation of its soul, but
not about having its say, then this should no longer be called hierarchical, but hierarchistic, in the bad sense. It was widespread
before the Council, but when one finds such conditions even after
the Council, one can only denounce it. We should work together
with others in one way or another so that it finally stops.

That was the purpose of a longish report I sent after my visit
to Angola in 1977 to Archbishop Agostino Casaroli, who was
responsible for the Vatican's foreign policy. A good two years
before, the curias general in Rome worried about their missionaries in Angola, had formed a working group to suggest to them
the right approach for the period of political upheaval. The liberation movement FRELIMO was making great advances. The
Portuguese government and with it the Portuguese bishops were
unwilling to give way. They viewed the freedom fighters, with
whom all the people sympathized, merely as rebels. We had at
one time also invited Archbishop Casaroli over and pressed him
to get Pope Paul VI to try to persuade the bishops there to put
themselves on the side of the future, so that the Church would
not be isolated and disgraced after the liberation. Archbishop

Casaroli showed a great deal of receptivity to this idea. In fact, the pope then invited two bishops from Mozambique to Rome for a discussion. But they were not capable of changing their way of thinking. Their reaction was simply: Everything is against us, and now the pope too is leaving us in the lurch. When the turnabout came, all those bishops—with the exception of a single one, who had recognized the signs of the time—had to resign; and they could thank their lucky stars that the new government gave them a safe-conduct back to Portugal and did not put them on trial.

In Angola things followed a similar course. But I found it tragic that even the new group of Angolan bishops had not yet, in my opinion, properly adjusted to the situation. And so I got up the courage on February 2, 1977, to inform Archbishop A. Casaroli more closely about that hierarchistic hierarchy:

Your Excellency, 33

After our meetings over two years ago in the "Mozambique group," I am now taking the liberty to communicate to you some of my impressions of a similar country, namely Angola. I have just spent three weeks there, giving two courses on pastoral theology to our brothers in Luanda and Uije. I also had the opportunity of speaking with Archbishop Eduardo A. Muaca of Luanda, with the Apostolic Delegate Archbishop Giovanni de Andrea, with Bishop Francisco dos Santos of Uije, with many confreres and quite a few representatives of the government on the local and regional level, along with a private advisor of the President, Dr. Augustino Neto. The following items are not designed to be accusations, but information for the benefit of the Church.

A. My Impressions of the Church in Angola

It seems to me that the bishops as a group are still too much in the grip of nostalgia for the past. They have not joined the people in taking "the great leap forward." They are still standing on the other shore of the Red Sea, as it were, observing from afar the people and the government, as they now make their way through the wilderness, so as to give them good counsel from the standpoint of faith—but counsel not sufficiently based on a serious analysis of the new situation as a whole.

They still think of themselves too much as "bishops," as if the bishops were the Church. Yet in "Lumen gentium" the hierarchy is not discussed until the third chapter, after the treatment of the Church as the people of God. It also seems to me that there is a lack of genuine dialogue with the main body of the Church, with the clergy, with lay people, with the theologians.

They have not yet overcome their innate antipathy to Marxism. Needless to say, we would all, strictly speaking, prefer a non-Marxist regime. But in the face of a fait accompli—in which the preceding government-church system had some responsibility—this sort of aversion is of little use. According to my informants, the government actually has the impression that the bishops have no clear notion of what is going on, but are rather clustered helplessly in a latent opposition, and for that reason do not have the people behind them. Metaphorically speaking, the cupola of the Church (the bishops) is no longer on top of the nave (the people).

Some Evidence for These Assertions

1. On the occasion of national independence a special edition of the church magazine, *O Apostolado*, was published in November, 1975. It contained 17 photos, all of them picturing nuncios, cardinals, bishops, or three church buildings, but not a single one of a representative, let alone a group, of the "people of God." This kind of clerical Church, cut off from the people, can hardly expect any sympathy in a "people's republic." A copy of this magazine is enclosed.

2. On the same occasion a pastoral letter was issued, which speaks in the Introduction of the many difficulties, indeed of the chaos, in the current situation, only to move on to the first chapter, where at great length it lauds the presence of the Church over the last five centuries—at a moment when the people are seeking to make a radical break with the colonial past and to build

their future.

3. When the government ordered the teaching of Marxism in the schools, the bishops reacted coldly and forbade all priests, brothers, and sisters to continue-working in these schools, which caused the government grave difficulties, apart from depriving the Church, at the same time, of the chance to make its presence felt there.

4. Last November a "pastoral communication" was read out in all the churches, accusing the government in the presence of all the people of failure to abide by the constitution. These accusations were necessarily generalized and expressed in public without first having a serious dialogue with the government. A respected person in the Church told me they could dare to speak so harshly just at that moment because they knew that the regime was having internal problems and so could not respond in kind. This sort of desire to profit from the weaknesses of the government reveals a not very loyal frame of mind.

5. The well known critical group of Basque priests and a Capuchin from Venice was not heard out by the bishops in a real dialogue that addressed their main concerns. Instead the critics were given nothing but grief and had their names reported to Rome.

B. My Interpretation

It is a ticklish and difficult job to give a just appraisal of Marxism as it de facto exists. Of course, if one counters Marxism, which has become a fact of life in many countries, merely by repeating the principles of "Diviniredemptoris,"[27] then we are burning all the bridges and all too quickly pronouncing ourselves martyrs.

It seems to me that the regime in Angola is by no means 100 percent Marxist, even if the president said in a speech this January that the year 1977 would be crucial for making Marxism-Leninism a reality. In a nation with a deeply religious spirit, whose people are more than 50 percent Christian, with many practicing Christians in high political office, a government cannot be simply anti-Christian, or it would have little success. The president and many other government officials appear to be striving for an authentic dialogue with the Church, provided that the Church is loyal and open and takes seriously the autonomy of the state (which is recognized in "Gaudium et spes"). But the government is dependent upon Russia and Cuba, on the one hand to control the country militarily in the struggle against the FNLA and the UNITA, and on the other for the battle against the white regimes in Rhodesia, Namibia, and South Africa. That is why as a quid pro quo the government "must" declare itself for Marxism. Besides it also finds Marxism fascinating because of its scientific aspect, which it sees as a weapon against the magical mentality of the people. If the regime can only get its own army, which it is now training, and if in the southern tip of Africa a political or military solution can be found, then there is hope that Marxism, while it survives as an intellectual discipline, will wither as an ideology. Beyond that I would venture to say that a dose of Marxism can only be useful in Angola, to make some Christians, whose thinking has been all too traditionalist, more aware and capable of giving an account of their faith.

The point, then, is to build bridges, to give the government a certain amount of credit, to offer to cooperate selflessly for the welfare of the people, finally to prove that religion is not opium, but a stronger stimulus to "revolution" than Marxism is. Only on this condition will the moment come—under certain conditions—to voice a protest in the name of justice. In any case, and especially in Africa, one can achieve a lot more with good human relations than with mere clinging to legal positions.

I would say that the bishops must learn something from the address of Paul VI to the communist mayor of Rome, a man who nonetheless represented legitimate authority. Without making any accusations, the pope spoke of "wishes for good cheer, orderly life together, and moral, civil, and social progress" (OR

January 3, 1977).

C. My Suggestions

1. It strikes me that it would be very useful if the bishops' conference appointed a commission (three bishops, six priests, and six lay people) with the charge of undertaking a serious analysis of the pastoral situation, with a concrete program that aims to establish priorities and change mentalities. The "Pastoral Letter on Evangelization in Angola" of June, 1976, gives a general orientation but not a concrete program.

2. Given the fact that there are currently in Africa at least ten countries under Marxist regimes (Ethiopia, Somalia, Mozambique, Angola, Congo-Brazzaville, Guinea-Bissau, Guinea, Mali, Benin, Cape Verde. . .) and that both Christians and their bishops are having trouble finding the right relationship with the government, I think it would be very helpful if a person such as yourself or Archbishop Cesare Zacchi[28] were to take an informational and inspirational trip to some of these countries, to get in touch with the new situation and, together with the bishops, to find an expedient response, which would evidently follow the lines of the Vatican's "Ostpolitik," as described by H. J. Stehle in his well known book.

3. I expect that the promotion (and with it his departure from Malanje) of Msgr. do Nascimento[29] and his vicar general offers a new opportunity to the Basque group to continue their work. But if this case should still be open, I would like to say a word in their favor. I have spoken with them, and I believe the Church needs such critical groups. I am convinced that they are not practicing a mere horizontal secularity, but are living up to the real meaning of integral salvation, of religion, which is incarnate in earthly realities. Their aim is to discover and bring out the evangelical values in culture, in politics (!), in the sciences, and in hope, as called for by "Evangelii nuntiandi."

Those are, your excellency, my frank and fraternal observations. I hope that with the restructuring of the Angola Bishops'

Conference, which was just announced, and especially with the
promotion of Bishop Manuel Franklin to archbishop (according
to my information he is the best of the bishops), my various
impressions and suggestions have already become anachronistic.
So much the better.

With best wishes, fraternally yours

Fr. Walbert Bühlmann
Secretary General for the Missions of the Capuchins

As I have already said, this letter received no acknowledgment.
But I learned afterwards that it was sent to the Apostolic Delegate
in Luanda and read there with indignation. How can this little
Capuchin presume to tell the bishops what they have to do?

A few months later that group of Basque priests, without any
further dialogue, was suspended by the president of the Bishops'
Conference, i.e., they were forbidden to exercise their priestly
functions henceforth. Thereupon they published a dossier on their
case and sent me three copies for dissemination as I saw fit. I
forwarded one copy to Archbishop Casaroli on January 10, 1978,
with the comment that "I refrain from any judgment on this."
Once again there was no acknowledgment.

2. A Controversial Cardinal

For yet another time I must speak of Cardinal Agnelo Rossi,
the prefect of the Congregation for the Evangelization of the
Nations or De Propaganda Fide. The matter was as follows. The
Italian missionary institute of the Saveriani, which publishes a
very dynamic magazine called *The Missions Today*, had organized
a four day seminar, from April 24-27, 1980, for one thousand
young people on the topic of "Non-violence and the New Society." Among the four main speakers were Archbishop Helder
Camara and myself. A few weeks before it was supposed to
take place, its organizers telephoned me to say that the whole
thing had to be called off, under heavy pressure from the Church.
They were unwilling to give me any further explanations over the

phone. So I contacted the superior general of the institute, Fr. Gabriele Ferrari, whom I knew well. We got together, and he told me how he had been pressured by Cardinal Rossi. I asked him to let me have this information in writing so that I could use it. Here is the document of June 12, 1980:

Dear Fr. Bühlmann,

You wished to hear from me the reasons why the meeting from April 24th to the 27th on "Non-violence and the New Society," to which you were invited to speak on the topic, "The Mission of the Church and the New World," could not be held.

It is very sad for me to recall those days, but since you asked me to, I will tell you in all candor, even though this will cause you some bitterness, that one of the weightiest objections troubling the cardinal prefect of the Propaganda Fide was the fact that you were one of the speakers and would be talking about the Church's mission. The cardinal kept stressing (although I tried to downplay your presence) that he could not approve of this because, he said (I am quoting from memory), Fr. Bühlmann does not represent the voice of the Church on the missions. I have to add that he was also uncomfortable with other speakers, among others the well known archbishop of Olinda and Recife, Helder Camara.

Seeing the cardinal's unyielding determination, I asked our provincial superior of Italy whether it might not be better to cancel the meeting. I was afraid that otherwise it could unleash needless and harmful polemics. As a matter of fact, on March 26, the day after my conversation with the cardinal, the cardinal of Bologna, in his role as president of the Bishops' Conference of Emilia-Romagna, likewise urged the provincial superior of Italy to call off the meeting. Thus we jointly decided to do this, even though this meant that we had to write off several million lire in preparatory expenses and to quiet the indignation of not a few registered participants. . . .

All this now has been over and done with for some time. But I was very sorry for your sake when I saw how you are judged in that office. I am sure that with your faith you accept this trial in the Franciscan spirit, and can even experience "perfect joy" in it.

I assure you that at all times you have my entire devotion and affection.

Fr. Gabriele Ferrari

Since the Saveriani are a missionary institute, they are also legally subject to the Propaganda Fide. Thus Cardinal Rossi could put greater pressure on Fr. Ferrari than he could on my superior general, because we Capuchins are subordinate to the Congregation for Religious.

Was I now to be content with an "experience of perfect joy"? I felt that no one should be allowed to get away with such an outrageous act in the Church, that this thing had to be passed on to the appropriate higher authorities in the Vatican, not only "for your information," but for investigation. And so on June 16, 1980, I wrote a letter to Archbishop Eduardo Martinez Somalo, substitute in the Secretariat of State, with copies to Cardinal Eduardo Pironio, prefect of the Congregation for Religious, to Cardinal Agnelo Rossi and also to Fr. Pedro Arrupe, by virtue of his position as president of the Union of Superiors General, because I thought the superiors general ought to know all the goings on in the holy city of Rome.

Your Excellency,

I am sorry to take up your time—busy as you are—with my case. But if it were only just "my case"! I believe that this case bears on the good name of the Roman Curia, and I feel obliged to inform you about the repeated cases of authoritarianism, of a lack of dialogue, of moral violence, of violations of human rights. Among these instances I myself had to put up with harassment for six years by a member of this Curia, specifically Cardinal A. Rossi.

[First I reported about the incidents we are already familiar with: How in 1974/75 I was fired from the Urbaniana University without any dialogue, on account of my book; how in 1976 my lecture at the Congress on Missiology was not published in the Proceedings; how in 1976/77 I had to do battle with very old-fashioned "experts" from the Congregation of the Faith; how in 1978 Cardinal Rossi, citing altogether flimsy complaints, forced my minister general to dismiss me from my post (although we later made peace); how in 1980, despite this peace, Cardinal Rossi forbade a congress from meeting because Archbishop Helder Camara and myself were among the speakers.]

This sort of procedure fits in well with a totalitarian system but not with the post-conciliar Church. If I and Helder Camara do not represent the voice of the Church, then I turn the tables on Cardinal Rossi and say that he can no longer speak in the name of the Church, since he wants to uphold ideas about the missions and concrete arrangements in the missions that have become totally anachronistic.

I refrain from passing any judgment on the person of the cardinal, who no doubt acts in accordance with his conscience and convictions. But he allows himself to be guided by an unenlightened zeal that is devoid of any knowledge of modern-day theology and missiology. Since he shies away from all dialogue with experts in the field, in his case one has to speak of ignorantia crassa," of callous and deliberate ignorance. And thus his authority, lacking competence as it does, turns into authoritarianism and indeed into repressive violence, as in this case of the banned congress and of other incidents I have reported.

In the world one would sue this kind of person and charge him with slander and misuse of authority. Must we in the Church simply keep silent and swallow everything? Pope John Paul II, who demands so emphatically that all economic and political systems respect human rights, cannot tolerate the repeated disrespect for these rights in the Church.

Up until now I have always tried, out of love for the Church, not to make a public scandal out of my case, although various newspapers and magazines have asked me to let them have the documents supporting it. But I raise my voice all the more loudly in the Church, and along with many others I do not despair that certain attitudes on the part of the Roman Curia will finally change.

Yours truly,

Fr. Walbert Bühlmann

By return mail Cardinal Rossi sent me a handwritten answer on June 19, 1980:

My dear Fr. Bühlmann,

Thank you for calling to my attention the letter from the superior general of the Saveriani and to your reply.

Once again, best wishes.

Agnelo Cardinal Rossi

Should that be called evangelical love of one's enemies or naivete and disagreeable ascetical manners?

With similar speed Fr. Arrupe sent me, on June 20, 1980, a sign of his understanding and sympathy:

Dear Father,

Thank you for sending me the copy of your letter to Msgr. Eduardo Martinez Somalo, and of the documents on the problems you have had in recent years with the holy Congregation for the Evangelization of the Nations.

I can imagine how much you must have suffered from this, but also how great your loyalty is, in clearly explaining your difficulties to your superiors and to the Roman Curia.

I hope that a cordial mutual understanding may grow out of this very unpleasant affair, and out of that understanding a great light for the missions and for the Church.

The paths of the Lord are always marked by the cross and suffering, which must be very great for you in this case, since it is about persons and concerns so close to your heart.

I recommend the whole matter to the Lord; and I pray that he may enlighten everyone, so that everything redounds to the greater welfare of the Church.

Fraternally in the Lord,

Pedro Arrupe, SJ, President of the USG

But otherwise there was no movement. In the Vatican everything was silent. Then, after six months, Archbishop S. Lourdusamy, secretary of the Propaganda Fide, invited my minister general to a discussion set for December 6, 1980, about my letter to Archbishop Martinez Somalo of the Secretariat of State, and my grievances against Cardinal Rossi. Archbishop Lourdusamy also wanted to learn what Fr. Pascal Rywalski thought about this thorny business. Fr. Rywalski had the courage to lay his cards on the table. I reproduce here the minutes of the discussion, drawn up by Fr. Pascal himself on December 8, 1980:

—It seems to me that the contents of Fr. Bühlmann's letter are founded in fact, even though some expressions would be improved by a somewhat milder choice of words.

—Similar complaints in similar language about other mission problems are often loudly voiced at meetings of the Union of Superiors General.

—The undersigned is not the right partner to be talking about this letter, even though he thanks the archbishop for inviting him to this discussion. There is a conviction on both sides that the discussion must take place when Fr. Bühlmann too is present.

—We are also agreed that it would be desirable for both parties once again to conduct peace talks together and to bind themselves to the promise that if new difficulties arise, they will negotiate directly and without delay, as Christian to Christian, man to man, and avoid condemning the other in the presence of third persons.

—These minutes would be incomplete, if I did not stress that the discussion went off very amiably, that Archbishop Lourdusamy represented the interests of Cardinal Rossi intelligently and with delicacy, while at the same time referring to the good relations that have always existed between himself and Fr. B¨uhlmann.

Fr. Pascal Rywalski

One month later I too got an invitation from Archbishop Lourdusamy. I was to come not during office hours, but in the afternoon to the private residence of the archbishop in the palazzo of the Propaganda Fide. Indian sisters served us tea and sweets. The discussion, carried on, like the first one, in a brotherly tone, repeated roughly the same points that had already been discussed with Fr. Pascal. In addition, the archbishop reproached me for speaking ill of the Propaganda Fide during my recent trip to the U.S.A. I answered: "I just told the truth. If that has ill effects on the Propaganda Fide, it's not my fault."

While on a lecture tour in America I had, in fact, been part of a weekend program at the Protestant missionary studies center at Ventnor. The director, my friend G. H. Anderson, had invited 30 interested persons, 15 Protestants and 15 Catholics, from far and wide, to whom I was to speak about the stages of my missiological development. At discussion time one of the first questions that came up was not about my new theology of the non-Christian religions, which had caused something of a stir, but about my experiences with Rome. And I had told the truth, because I felt that only the truth liberates, and that mature Christians are not shaken by it, but find it deepens their understanding of the Church. Among the guests was the national director of the papal mission operations, Msgr. W. J. McCormack, who naturally sent a report afterwards to Rome.

After my previous experiences I could not face the thought of renewed "peace talks" with Cardinal Rossi. What is the use of fine words in the face of the opposite kind of actions? Of course I forgave Cardinal Rossi. After all, we spent another two years alongside each other, until after twelve years of service at the curia general of the Capuchins I asked, of my own accord, to be relieved, and then returned to Switzerland; while Cardinal Rossi too, when he reached 70, left the Propaganda Fide and was appointed president of the administration of the patrimony of the Holy See. Now that Archbishop Lourdusamy had intervened, did the whole affair have to be looked upon as closed? I found Cardinal Rossi's actions too grave to be settled by an amicable conversation over tea. I kept waiting for some kind of arbitrator's decision from the authority I had appealed to. But when the people there did not breathe a word, I was stubborn enough, just about a year later, on June 24, 1981, to write one more time to Archbishop Martinez Somalo:

Your Excellency,

It is now a year since I sent you a letter, of which I am enclosing a photocopy. I have never received an answer to it, not even an acknowledgment that you got it. I don't know how I ought to interpret this sort of thing. Is Mother Church so anonymous that she doesn't deign to answer her sons when they present their difficulties? Or so diplomatic that she does not want to say that any party is right or wrong? Or so spiritualistic that she wishes to test the humility of her sons for their greater self-sanctification?

However that may be, in the eyes of Cardinal Rossi, I belong together with Archbishop Helder Camara to those people who cannot speak in the name of the Church. In the meantime, Archbishop Helder Camara has been rehabilitated by the pope in person, when the latter embraced him in Recife in front of the people and thanked him for everything that he had done in his life.

I have a legitimate interest in knowing whether the Holy See sustains Cardinal Rossi's verdict against me or is rather giving me a sign of a certain vindication. Basically I wish to do nothing more than represent a credible post-conciliar Church, "which again gives us hope, for which it is worth while to put one's hand in the fire," as many readers of my books and people who have heard my lectures keep telling me.

Respectfully,

Fr. Walbert Bühlmann

After the summer vacation, on September 10, 1981, I received in the mail an envelope from the Secretariat of State:

Reverend Father,

I write in reference to a letter of June 24 of this year, with which you sent me a photocopy of a previous message, dated June 15, 1980 was addressed to me and, for their information, to their Eminences Cardinals E. Pironio and A. Rossi, as well as to Fr. P. Arrupe, the president of the USG.

I am anxious to assure you that I read your messages to the Secretariat of State with proper attention and then entrusted the Congregation for the Evangelization of the Nations with your case.

I am, Father, your most humble servant in the Lord,

E. Martinez, Substitute

That was all, then. The higher authorities simply pass on the letter and wash their hands in all innocence. In the world a similar case would not run its course so innocuously. In the Church, too, love should not exclude justice, even when high-placed personalities are involved.

Part Five

The Rites Controversy Is Only Just Beginning

(Negotiations with the Congregation for Divine Worship)

1. "You Are 100 Percent Right"

Nowadays we can hardly still believe that Catholics on all continents for so many years had to hold their services in the Latin language—and actually did hold them, with unquestioning obedience. When, in the 1930s, Romano Guardini began to celebrate a more meaningful liturgy in German (with student groups, behind closed doors), he was repeatedly forbidden by the bishops to continue. But he went on nonetheless. Pius Parsch of Klosterneuburg was a similar pioneer.

In 1959 the first study week on the missions and the liturgy took place, led by P. J. Hofinger in Uden (Holland). The participants agreed on the following desiderata:

—That all singing by the congregation or choir be permitted in the language of the country.

—That the readings by the priest be permitted directly in the

183

language of the country.

—That the pericopes from Scripture be increased in number and divided into a cycle lasting several years.

—That the intercessory prayers of the faithful be re-introduced in a suitable form.

—That the service of the divine word be celebrated not at the altar but from the sedilia and the ambo.

—That the whole mass be simplified and its structure made clearer.

Now this is a peculiar feature: As convinced as people were of the rightness of these desires and demands, they were still inhibited and even afraid to announce them in the proper place, in Rome. Should they even pass them on to Rome? Wouldn't that unleash a still more rigorous opposition to the new efforts?

Then came the Council, and in a flash all these things became a foregone conclusion. For many Catholics the reformed liturgy is the peculiar trademark and distinctive sign of Vatican II. The Roman Curia, of course, played a recalcitrant role in the process. Practically every change had to be wrested from it piece by piece. First they allowed the intercessory prayers in the mother tongue, then the readings from Scripture, and finally the Eucharistic canon. The Constitution on the Liturgy had provided that a certain variety of Eucharistic prayers might be used, but they had to be approved in Rome.

Thus it came about that many bishops' conferences sent such adapted models to Rome for approval—and kept waiting for the green light. Instead, in June, 1973, a letter was issued, stating that the pope had decided not to allow a single one of the new prayers. In this he was following the unanimous opinion of the plenary assembly of the Congregation for Divine Worship.

I was deeply incensed by this, especially for the sake of the young churches. I expressed my chagrin to Msgr. Scalzotto, the undersecretary to the Propaganda Fide: "What part did the Propaganda Fide play in this decision? Why didn't it defend the interests of the young churches?" Answer: "Just don't get excited, Father! One accepts the decision, and after a while one asks for and gets a dispensation for individual cases." —"That sort of Italian mentality is not our cup of tea. We want a straightforward solution, not one that creeps in through the back door."

Then I wrote a letter to the prefect of the Congregation for Divine Worship, Cardinal A. Tabera Araoz. But instead of sending the letter through the mail, I handed it myself to the secretary of the Congregation, Archbishop A. Bugnini. I did not yet know him personally, but I was aware that he was an expert in liturgical scholarship, and it is always interesting to speak to experts. After I had introduced myself, I asked him, first of all, to read my letter to the cardinal, dated June 27, 1973:

Your Eminence,

Loyal as I am to the pope, I take the liberty of expressing to you, not as the secretary general for missions of the Capuchins, but as a simple Christian, my uneasiness over the brief, "Eucharistiae participationis." I have a certain knowledge and practical experience of Africa, Latin America, and Asia; and from this standpoint I can only submit the following reflections:

1. For too long we have imported to the southern continents, and had people there praying what I would almost call prefabricated prayers. And yet in those places spontaneity and creativity, which are gifts from God, abound. In his standard work on prayer F. Heiler stresses spontaneousness as an essential, characteristic note of the non-European peoples. The enormous success of the independent churches ("sects") in Latin America, Africa, and Asia is likewise traceable in large part to the spontaneous praying that goes on at their meetings.

2. For too long also we Europeans have made our decisions for the rest of the world. During the period of European hegemony this was tolerated, but today in the polycentric world, and with

all the political and cultural nationalism, it seems to me that it has become anachronistic to decide everything in Rome for the other continents.

3. If the Holy See, as the brief says, was driven "by pastoral love for unity," then I would see unity not so much in a compulsory uniformity, but in union in the same love and the same faith, even though external forms may vary—obviously, all that would be under the supervision of the bishops. It is not necessary to limit freedom in this way to put a stop to real abuses that occur. With the same motive of serving unity Latin too had been imposed on people for centuries. Today we understand that unity does not depend upon Latin.

4. If this decision was urged "by bishops, priests, and a great many believers" (commentary by A.B. in the OR of June 15), then I fear that these individuals represent only a part of the Church, namely the so-called traditionalistic part. Not a few of them would be only too happy to suppress any movement in the Church and to hold on to Latin. But the younger, more spontaneous part of the Church, which stands closer to the realities of life, was not heeded, I think, because these people do not write to Rome. But now they find themselves in a conflict of conscience, forced to choose between fidelity to the authority of the Church or to the cultural heritage of their homeland.

This past winter I have several times attended the "Indian liturgy" . . . . I am also well informed about the African Eucharistic prayers that are used in various places. And all this is now to be banned!

I apologize for having spoken so freely. But I believe that this is no offence against loyalty to the Church—quite the contrary.

Yours faithfully in the Lord,

Fr. Walbert Bühlmann

I had the impression that Archbishop Bugnini read the letter sympathetically. When he was finished with it, I at once began to harp on the same theme: "The four canons in the Roman Missal are well and good. They can and should serve everywhere as models. They are the norm. But if they are to be binding and exclusive laws, they become dubious. Since they are to be prayed everywhere, they necessarily remain general and abstract. They are not a language of the living people of God, which differs from region to region. The two cardinals from the Third World who were present at the plenary assembly cannot be considered advocates of those churches. Cardinal Gracias of Bombay has such a western frame of mind that he speaks only English and no Indian language, and Cardinal Rugambwa of Dar es Salaam is so diffident and loyal to the Church that he never opens his mouth."[30]

My interlocutor listened to me with interest. Then he said: "Father, your ideas deserve consideration. You are 80 percent right. But still other viewpoints must be respected. Of the roughly 400 Eucharistic prayers that were submitted to the Congregation, only 16 were judged to be in full harmony with objective faith. The liturgy must not be left in the hands of ignoramuses. The Holy Father has simply decided this way, and so there is no more room for discussion. Now it is very important to give the people a deep catechetical training and prepare them for further changes. And there is so much unrest prevailing in the Church these days. If there is more peace and quiet in twenty years, then we can also give more freedom." —"In twenty years you won't have to give this freedom any more. I don't think the young people will go on participating in the old people's liturgy for another twenty years. You help yourself to the freedom or you stop going to church. If the little groups don't get permission to develop more creativity, they will get tired and abandon the whole thing . . . ."

Now the ice was breaking. Archbishop Bugnini looked me in the eye and said: "Now I'm no longer speaking to you as the secretary of the Congregation, but as Fr. Bugnini. Now I can tell you: You are 100 percent right. I agree completely with your remarks. But we have to take the time factor into consideration.

When I was still secretary of the Liturgical Council, I could work freely and had direct access to the Holy Father. That was a beautiful time. Back then I presented to him ideas exactly like yours, and he appreciated them. But now I'm caught in the structure of the Congregation. A few powerful men set the tone, and they have little understanding of what liturgy is really about. They act more from 'political' considerations. I can't run full tilt against these men. I too think that different peoples should express themselves with the means provided by their own cultures. I always said that liturgical reform had to take place in three steps: first, by creating a simpler, more understandable, clearer, richer liturgy; second, by translating this liturgy into the various languages; third, by inculturating the liturgy and thereby making it more diverse. Now they will no longer allow this step. When I was returning from the World Eucharistic Congress in Melbourne, I paid a visit to the Apostolic Nuncio of Bangkok, an old college friend. He spoke about the tiny minority of Christians, who don't even make up 1 percent of the population. So I asked him how our religion was viewed and esteemed in the country. His answer: 'Christianity is considered a foreigners' religion.' That is wretched. But sometimes that's the way it is. It takes time and patience."

We bade one another a friendly farewell. I stressed again that my letter, once it had been examined by the proper authorities—even if in the meantime nothing was changed—should go into the archives. There it could lie alongside the letters of the conservative Church, to document the viewpoint of the post-conciliar Church.

Soon afterwards Archbishop Bugnini was shipwrecked on the rock of his attitude as an expert and vocal critic. Under pressure from those "powerful men" he was fired without notice, without explanation, without a word of thanks. He remained idle for four months in the house of his religious community. I paid him a visit around this time and found out that the "rumors" about the manner of his dismissal, almost unbelievable as they were,

were true. Finally he was sent as Apostolic Nuncio to Teheran, "damnatus ad bestias" one might say (condemned to be thrown to the beasts) where he could not even celebrate a decent liturgy because there were almost no Christians there; where he could not continue his liturgical scholarship, because he had no proper libraries to work with. Not long afterwards he died from the after-effects of an operation.

2. "Your Legislation Stifles All Hope"

We can never sufficiently appreciate how good it is that we now live, intellectually speaking, in a contemporary world picture and no longer in the medieval one that lingered until a few decades ago. In that historical frame of mind we Catholics were convinced that we alone possessed the true religion and culture, and that all other people were "heathens, idolaters, unbelievers, and savages." For over a thousand years we not only condemned the Jews, the pagans, the Muslims, and the heretics, but we even waged war against them.

The Council and post-conciliar theology effected a transformation in all this. Today we no longer repeat the axiom, "Outside the Church there is no salvation," as it was traditionally understood. Instead we may expand the principle and say, "Outside humanity there is no salvation" (E. Schillebeckx), i.e., whenever and wherever human beings were and are, they were living in God's grace and love. God raised up prophets and mystics among them, and gave them inspiration and revelation.

Pope Paul VI loved to set up concrete signs of this new evaluation. Thus at Pentecost in 1964 he announced that he was establishing a new Secretariat for the Non-Christian Religions, and he stressed that this had come about entirely because of the conciliar atmosphere of unity and of the new understanding among all believers. How often in the past had not ignorance, prejudices, and even a more or less bad faith distorted and disfigured both sides. We had seen only vices in one another, where a more loving vision could have discovered all sorts of natural virtue.

In the same year the pope took his sensational trip to the Eucharistic World Congress in Bombay. There on December 3, the feast of St. Francis Xavier, he had a meeting with representatives of Hinduism, Islam, Buddhism, and Parseeism. He spoke of these religions with deep reverence; and everyone could sense that his words came from the heart: "This visit to India is the fulfillment of a desire that has long been in our mind. Your land is the home of old cultures, the cradle of great religions, the domicile of a people that has sought God with tireless zeal, in deep silence and contemplation, in hymns of ardent prayer. Seldom has such a holy longing for God been expressed with words so full of the spirit of Advent as it was in the words of your holy books, which were written many centuries before Christ and which implored: 'From the unreal lead me to the real; from the darkness lead me to the light; from death lead me to immortality.' This is a prayer that belongs to our time as well. Today more than ever it might well spring forth from our hearts . . . ."

In the wake of this new spirit there were all sorts of conferences between Christians and representatives of the other religions, often organized in concert by Rome and Geneva, by the Vatican and the World Council of Churches.[31] In the meantime in India a Catholic Indian liturgy was worked out, with Indian symbols such as oil lamps and flowers, in Indian languages and with allusions to the religious heritage of India. Occasionally too the most beautiful texts from the sacred books of Hinduism were brought into play. This was done on a trial basis, with permission from the bishops and from Rome. Logically the next thing to do was to give this practice theological legitimation. And so in 1974 a seminar was held in Bangalore, with 32 experts and a number of bishops discussing the status and function of the sacred scriptures of Hinduism. Among the participants was Cardinal Joseph Parecattil, president of the Indian Bishops' Conference, who was in complete sympathy with the project. The group had assigned itself no easy task. Each of the participants in advance of the meeting, had to write a paper on the subject from the vantage point of his own specialty, whether scripture studies, dogmatics, patrology, liturgy, comparative religion, philosophy of language, etc.

Building on these contributions the group was increasingly drawn to the idea that God has revealed himself to all people and nations, even though in different ways and on different levels. In all that, one could already hear the word of God. The holy Scriptures are simply the reflection of this faith experience, a manifestation and sign of God's activity in the world. The revelation of Jesus Christ is not an isolated event; in him the final, definitive "word of God" was spoken, and the unsurpassable high point of divine revelation and salvation history. One cannot deny that those Indian scriptures are also inspired in an analogous sense. It is interesting to know, by the way, that the Old Testament has incorporated some non-Jewish texts—wisdom sayings, prayers, and stories (Ruth, Job)—into the canon. Christians are in a position to read extra-biblical texts "anew," and to discover in them a connection to Christ. The fact that the representatives of those religions might not accept these interpretations doesn't prove anything, since the Jews likewise did not accept the "Christian" interpretation of the Old Testament.

Having argued in this way, the group came to the conclusion that the finest texts of these holy books could also be used in the Christian liturgy, not in place of the Old Testament, but rather to complement it, and to make Christians aware of the analogous case of God's salvation history in India. The conference rightly stressed that this had to be done in a pastorally prudent manner, at first only in small groups. Homilies would have to awaken understanding for this sort of thing, pointing out the greatness of the power of God's Spirit. The participants had very high hopes for all that this new orientation might accomplish for Christianity's encounter with Hinduism, after centuries of merely living alongside one another.

The whole seminar filled up a 707 page report, including a

deliberately detailed final declaration of 32 pages, since it was assumed that only a few readers would be likely to read through the whole book. The report was immediately sent to Rome and to all the bishops of India. There was some nervous waiting and wondering: Would the bishops, would Rome, take the trouble to read and study it, to understand the novelty of the situation and the challenge it presented? Or would they simply continue on the same track and issue a biased statement rejecting the report? Months went by, the calm before the storm.

Then on June 14, 1975, the answer came from the Roman Congregation for Divine Worship. One might have understood if the answer had acknowledged the zeal of the conference participants, if it had said something positive about the scholarly results of their work, and then had urged them to do further study and exercise more pastoral care, in view of the many people who were not yet so advanced in their thinking. Instead of this, in curt, dry language the whole experiment was called off. After two introductory sentences the text read: "With the intention of guaranteeing in a peaceful and disciplined fashion the peaceful and harmonious development of liturgical adaptation in India, this Congregation respectfully asks the bishops' conference be solicitous in undertaking the following steps:

— Publication of texts that include non-biblical readings for liturgical use is to be stopped;

—The publication and distribution of the New Orders of Mass with Indian canons is to be forbidden;

—The bishops' conference should publicly announce that the use of nonbiblical readings in the liturgy and the use of the Indian Eucharistic prayer are no longer allowed, neither in solemn nor private celebrations of mass;

—That every initiative in this area must first be arranged with this Congregation and no actions be undertaken without first obtaining the necessary written permission."

At the conclusion of the brief there was another appeal to Indian Christianity, "which in the long centuries of its tradition has shown so much fidelity to the Church." The brief struck like crippling thunderbolt. The invocation of "India's centuries long fidelity to the Church" sounded like irony, because out of this "loyalty to Rome" the Catholics of India had led a ghetto existence up until modern times. With their Latin mass and private chapel piety, they constituted a foreign body in the country. It is understandable that not all Christians immediately agreed with this new interpretation of Hinduism, and that not a few bishops and strong lay groups—Indian Lefebvre Christians!—wished to cling to their old Mass. But it was painful to see it was precisely this group that won a hearing in Rome, because evidently the same sort of conservative attitude prevails in the control room of the Church itself.

I was unwilling to resign myself to this situation, and asked for an audience with Cardinal James Knox, who had meanwhile replaced Cardinal Tabera as prefect of the Congregation for Divine Worship. I knew this Australian cardinal from East Africa and India, where I had visited him when he was an Apostolic Delegate there. Later he became archbishop of Melbourne, then cardinal, and finally he was called to the Roman Curia in the course of its internationalization. His reputation as an arch-conservative had preceded him.

He gave me a friendly reception, and we exchanged some memories from East Africa. Then I went right to my point: "Your Eminence, I am very taken aback by your letter to India, in which you strictly forbid the Indian liturgy that has been in use up till now. The texts from the Council, *Sacrosanctum Concilium* and *Ad gentes* talk about the inculturation of Christianity, especially in the liturgy, as possible and desirable. Ten years later, in *Evangelii nuntiandi* Pope Paul VI demands that the Gospel be translated not only into many languages but into many cultures. He says that inculturation not only may, but should, take place, and that means in theology, liturgy, and church structures.

These documents awaken hope, and then your concrete legislation comes along and stifles all hope. I find that your letter to
India runs contrary to the documents mentioned."—"Father, you
must understand, nowadays we have to fight against the right and
the left: against the right, against the Lefebvre people, who want
to hold on to the Latin liturgy; and against the left, against priests
who think everyone can make up his own liturgy."—"I don't at
all mean that every priest should make up his own liturgy, but
countries and continents should be able to have their inculturated
liturgy under the supervision of their bishops. Let me just remind
you of the sad story of the Chinese and Indian rites controversy
in the 16th and 17th century, when that attempt to inculturate
Christianity was strictly forbidden. The Church of Asia was badly
damaged, and it has remained a foreign body in those countries
till this day. For centuries we have condemned those religions out
of ignorance and theological narrowness. Now, when we finally
see the working out of God's salvation on a larger scale, and
we would like to use the finest texts from the sacred books of
Hinduism for the education and enrichment of Christians in our
liturgy . . . ."

—"So long as I'm around, that will not happen!"

I observed that with that kind of attitude all talk was unnecessary. In these palaces of the Vatican the old solution still held:
"Sic volo, sic jubeo, stet pro ratione voluntas" (Thus I will, thus
I command, let will stand in the place of reason.) I now understood why Cardinal Knox was characterized as mulish and obsti-
nate even in certain Vatican circles.

He has died since then. But the Indian liturgy is coming to
life again. It will reach the goal. But it is tragic that initiatives
and efforts meet with nothing from Rome but obstacles instead
of encouragement and guidance. What good do all the beautiful speeches and documents do in the face of such a pigheaded
attitude? In November, 1982, on the 400th anniversary of the
arrival in China of Matteo Ricci, Pope John Paul II delivered a

grandly designed address at the Gregorian University in Rome in the presence of the Chinese legation. He had moving words of praise for this pioneer and prophet, who wished to harmonize Christianity with Chinese culture. But he never mentioned that this bold experiment was forbidden by Rome for 300 years, so much so, that all missionaries to Asia had to swear an anti-rites oath. Even though the oath was suspended during the 1930's, the anti-rite mentality is still holding its ground in Rome, now as ever, as soon as any concrete questions come up. Karl Rahner was right when he said: "The rites controversy is only just beginning."

Part Six

Confronting a Changed World

(Negotiations with the Congregation for the Eastern Churches)

The following report does not relate to me personally and does not grow out of my private initiatives, but is a matter of official business. Therefore I do not have the supporting documents at my disposition, which are in the appropriate archives. Hence I have to rely on my memory. In presenting this case I want to make readers aware that I had not simply provoked the Roman Curia as an individual, but that even in official negotiations people have had to suffer under its ponderous paws.

In the spring of 1974 the assistant general of the Capuchins, Fr. Bonaventura Marinelli, and myself went on a visitation of our Italian and French confreres in Turkey. They lived in difficult posts scattered along the coast of the Black Sea, in Trabzon and Samsun, on the western side of the country, in Istanbul and Izmir (the old Smyrna), and on the southern coast, in Mersin, Adana, Iskenderum, and Antakya (ancient Antioch), where Jesus' disciples were for the first time called Christians, and where Paul started out on his first missionary journey. We had to travel hundreds of kilometers to seek out our people and to give them a little bit of the experience of community. Turkey is a very difficult region for the Church: Among a population of 45,000,000 there are only 17,000 Catholics, or .037 percent of the total. Fifty years ago it was still around 50,000, but a large part of these were foreigners, who have in the meantime emigrated. Nevertheless, the church structures have remained as they once were. For example in Istanbul and Izmir one finds close together three churches of three different orders, although one church would do. This is because the orders don't talk to each other, but also because the government permits no changes. In Trabzon around the turn of the century there were about 400 Catholics and a Capuchin monastery with a very beautiful church. Today the father who watches over the house and church is the only Catholic in the whole area. One thinks back with melancholy to the time of St. Paul and the first Christian centuries, when Asia Minor was a center of Christendom and several councils took place there, in Ephesus, Constantinople, Chalcedon, and Nicaea. Today the missionaries there strike one as resistance fighters in hopeless positions, because the few native Christians are still emigrating, since the religious and social climate in their own homeland makes them uncomfortable.

The Apostolic Nuncio in Ankara functioned at the same time as the Apostolic Vicar of Istanbul. Thus as the bishop he had a number of parishes under him. But there were widespread complaints that he didn't trouble himself about them and never visited them. By way of excuse he said that as a member of the diplomatic corps he could travel only with difficulty. People still remembered the pastoral and brotherly visits of the erstwhile nuncio, Angelo Roncalli, later Pope John XXIII, that did so much good. During our visit to the nuncio, Salvatore Asta, we told him frankly that the missionaries felt lonely and abandoned, and that he ought to visit them more often. He replied, "I'm still busy writing a book about Turkey. I'll visit them more often when it's finished."

When we got back to Rome, we drew up a report for the leadership of our order. We also brought a copy of it to the Congregation for the Eastern Churches. The then prefect, Cardinal Philippe, listened very attentively to our explanations, and immediately agreed with our idea of calling together representatives of all the curias general that have missionaries or sisters in Turkey, to discuss the common problems and, working in common, to find possible solutions for the changed situation. Then he called in the "minutante" (drafter of the minutes), the consultant for Turkey, Msgr. L. Marinelli. When we repeated to him our proposal and the reasoning behind it, he answered: "We've known about that all along. Turkey is just Turkey. You can't do anything there, just grit your teeth and hold on." Instantly the idea of a meeting evaporated.

So Fr. Bonaventura and I convened the people in charge ourselves. Msgr. Marinelli got wind of it by accident and was immediately on the telephone: "What are you doing there without us?" —"If you don't do it, we will!" He wanted at least to be on hand, which was just fine with us. Twice we had nothing more than a useful exchange of ideas and information. The third time we got down to concrete requests:

—We proposed through our curias general that in Turkey as in so many other countries, a "Union of Higher Superiors" be founded, so that they could meet, talk with each other, and solve their common problems in common. This was soon done.

We asked the Congregation for the Eastern Churches, as well as the Secretariat of State:

—That the function of the Apostolic Vicar of Istanbul be separated from the nunciature and entrusted to the right sort of person. This happened with surprising speed. As early as November 15th of the same year the Capuchin P. G. Dubois was appointed to this post.

— That documentation be put together in the European countries about how the Turks were treated here in matters of religious freedom. The result was to be submitted by the nuncio in Ankara to the government there, so that as a quid pro quo, Catholics in Turkey would get more freedom of religion. We never heard whether this was carried out or not.

—That the solitary priest in Trabzon be withdrawn, and the church and house put to a different use. Here the answer was a categorical no: The Church never gave up a station, especially not in Muslim countries. The heroic man had to stick it out until exactly ten years later, after repeated attempts, the permission to leave was finally given.

At all events, these three meetings proved fruitful. In the end Msgr. Marinelli admitted: "This has been a new experience for me, to see how you get together, take counsel together, and come to concrete decisions." Unfortunately, this meeting and joint, brotherly consultation, which is taken for granted elsewhere, is much too seldom practiced in the Vatican. There the bureaucratic principle prevails that the authorities decide and the others do what they're told. Around that time I once met a coworker at Radio Vatican and asked him whether the people in charge of the various language programs met every few weeks or months and agreed on what the crucial points were that they wanted to communicate to the world. His answer was: "That sort of thing isn't customary in the Vatican. Everybody muddles along with his own business. Meetings are quickly suspected of being conspiracies."

Part Seven

Do the People in the Vatican Read Books?:

(Negotiations with the Congregation of the Clergy)

Finally I have a cheerful story from the Vatican. In April, 1979 I got a letter with twenty dollars from a priest in Chicago, asking me to present a copy of the English edition of my book on the Third Church to Cardinal John Wright, the prefect of the Congregation of the Clergy, with fraternal greetings. I did as the writer requested, simply leaving the book, along with the letter, with the porter of the Congregation. Two weeks later I could not believe my eyes when I read the Cardinal's answer:[32]

Dear Father,

You were so kind as to send me your book on the Third Church. I can tell you that I read it through almost in one sitting. It has greatly excited and enriched me. Even though I am not quite in agreement with everything you say, on the whole I thought very highly of it, and I would feel happy to have inspired such a book.

With cordial best wishes, yours truly

John Card. Wright

This was really a surprise. On account of this one experience I had to correct my judgment that the people in the Vatican don't read books. I proudly showed the letter to my confreres.

At that time I was busy working out a lecture on the first six months of Pope Karol Wojtyla. Then I got the idea to use the contact I had made with Cardinal Wright, who was known as an affable man, to get some background information. I called him up: "Your Eminence, I am Walbert Bühlmann, secretary general of the Capuchin Missions. First of all, my deepest thanks for the lovely letter that you responded to my book with." —"What letter? What book?" I realized at once that something had gone wrong, but I didn't get flustered: "No matter. But it would be a great help to me if I could have a talk with you." It was set for the coming Friday at 11 o'clock.

I knew that the Cardinal had had a leg amputated a year before and had to be carried into his office every day. But he stayed on the job until death released him. That is how reluctant they are at the Vatican to make replacements. When I entered his room, I saw my book on his desk.

He began to say at once, as if unwillingly, "First of all, I don't like the title of your book. I believe in one Church, not three Churches. . . ."—"Your Eminence, let's not argue about the title. Some like it, some don't. But the book's main theses are worth noticing. . . ." I told him in five minutes what the book was about, and he listened attentively: the whole thing was news to him, he had not read the book. After a while he asked me whether I had known Bishop Hilarin Felder—a Swiss Capuchin, a friend of Pope Pius XI, on behalf of whom he had had to visit my seminaries and religious houses, including the papal universities in Rome. "Yes, I was with the old bishop in the monastery at Freiburg for the last ten years of his life." We swapped stories about the dead man, laughed a lot, and parted good friends. The cardinal's secretary wasn't there—a diplomatic absence, because naturally he didn't want to admit that he was the only one who had read the book, and had gotten the cardinal to sign it. Even that way I was glad about the whole thing.

Part Eight

Models of Administration and Inspiration

(Negotiations with the Secretariats for the Unity of Christians and for Non-Christians)

If you want to know what post-conciliar church administration could and should be, where, in keeping with the wish of John XXIII, the windows have been opened and fresh air let in, you can experience it in the two secretariats named in the title. Here too, of course, one passes over stone floors and through high-ceilinged corridors, but once you have the man you are looking for, you notice at once that here you are dealing with an expert, with someone who combines practical experience in his special field with knowledge of its literature, with someone from whom you can get information and to whom you can give it. I always liked to go to these secretariats from time to time, and I have always come back enriched.

1. The Bible, the Common Bond of All Christians

It is no accident that the first president of the Secretariat for the Unity of Christians was not a dogmatic theologian nor a canon lawyer, but a biblical scholar. This was Cardinal Augustin Bea, who also, as we know, had a strong influence on the thinking of Pope John XXIII. People who come to a job from the Bible think in broad terms as God does, work for unity, as God does, and do not let themselves be trapped by human structures.

From the beginning of my life in the Capuchins, well before the Council, I too practiced ecumenism, taking it for granted, in the spirit of the Bible and the Franciscans. In 1946, when I was working on my doctoral dissertation on Christian terminology in the mission languages—and hence was investigating the problem of how technical biblical terms can be translated into the modern languages—I once spent three weeks constantly visiting the Protestant Mission House in Basel, to use the library. People were surprised, because I was the first Catholic to cross their threshold in the almost 150 year history of the house. And so I struck up a number of friendships. After finishing the doctorate and living in Africa for three years, I returned to work in Switzerland, where I was repeatedly invited by the Basel Mission to give lectures to the missionaries on leave. In the discussions that followed the question was stubbornly repeated: "Why don't you Catholic missionaries translate the Bible into the languages of the missions?" In 1959, when I asked my friend from this Basel Mission, F. Raaflaub, later president of the Swiss Evangelical Mission Council, what he knew about the efforts by the Catholic missions to translate the Bible, he told me: "If you ask me about the Catholic Bible in the mission languages, I have to say, 'It doesn't exist.' "

This prompted me, together with Prof. J. Beckmann, the editor of the *Neue Zeitschrift fur Missionswissenschaft*, to start a long series of articles on the Bible in the Catholic missions. Co-workers from the three southern continents were asked to contribute to it. The results showed that on this score we Catholics could actually point to a varied achievement in the past and present, even though we had admittedly not done as much as the Protestant Bible societies. In the introductory article I called attention to the ecumenical desirability of the different churches' trying to issue joint editions of the Bible, instead of using the Bible to compete with each other.[33]

Shortly thereafter, in the spring of 1962, I found myself once again on a long stay in Africa. In Dar es Salaam I had learned that the Catholic Church, which had already had a Swahili New Testament available for some time, was now about to print an Old Testament as well, translated by a group of missionaries and African priests, none of whom unfortunately had mastered the original languages of the Bible. A few Protestant scholars who were able to take a look at the text judged that it was a poor Swahili, which wholly failed to exploit the rich possibilities of the language, and that in many cases the original text had not been rendered well, either. The bishops were caught in an impasse, and so they did what one always does in this kind of situation: they appointed a committee to study the case. At that point I arrived and went to work immediately. First of all I spoke with the secretary of the bishops' conference, F. Robinson, then with the archbishop of Dar es Salaam, E. Maranta, and asked them whether the moment might not have come to take a new approach. Instead of bringing a bad Bible out on the market, it would really be better to adopt the new two-volume Protestant Bible. Both men saw that as a good way out of the difficulty. Then I flew to Nairobi just to submit this idea to the Apostolic Delegate, Guido Del Mestri. He thought it was "excellent, perfectly in line with the thinking of Pope John XXIII." Then I went in a private capacity to the combined "Christian Secretariat" of the Protestant Churches and asked what their reaction would be should the Catholic Church ask to adopt their Bible. Their answer: "We would be very surprised, but very delighted too." This request was in fact made to them, and thus the first joint Bible project in Africa took place. In *Dei verbum* the Council had not only allowed but strongly recommended ecumenical cooperation on the Bible. Since then we have not only gotten a "Unity Bible" in Europe, but in Africa and Asia at the present time there are something like 80 joint

Bible projects in operation. With this launching of the first ecumenical Bible in Africa to my credit, I introduced myself on my
first visit to the Secretariat in Rome, and immediately established
good contacts with W. Abbot, B. Meeking, and later also with
P. Duprey. In March, 1974, I was invited by this Secretariat to
a three-day seminar, along with Congar, Lyonnet, Grasso, etc.,
to give a specifically Catholic answer to the notion of "salvation
today," as it had been first discussed at the Bangkok conference
of the World Council of Churches. I often thought to myself when
I paid a visit to this Secretariat: This is the way it ought to be in
all the Vatican bureaus.

It's too bad that this Secretariat cannot proceed at its own
tempo, but is often slowed down or simply passed over by the
Congregations. It was hardly being allowed to speak for itself
when the letter of John Paul II appeared in September, 1985,
in response to the American Lutheran Bishop James Crumley.
"We should," the letter said, "make the beginning of the third
millenium the beginning of a special time of effort to achieve full
unity in Christ." This represents a typical delaying technique. It
would have been much more meaningful to say that we should
use the remaining years of this millenium as a deadline, so as
to overcome the split with the Eastern Churches (dating from
the 1054) and with the Reformation churches (dating from the
16th century) sometime before the end of this calamitous second
millenium. In that way we could face the world of the non-
Christian religions and the world of both eastern and western
materialism and atheism as the one Church of Christ amidst all
the diversity.

Then a dramatic incident occurred. On the first page of the
Osservatore Romano for February 25-26, 1985, a book that awakened many hopes, H. Fries and Karl Rahner's *Unification of the
Churches—A Real Possibility,* with an overview, "Agreement and
Criticism," by H. Fries (Freiburg im Breisgau) was given a very
rough going over. The reviewer, Daniel Ols, OP, described it as
a topsy-turvy treatment of Catholic dogma, with grave errors and

dangerous illusions. At the time I happened to be back in Rome and asked people at the Secretariat for the Unity of Christians what they had to say about this affair. They replied that they hadn't been consulted at all. Once again a typical performance: The Vatican has a special secretariat with expert advisors on the subject of ecumenism, but it goes over their heads and lets a man (or was he assigned to the job?) totally unknown in ecumenical circles, with no experience of the subject, have the front page of its official newspaper, to deliver this low blow to a pair of tried and true authors. This is the "structure of the congregations," to which the scholar A. Bugnini had already been sacrificed.

2. Dialogue with "Believers in Other Religions"

The same positive judgment holds for the Secretariat for Non-Christians. In studying missiology I personally had always been interested in the related sciences, and had tried to build bridges to them, first with ethnology and linguistics, then with the socio-political development of the Third World and its effects on the Church. Later I became increasingly involved with the non-Christian religions and their followers, who still make up two-thirds of the human race. Apart from lectures and articles, I have written two books on this, one that is more a reportage on interreligious congresses,[34] the other an attempt at a synthesis.[35] In one of the latest studies from the U.S.A. this book is frequently cited as a typical expression of what people in open-minded Catholic circles think about the subject.[36]

In contrast to the Propaganda Fide and to the Congregation of the Faith, which took offense to my book precisely because of its theme of ecumenism and the non-Christian religions, I received a great deal of understanding and encouragement from this Secretariat, both from its former secretary, Fr. Rossano, now suffragan bishop of Rome, and the current one, M. Zago. The latter assured me that my book was quite in line with the thinking of the Secretariat and that he had already given it to other people to read. When he was reappointed secretary, and I congratulated him on that, he wrote back to me on April 13, 1983:

Carissimo Fr. Bühlmann,

Many thanks for the good wishes you sent me on my appointment as secretary. I have always greatly prized my friendship
with you, as I have your competence, your creativity, and your
honesty. I hope that you can long continue to stir up the waters,
so that the kingdom of God may move forward. Pray for me too
that I can promote the spirit of Vatican II, which is the spirit of
the Gospel. I send you my best wishes, and assure you of my
prayers.

Fraternally yours in Christ and in the Immaculate Virgin Mary,

Fr. Marcello Zago, OMI

The same sort of friendship bound me to Fr. T. Michel, a
specialist in Islam, and to the president of the Secretariat, Archbishop J. Jadot, who was previously active for twelve years as
the Apostolic Delegate in the USA, and had deserved well of the
Church there by renewing the American bishops' conference with
young, pastorally minded bishops.

This friendship also led to my being entrusted in October, 1983
with sketching out a document on dialogue with the non-Christian
religions. I was also asked to turn in my own comments, and my
frank criticisms. I felt no inhibitions about writing as follows to
Archbishop Jadot on October 29, 1983:

Your Excellency,

Many thanks for the trust you have shown by presenting me
with the still confidential document on dialogue and the missions,
with the request for my comments on it. Much as I respect
your Secretariat, in fact precisely because of this respect and the
sympathy that I sense toward me on the part of your bureau, I
am taking the liberty of doing a radical critique in the hope that
before—or after—the next general assembly a second edition can
be put together that will be more trenchant and solid.

My general impression is that the document, as it stands, is not at all satisfactory. The criterion followed according to no. 4, that "no [attempt should be made] to do theological research, but simply expound the teaching of Vatican II and the Church's magisterium," condemns the document in advance to offer nothing new. Consequently it cannot lead us out of the impasse, the dilemma opposing dialogue and the missions. But that was ultimately the purpose for composing such a document in the first place. Thanks to that criterion the document becomes a "book of sentences," a piling up of authoritative texts, which are, however, often neither complete nor conclusive, theologically speaking. If they were, we wouldn't be in the impasse we are. So we have to go beyond the official magisterium. As the document now stands, it will be received as a typical "Roman document." It will, perhaps, be read—and put aside, because it strikes the reader as too general, too unfinished, too removed from real life . . . ." [I then offered many specific criticisms and finally submitted a new outline.]

The document appeared around Pentecost, 1984, on the occasion of the 20th anniversary of the Secretariat. It had been made significantly better and more theological. Needless to say, it no longer spoke of "pagans and unbelievers," but of "believers in other religions," which conveys a good deal more than "those of a different faith," where the accent is on "different" instead of on "faith." At bottom, however, it remains a compromise. One can sense the precautions that had to be taken with an eye to the other Roman Congregations with a less open-minded attitude. Thus, after justifying both the missions and dialogue, it aptly says of the relation between the two: "Dialogue is above all a style of action, an outlook, a spirit that shapes behavior. It includes attentiveness, respect, and open-mindedness toward others, to whom one leaves room for their personal identity, their forms of expressions, and their values. This sort of dialogue is the norm and necessary style for all the Christian missions and each of their parts, whether it is a question of simple presence with the testimony of the mis-

sionary's life or the providing of services or direct proclamation
of the Gospel." The expression "simple presence" implies but
does not say clearly enough that there can be and are situations
where for a certain time we must carry on nothing but dialogue
and set aside any plans for making conversions. The Propaganda
Fide would not swallow that sort of thing, because the people
there still do not recognize that it is good and valuable in itself to
conduct a dialogue through conversation, prayer, and work with
men and women who, it is true, do "not yet" live in the Church,
but "already" live in the kingdom of God.

The obvious tension between the secretariats and the congregations is not merely an accident, but has deeper roots, in that the
latter stress ecclesiology, the former Christology. The congregations think in a more introverted, internal-ecclesiastical way, and
are bent on the sacramentalization of Catholics, while the secretariats are intent on the evangelization of all people. The congregations, as we have already sufficiently noted, still drag a lot of
preconciliar ballast along with them; the secretariats proceed in an
exemplary postconciliar fashion. In 1982, when Pope John Paul
II presented his outline of curial reform at the second meeting of
the cardinals, there were stubborn rumors going around that he
had had a notion of dissolving the postconciliar secretariats—in
other words, of integrating them into suitable Congregations and
thereby stifling their special functions—but that the cardinals had
managed to dissuade him from this idea. At the third meeting
of the cardinals in November 1985 people thought for sure that
the secretariats would now be declared "councils," which would
constitute a downgrading in the hierarchy. Thus the tug-of-war
between authority and competence goes on. When will we finally
progress so far that the Vatican takes seriously the competence
of the specialists who know contemporary theology and recognize
the signs of the time—without in any way losing its authority but
rather making it credible and acceptable?

3. Gandhi Should Be Canonized

In April, 1983 the hit film *Gandhi* by Richard Attenborough
was showing in Rome and in many other cities of the world. I
had already seen it twice. I called up Cardinal B. Gantin, the
president of the papal commission "Justitia et Pax." A few years
earlier I had invited him to see the film, *Jesus Christ Superstar*,
with me, which he greatly liked. Now I encouraged him to come
see *Gandhi* with me, since I thought it was tremendous, both
for the acting and for the message, and, with its ideas of equal
rights, of the brotherhood of all people, of respect for other
religions and of non-violence, closely connected to the efforts of
his commission. Though he was short of time, the cardinal came
and was very impressed. I then suggested he should really ask
the pope to say a word in recognition of this film and its message
at His Angelus homily. The cardinal replied: "That would sound
like publicity for the film." Myself: "No harm in that. Since
Rome already issues condemnations of bad films, it could say
something in recognition of this extraordinarily good film." But
the idea came to naught.

The next day I went to Archbishop J. Jadot and tried to convince him that he and all the people in his Secretariat for Non-
Christians had to see this film. After that, I thought he should
make an attempt to get the Congregation for Canonizations to
study the question of whether Gandhi might not be canonized.
That wouldn't mean that he had been pocketed by the Catholic
Church, but that the Church was making quiet reparations for all
the injustice that we have done to non-Christian religions over the
centuries. We would be thereby officially acknowledging that a
non-Christian too could be a model, showing us Christians how
to live. Archbishop Jadot liked the idea, but he answered: "That
one you'll have to launch. This sort of thing can't come from
above, it has to come from below." So I sent off a press release
about the proposal to the Italian, English, and German newspapers. I wanted to shock readers a bit with the notion and to give

them some food for thought. I added, of course, that if this suggestion was to have any prospect of success, then it would have to be accepted and advanced by the Church of India. In all likelihood, a whole lot more water will have to flow down the Indus and the Ganges before we get to that point.

Part Nine

Getting Rid of the Roman Curial Style
(Negotiations with the Secretariat for Non-believers)

I had less to do with this Secretariat. It made smaller waves than the two other Secretariats because its job was significantly harder, but also, perhaps, because they had not found the right tone, as the following episode illustrates.

Our curia general received a letter from this Secretariat dated February 13, 1975. Although it has no importance in itself, I want to quote it as a typical example of the Roman curial style:

Most Reverend Father,

This Secretariat wishes to manifest to *your most reverend Paternity* its lively gratitude for the kind answer that was given at

---

Translator's note: Bühlmann's chapter title may well allude to the immortal jest by the renowned Venetian historian, Fra Paolo Sarpi (1552-1623). Attacked by a gang of papal assassins and stabbed in the forehead with a dagger (he eventually recovered), Sarpi coolly remarked "Conosco lo stilo della curia romana." (The Italian word *stilo* means both "style" and "stiletto"): "I recognize the style of the Roman Curia." -Th the time to our brief Prot. n. 002683/74 of May 22, last year, with regard to the determination of the special matter and the territorial circumscription that you proposed for a more effective and fruitful development of the relations of your order's institute with the same Secretariat.

Among the various initiatives which this *holy dicastery* will be undertaking shortly is that of taking a deeper view of the problems involved in the so very widespread phenomenon of religious indifference, which in a secularized world like ours causes not a little concern to those who bear the pastoral responsibility for the people of God.

In order, therefore, to acquire the broadest imaginable knowledge from those competent to deal with such a problem, and then to call the attention of the *holy hierarchy* to the collected findings, while rendering it open to a sure orientation of the appropriate pastoral activity, we here have considered the collaboration of *your Paternity* in the study of the above-mentioned phenomenon as especially valuable. [There follows a detailed, ten line invitation to a discussion of this theme for March 13, at 4:30 P.M.]

In the certainty that *your Paternity*, interested as you are in a balanced assessment of the consequences and peculiar features of a phenomenon that is so complex and for that reason so important these days, will not deny us at this session the esteemed help of your competence and experience, we present to you even now the special expression of our deep gratitude.

We meanwhile take the opportunity to assure your most reverend Paternity with deep religious respect that we are your humble servants,

Ant. Mauro. Vice President
P. Miano, Sec

The reader will doubtless have noticed already that this letter, with its complicated style, is so swarming with convoluted expressions that it makes a normal Christian's head spin. At the meeting itself we were first ushered into the presence of the president of the Secretariat, Cardinal Franz Konig, who stays only occasionally in Rome, and offered a lecture on the phenomenon of secularization, in rather negative tones, as the destruction of so many religious values. In the discussion I asked leave to speak and said: "We bemoan secularization and do it in a way that is one of the reasons why many people don't take the Church seriously any more. In the letter of invitation, for example, we ordinary men were addressed as 'most reverend Paternity.' In the official Vatican style, seen also in the *Osservatore Romano*, discriminating distinctions are drawn, and the Church continues to be divided into lay people, who get no title; Venerabili (religious brothers); Reverendi (ordinary priests): Molto Reverendi (provincial superiors); Reverendissimi (superiors general); Le Loro Eccellenze Reverendissime I Monsignori (bishops), and finally Le Loro Eminenze Reverendissime I Signori Cardinali (Cardinals). We have evidently completely forgotten that the New Testament speaks of brothers and sisters, and that the communists call themselves comrades. Why does Rome set such great store by titles that we others laugh at? I would like to move that this Secretariat in particular, which has to deal with the Marxist comrades, make an attempt at the Secretariat of State to get rid of this Roman curial style."

Loud applause. Afterwards a co-worker of the Secretariat told me that they were totally in agreement with me, but the vice-president, Archbishop Mauro, was very attached to this style. This party-line Archbishop was later appointed papal delegate for the basilicas of San Paolo fuori le mura in Rome and Sant'Antonio in Padua. But the curial style goes on luxuriating merrily in the Vatican and lets the world be the world. After all, the Church mustn't adjust to the world in everything.

Part Ten

How Necessary is Special Dress for Priests and Religious?

(Negotiations with the General Vicariate of Rome)

At the "révision de vie" with the pope I had already pointed out that so much weight ought not to be put on priests' and religious' wearing special dress, since the question took on an altogether different look in different countries and continents. This fraternal admonition evidently failed to have the desired effect. Things did get somewhat quieter on the subject, but in October 1982, at the beginning of the new academic year, the pope wished to resolve the question once and for all, firstly for Rome, as the exemplar, and then for the other countries too.

In the *Osservatore Romano* for October 19, 1982, (it always comes out on the evening before the publication date) there was a letter on the front page from the pope to Cardinal Ugo Poletti, the vicar general for the archdiocese of Rome, asking him to see to it that the sacred character of the Holy City be preserved, and that as a sign of this all priests and religious were to wear their habit when they went outside. There followed a text that expressed this wish in the form of a law that was to take immediate effect,

216

signed by Cardinal U. Poletti, and additionally by Cardinal S. Oddi, the prefect of the Congregation of the Clergy, Cardinal E. Pironio, prefect of the Congregation for Religious, and Cardinal W. Baum, prefect of the Congregation for Catholic Education, which was in charge of the papal universities.

I didn't get much sleep that night. My brain was seething. I simply couldn't get it into my head that they were making problems where none were, while they weren't taking the real problems seriously enough and tackling them directly. In the morning, right after breakfast, I wrote the following letter and sent it out, so that the four cardinals named above had it on their desks before noon:

Your Eminence,

As I will soon be leaving Rome to return to Switzerland after serving for twelve years at the curia general of the Capuchin order and all over the world, I can take the liberty of presenting to you with all "parrheaia" (frankness) my reflections on the new regulation: It is now obligatory, by the highest authority of the pope and three Roman Congregations (the only thing missing is a reference to divine law), for priests and religious to wear their particular habit at all times. I foresee that three kinds of reaction will emerge to the new decree:

—Some people will have no problem performing an act of obedience out of love for the Church.

—Others will tell themselves: Don't get excited, let time pass, this order will have the same fate as *Veterum sapientia*.[37]

—Still others will raise serious critical questions, for example:

1. We are all agreed that many things are wrong with the Church and with the city of Rome. But do you seriously dare to believe that things will improve if 10,000 people, instead of 5,000, walk through the streets of Rome in their habit? Things will get better, and a believable witness will be given, through the efforts of groups like that of S. Egidio.[38] Whether these people

wear religious dress or not is immaterial.

2. You remember that twelve years ago a poll of the Roman population showed that the monsignori from the Vatican were the least sympathetically viewed of all priests. . . . Why then impose on the whole clergy the pattern of thinking and dressing proper to these eminences and excellencies?

3. What would Jesus say to these five church laws about clothing, he who could not bear the caste of Pharisees, with their religious garments? "They make their phylacteries broad and their fringes long" (Mt 23:5). Jesus, however, did not say, "By this shall men know that you are my disciples, that you wear the Roman collar," but "that you love one another."

4. On the same front page of the *Osservatore Romano* there is an appeal by the pope in favor of "solidarity among the nations to overcome hunger in the world." Why does this appeal remain so general, and consequently without effect; and why are no concrete rules made on this issue, instead of the question of dress, for the clergy and Christian people?

5. Why impose such rules on grown-ups, professors and students, and measure their loyalty to the Church by such external laws? Isn't that an enormous affront to freedom of conscience?

6. You speak of these "wonderful young people" who gladly wear religious dress. But aren't they mostly traditionalists, verticalists, integralists, so much from the mold of Archbishop Lefebvre, who have become world-weary and instead of doing their utmost for a just world, take flight into the Church, into the habit, into prayer?

7. Is this victory of the Church's right wing a genuine or rather a Pyrrhic victory, which increasingly isolates the Church from the world, which makes its agenda without the Church? How will this arrangement, this introversion be judged by history? Perhaps the way the anti-modernist campaign in the beginning of this century is judged today?

8. How can the primate of Poland, Cardinal Glemp, and Pope Wojtyla speak out so clearly in favor of Solidarity and against the system of oppression, while people in the Church dictate laws, without ever consulting the rank and file, that trample on the sentiments of the rank and file?

9. After so many questions, whose answer to many observers is clear, would it be surprising if a good part of the seminarians, the professors, the clergy and religious continued, as before, to go their own way, following the Gospel and their consciences, or even expressed their dissent in a public demonstration? Isn't it true that the right to free expression of one's opinion and even dissent are human rights that are valid in the Church?

I originally intended to distribute this letter among the mass of students and professors of the papal universities. But then I reconsidered and preferred not to influence them in any way, but to leave them their full freedom and await their spontaneous reaction. We shall see. But I would ask not to condemn too readily those who in the distress of their heart raise questions like those above.

Despite all the difficulties of your office, I wish you "Pace e Bene!"

Fr. Walbert Bühlmann

I also sent copies of this letter to the two Secretariats of the two Unions of Superiors General. From there it swiftly made its way to the many curias general and from there to the many houses of study. For a while it was the talk of the day among the students. Anyhow, for all its probing questions it remained polite. Afterwards the seminarians turned out caricatures and fictitious replies from Cardinal Poletti, some of them very ironic and satirical. The Church's highest authority took a dangerous risk for a problem that wasn't a problem—and lost both the battle and some prestige. The effect of the brief was almost nil. Toward the end of the semester, one could see that, now as ever, around 80 percent of the theology students at the papal universities went out in civilian clothes.

The reaction of the four cardinals who received the letter was interesting. There was no sign of anything from Cardinal Baum. On October 25 Cardinal Poletti sent a short hand-written letter that expressed all his embarrassment.

Reverend Father,

I scarcely know what answer I should give, humanly speaking, to your numerous questions.

You are a Franciscan: In a moment of silent prayer come face to face with your revered father, St. Francis.

I greet you respectfully, yours truly

Ugo Card. Poletti

On October 20—i.e., right away—Cardinal Oddi took the trouble to write a long, sympathetic, moving letter, so much so that I almost repented having voiced my protest. But upon closer inspection I found in Oddi's answer a number of fallacies. It is by no means true that I am ashamed of my Franciscan habit, or that I disdain the merits of the Franciscans in history. But if at certain times the brown habit had its meaning, as a sign of renunciation of the world, it is not self-evident that people understand it that way in every milieu today, or that it has to be prescribed by church laws. Furthermore, when I speak about "traditionalists, verticalists, integralists," I am not referring to the habit of St. Francis, but to a part of today's youth. But let's read the letter itself:

Dear Father,

I have read with attention your letter on ecclesiastical dress, and I can understand your state of mind, which is why you have raised many problems. On some of them, for example with respect to hunger, I could find myself in agreement with you, even though they have no relevance to the actual point at issue. I have no wish to deliver to you here a treatise on the habit, but only to speak to you in brotherly fashion about the question,

out of the great reverence and warm feelings I have for your
Capuchin order and for all Franciscan orders. In fact the Lord
granted me an undeserved grace in my life, in that I get to busy
myself with the Franciscan shrines in Assisi, and hence I take
part in all the important festivals of St. Francis. I was especially,
immeasurably moved by the raising of the body of the Poverello.
I have entrusted to him not only my priestly work, but my whole
person.

Father, I think that you too were moved at the sight of St.
Francis' habit, which is so poor and humble, and which is preserved in Assisi with so much loving care. So many holy and
humble brothers, Franciscan and Capuchin, have knelt before this
revered relic, and have then gone out all over the world, wearing
the habit of St. Francis. In that way this habit has become the
banner of Franciscan evangelization and service to the poor. I
cannot forget my excitement, when I entered the Capitol building
in the United States and discovered there the robe of St. Francis
in the form of the only Catholic priest who has a statue there,
namely Father Serra.[39]

I assume that you are Swiss. In many churches of Switzerland
too I have found this sign of evangelization and service. Father,
can you look at the relic of the habit of St. Francis and really
have the courage to quote the passage from Matthew 23:5, as
you do in your passionate letter? In the face of the robe of St.
Francis, which you are called to wear—can you really speak of
the "victory of the right wing," and of "traditionalists, verticalists,
integralists," as you do in your letter? In view of the humble robe
of St. Francis—do you really have the courage to say this is the
"pattern of dressing proper to those eminences and excellencies"?

Father, let's be clear on this: what the pope wants from you is
purely and simply to wear the habit of St. Francis. Do you think
perhaps that St. Francis would have refused to carry out a wish
of the Holy Father?

We live at a time of tensions, and tensions are sown in our midst as well. If you are willing to receive it, I give you my blessing, so that you can accept this word of the pope in peace and joy.

With priestly respect,

Silvio Card. Oddi

The letter from Archbishop A. Mayer, the secretary of the Congregation for Religious, now cardinal-prefect of the Congregation for Divine Worship was a nasty one. The cardinal in charge, E. Pironio, was evidently absent at the time. He would in any case have sent a different answer. For as a man of dialogue and a Latin American he knew very well that in his homeland the cassock and traditional religious dress have been from earlier days a sign of identification with the political regime, and therefore are for the most part no longer worn. It may be too that Archbishop Mayer, who was generally regarded as the strong man of the Congregation, simply took over the job of responding to me on his own. On October 26 he wrote not to me but to my superior general, to bring charges against me:

Reverend Father,

The letter, which is enclosed here in a photocopy, has come to our office. It was written on October 19 by Rev. Walbert Bühlmann from your order and concerns the new regulation on the wearing of ecclesiastical dress in the diocese of Rome, which was issued by his Eminence, Cardinal Ugo Poletti, at the behest and with the agreement of the Holy Father.

This Holy Congregation expresses its particular astonishment at the conceit and arrogance with which a son of St. Francis has taken the liberty of criticizing the decisions of the Church's authority, especially since they come from a direct intervention of the Supreme Pontiff, the Bishop of Rome, and basically do no more than lend emphasis to the already existing legislation.

On the other hand, it is enough to read carefully the documentation that appeared in the *Osservatore Romano* to understand the reasons that have determined this regulation, without taking refuge in a line of argument that lacks any serious foundation, and above all to prompt every priest and religious to eager, childlike obedience.

I take the opportunity to declare myself, with devout wishes, your humble servant in the Lord,

A. Mayer, Sec.

The actual effect, or better, lack of any effect, of this regulation showed that the majority of today's priests and religious understand "childlike obedience" to the Church differently nowadays from the way people did in the "good old days" of feudalism. It would be good to take note of this, so that the Church could be governed in a more realistic and efficacious manner.

Part Eleven

Upgrading the Bishop's Synod in Rome

(Negotiations With the Bishops' Conferences in the Third World)

For forty years I have been busied myself with what were then the missions and are now the young churches. I have experienced their ascent, made people aware of their numerical importance in. my books, and rejoiced in their growing sense of themselves. Naturally, I also grieve with them over their problems. By that I mean, not their economic and political problems, some of which are quite dramatic, but that in the Church the powers that be are not yet ready to set them free from western hegemony and that financial support from Rome is used to exert pressure on them, so that they don't get out of line. For years, then, I have labored to play the role of interpreter and advocate of the young churches among the western members of the Church and at its summit in Rome. I have tried to lend support to their own efforts to win understanding for their individual character.

With a view to the extraordinary bishops' synod of 1985 in Rome, to which the presidents of the bishops' conferences, not elected delegates, were invited, in order to draw up a balance sheet on the twenty years after the Council, I thought it might be useful to provide the participants from the Third World with information that concerned them, and through them effectively to change the structure of the synod. The point is that while the constitution of every state can be changed, from case to case, by parliament or through a popular referendum, and so can be adapted to new realities, there is no such possibility in the Church. Even its highest authority, the synod of bishops, can really introduce no new postulates: They run aground on existing canon law. It has no right to pass any resolutions at all, unless the pope explicitly confers this power on it (canon 343). But the pope will evidently confer this power only if he is convinced in advance of the justice of the expected resolution. Thus the synod, with its purely advisory capacity, will always mark time and increasingly awaken feelings of frustration among its participants.

There are, in fact, two models for dealing with free men and women. In his plan of creation and salvation God himself has chosen the risk-model. By remaining hidden as the First Cause and allowing free play to "secondary" causes, he accepts the fact that many things will go awry, well knowing that in the end he *will* reach his goal, through all the good and evil. The Church, by contrast, seems to lack the courage to follow the example of "divine powerlessness." It opts for the security-model. It keeps all powers of decision for itself, and in this way it becomes a power structure that degrades the 800 million Catholics and 4500 bishops to figures that have only to carry out the decrees promulgated from on high.

In order to make some sort of change, if possible, in this situation, I sent the following letter in July, 1985 to the majority of the bishops' conferences from the Third World, 20 in English, 12 in French, and 11 in Spanish:

Dear Bishop,

As the author of the book *Where Faith Lives*, I am taking the liberty of submitting to you some reflections that might perhaps be of use to you at the coming bishops' synod in Rome. . . .

I shall limit myself here to the matter of the Third Church, which, after the "First Church" of the first millenium, the Eastern Church; and after the "Second Church" of the second millenium, the Western Church; now steps anew onto the stage of history as the "Third Church" of the coming third millenium, or as the Southern Church. All these three Churches together form now what is the first World Church in the real sense.

All the leading councils belonged either to the Eastern or to the Western Church. Vatican II enters the history books as the first council to see the Third Church assembled here and now as a body. In the years before the Council John XXIII had speeded up the appointment of African and Asian bishops so that he could see the many-colored faces of the young churches present at the Council.

At the time people could not yet discern the actual importance of the young churches, because the western churches were still unmistakably in charge and had a numerical superiority. In 1900, 77 percent of the Catholics lived in the western world. Around 1970, however, though many observers were blind to it, suddenly 51 percent of the Catholics already belonged to the southern world: Latin America, Africa, Asia-Oceania. By 1980 the proportion had risen to 58 percent. Thus it is easy to foresee that by the year 2000, not long from now, around 70 percent of Catholics will be at home in the southern or "Third Church."

Though the Council was not yet able to foresee this development, it nonetheless had a prophetic presentiment of it, and it elaborated principles to do justice to the newly evolved Third Church, namely the principles of the local church, collegiality, and legitimate pluralism. The problem, however, lies entirely in translating them into practice. The Church's ruling class displays a peculiar fear of genuine pluralism and basically permits only the Roman model of unity to prevail. A few examples will substantiate this statement:

—In the area of the liturgy India had created a supplementary "Indian liturgy" with Indian language and symbols. In 1975 Rome sent a letter strictly forbidding the celebration of this liturgy, since the time for experimenting was past. At the same time Zaire had drafted its liturgy, a two hour melodrama with full participation by the people, a true celebration not the mere repetition of a rite. Despite the repeated requests of the bishops it was not approved by Rome and was not even allowed to be put on for the pope. But in many churches in the towns and country it is celebrated anyway.

—In the area of theology Latin America has had the courage to develop for the first time a non-European theology. People have been very happy with it because in contrast to traditional scholastic theology and Catholic social teaching, which were well known there too, but remained mere "doctrines," it actually changes lives and has brought millions of poor people a new self-awareness and new hope. We know that for months now liberation theology has come under crossfire from Rome, and that one of its most prominent spokesmen, Leonardo Boff, was placed under a total ban against speaking and writing.

—In the area of discipline not enough allowance is made for the young churches and their concerns. At the bishops' synod of 1980 five African bishops, each in the name of his bishop's conference, asked for more understanding of their "African path to marriage." The answer they received in the concluding document was at bottom no answer, as it merely repeated the already familiar general principles. The "Third Church" is also still not represented in the Church's central administration in a manner commensurate with its strength. In leadership positions in Rome we find only one Asian, two Latin American, and two African cardinals, and at the most recent naming of cardinals two Asian, two African, and three Latin American bishops were chosen, but in return so were five Italians (although Italy by itself already has more cardinals than all of Latin America), 21 in all from the western world and 7 from the South. Rome seems to be afraid of the Third World, and is still expanding the historical hegemony of the western Church.

At the episcopal synods in Rome, on the other hand, the bishops of the young churches are predominant simply because they represent more countries. But the tragedy lies in the fact that these synods have only an advisory character. Afterwards everything falls into the gears of the Roman Curia and there gets processed in accordance with Roman criteria. If at the coming synod only one thing was accomplished—something many bishops would like to see—namely that the synod itself acquired a legislative character, then many things would change. For the experience of the last synods has shown that pastorally minded bishops are speaking there, are presenting their analyses, and offering their suggestions. Hope is awakening. People are saying in the World Church, "Look! Listen! Something of the conciliar mood is coming back." But a year later when the final document comes out, all hope is stifled once again and the status quo is confirmed.

Thus the synod ought to get the power to make the most important decisions for the Church—always acting together with the pope. Only then would it be a real expression of collegiality. Then it would be a kind of mini-council, a sort of ongoing-council. Then, as at the Council, new ideas and new blood would continually be infused into the organism of the Church, something that right now is badly needed, because only the Roman Curia, not the bishops of the world, is running the World Church.

It was a bad omen, and a rude awakening for me, when with one exception, from Latin America, none of the bishops reacted to the letter. Because of overwork? Laziness? Or, as I particularly suspected, because of fear of compromising themselves, since the letter was quite frank and open? At the synod itself the idea of legislative power for this body made no big splash. True, the Swiss Bishops' Conference, as stated at its press conference on November 21, 1985, stressed in a petition to Rome that it would be desirable to transform the synod from its present consultative authority into an autonomous body with definitive jurisdiction, although at the same time the Conference expressed its misgivings that this might be detrimental to collegiality with all bishops. The answer to that, of course, is that the synod would not pass resolutions as the result of sudden whims, but that all matters on the agenda would be publicized and consulted on in advance at the local bishops' conferences. In Rome, on the very first day of the synod, Maxim Hermaniuk, the Ukrainian metropolitan and archbishop of Winnipeg, caused a sensation with his idea of a "permanent bishops' synod." In the interests of genuine collegiality and dynamic leadership he proposed that together with the pope twenty bishops elected by the synod, plus five named by the pope, should decide all the questions in the life of the Church that have hitherto been decided by the pope together with the Roman Curia. This permanent bishops' conference would exercise the legislative power of the Church, while the Roman Curia would keep the executive power. So this would be a variant of the idea I presented above, and it grows out of the same intent, that the Church should be led not by the Roman Curia but by the bishops of the world.

The synod would not let itself be driven by this initial impulse. Suddenly and unequivocally another trend appeared, not to improve and upgrade the Church's central leadership, but to give much more authority and "say" to the local churches and the bishops conferences, in other words to break free from exaggerated centralization.

Whatever may concretely happen now, the message has been delivered. We must not let up, always coming back to our purpose, until things finally progress to the point—even if we don't get there before the year 2000—where the Council's ideas of episcopal collegiality, legitimate pluralism, and a basic pastoral approach are taken completely seriously, and in such a way that Vatican I is completed, not just theoretically, but practically and in fact, by Vatican II.

Part Twelve

Conclusion: Dreaming of the Church's Future

What we have seen in the previous eleven chapters constitutes a fragment of the 20th century Acts of the Apostles, a historical process full of tensions and confusion. To be sure, we have been looking only at the dark side of the picture. We ought now to move to the bright side. If we did, we would be amazed at the awakening of the young churches, at the liberation of the poor, at the dialogue with the non-Christian religions, at the new religious quest by the intelligentsia and many young people in both East and West—in short, at the winds of the Spirit that we can feel blowing inside and outside the Church. Needless to say, one would have to say many good things even about the Roman Curia, just to fill out the picture. But the gloomy aspects, which had to be shown for what they are, also form part of the reality of the Church. We can now draw from them the following conclusions:

—My working hypothesis seems to be confirmed. I maintained in the first part that the Roman Curia's way of thinking and acting is in line with neither the Gospel nor the Council, and that during ten important post-conciliar years too many members of the Curia were horribly incompetent, incapable of dialogue, and dictatorial. The truth of this could be read with increasing clarity in case after case that I cited.

—These were only the personal experiences of one man. It may be that I probed and poked away more than other people. But I could have amplified my account with a great many more similar details, which would make the whole business still more disgraceful.

—This kind of body is risking the loss of its authority. Even though the bishops and bishops' conferences have thus far tried, "for unity's sake," to abide by the Roman decrees, one cannot hold it against mature Christians, priests or laypeople, if they no longer accept this kind of authority in advance and blindly obey its regulations, but decide on a case to case basis how they want to react. No one should say that this is an open summons to passive resistance or even to disobedience to the Church. First of all, it is not a summons, but the mere stating of an accomplished fact. We have already seen that in West Germany only a bare quarter, 23 percent, of Catholics trouble themselves about promulgations from Rome. To that extent only this minority remains "Roman Catholic." Secondly, the Roman Curia is not, thank God, identical to the Church. It merely has a function to play in the service of the real Church, the people of God. Thirdly, an authority without competence and without regard for human dignity and freedom of conscience leads by itself to the brink of absurdity. We can only wait till the time is ripe and the pressure has increased so that some day the Curia gets totally reformed.[40] Fourthly, we can appeal to the present pope, who in 1969 as Cardinal Wojtyla said: "Conformism means death for any community; a loyal opposition is necessary for all communities." That is true not only for Poland and for all states, but for the Church as well.

—Until we get evident signs of a radically reformed Curia, we can think meaningfully and hopefully about this Roman Curia only in dreams.

The old saying that dreams are idle ("Träume sind Schäume") is not true. In the Old and New Testament they play a great role as modes of interpretation and stimulation. In the history of religion they have been considered by all peoples to be revelations from the gods. In the field of depth psychology Sigmund Freud thought he saw in them a fictional form of wish fulfillment and Carl G. Jung saw the self-portrayal of the person in wishes and mental sketches.

What we have in this case is not sleeping dreams but waking dreams. Paul Zulehner's remark is a propos here: "Anyone who doesn't have the courage to dream doesn't have the strength to fight." At a time of much worse depression and despairing acquiescence than today, when the people of Israel were living in the Babylonian captivity and could no longer muster any courage to believe in a better future, the prophet Isaiah came on the scene and spoke in Utopian visions of the wilderness exulting and shouting for joy, of streams gushing forth and watering the earth, of the eyes of the blind being opened and the tongues of the dumb singing out, of the lame leaping like a hart, of those ransomed by the Lord returning full of jubilation to Zion, everlasting joy on their heads, joy and gladness in their hearts (Chapter 35).

To this day these biblical visions keep awakening hope against all hope. For hope is the last thing a human being should give up. One can never think grandly enough of what can and will come. In a depressed mood our wings get broken, and we no longer even do what we could and should. Only in an atmosphere of hope do the inspirations come and the forces grow that we need for every great undertaking. In this sense the following three dreams are likewise to be understood as an expression of hope.

1. THE STRUGGLE WITH THE ANGEL OF THE CHURCH

The exegetes are divided over whether Jacob's wrestling with the angel is a real, external event or a visionary dream. However that may be, we read in Genesis 32: 25-32:

> And Jacob was left alone; and a man wrestled with
> him until the breaking of the day. When the man saw

that he did not prevail against Jacob, he touched the hollow of his thigh; and Jacob's thigh was put out of joint as he wrestled with him. Then he said, "Let me go, for the day is breaking." But Jacob said, "I will not let you go unless you bless me." And he said to him, "What is your name?" And he said, "Jacob." Then he said, "Your name shall no more be called Jacob, but Israel, for you have striven with God and with men, and have prevailed." Then Jacob asked him, "Tell me, I pray, your name." But he said, "Why is it that you ask my name?" And there he blessed him. So Jacob called the name of the place Peniel, saying, "For I have seen God face to face, and yet my life is preserved."

I had spent two days giving lectures at the general chapter of a missionary society in Rome, opening up to the participants the new horizons of the World Church and presenting to them the postulates that should shape the Church's path to the year 2001. The reactions had been good. My audience came from a pastoral background and felt strengthened in their own thoughts, expectations, and attitudes. There was a widespread sense of pain that initiatives and dynamic direction no longer come "from above," as the Council's decree on the missions had wished. I encouraged them to follow with the local churches along the path pointed out by the Gospel and the Council, to seek new solutions from life, and in this way to set the course for the next (the third) edition of the code of canon law, because, I said, life is always ahead of the law, and from time to time the law has to catch up with life again.

Now I was strolling, at once happy and tired, on my way home through the park of the Villa Borghese. Fresh air and birdsong have often enough had an inspirational effect on me. As I sauntered along, I suddenly felt as if I were entranced. I don't know whether I was fantasizing or dreaming, but in any case it seemed to me as if my way was barred by a powerful man dressed as a student of karate. He silently challenged me to combat.

When it comes to muscle power, I have never been a daredevil. But now there was no way to escape. We were already mixing it up, and to my surprise I saw that I could hold my ground against my opponent. We gripped one another, pushed, lifted, and threw one another, but we both kept getting up, ready for a fresh assault.

Suddenly it dawned on me that my opponent was the angel of God, more precisely the angel of the Church, and that he wanted to give me the opportunity of marking off my position in the Church. So I began to fight with words instead of with holds. Now I got visibly stronger and I marveled at my own courage. I talked and talked, as if to a wall, into an airless room. And yet I never doubted that I was saying important things in the right place.

"Have the members of the Church been struck blind? They can't help recognizing the open secret that Christendom's center of gravity has shifted from the west to the south, into the Third World: in the year 2000, 70 percent of Catholics and 60 percent of all Christians will live in that world. But the churchmen see that only as an extension of their sphere of power. They imagine that the western Church, in the forms that have evolved through history, is the only conceivable kind of Church, as if God would be content with a single species of bird, fish, or mammal. Instead he has fashioned an incredible variety of creatures, so that our wonder will never cease. Why then should a Church made up of creative individuals have only one form? On the contrary, we must postulate for the future many kinds of liturgy, a Roman, of course, but also an Indian, a Zairean, a Brazilian, and only together will they give us a notion of the harmony and variety of the chorus of humanity responding to God. We also have to give the green light to many theologies. No longer can one continent, the West, produce theology while the other continents merely consume it. The many churches of the various continents each have to set its own priorities and give the Gospel flesh and form in its own cultural sphere. Just as no group of astronauts can claim to have explored all of outer space, so even the different theologies of the different continents all together can provide only a feeble reflection of the immensity of theological space."

I noticed that my partner had grown tamer and let me talk without impeding me. So I got the courage to go on spinning out my thoughts. "I also believe that for all the trend toward unity in essentials, I mean in faith in Jesus Christ and his Gospel and in the same active love, we ought not only to tolerate but to promote a great multiplicity of forms in secondary matters. There are already two very different models of the Church. The Eastern churches and similarly the Reformation churches developed Christology and pneumatology more, while we in the Catholic Church were more intent on ecclesiology. They follow more the synodal or collegial principle, we the monarchical principle. They stress freedom in the Spirit more, we stress authority and obedience. Thus, as there already are de facto two complementary models of the Church, in the future there could and should be an Asian, African, and Latin American model. Together they would express, even though only feebly, the abundance of the Church's being."

Suddenly the angel of the Church seemed to be getting weak, but not as though he had let down his guard. He was not to go down for the count. I kept on talking at him: "All these are ideas that are reasonable to half-way reasonable people. But the men of the Church act as if they were blind. The air in their offices doesn't seem to agree with them. Any decent physician knows that he has to continue his education all through life, since medical knowledge doubles approximately every seven years. But they remain stuck fast in their handbook-theology. They won't listen to reason; they think they already know better about everything. When they meet experts in any field they have only defensive reactions. The gap between authority and competence keeps growing wider and wider. This creates malaise, antipathy, and, what is even worse, apathy and resignation in the Church. But anyone who despite everything refuses to be paralyzed and wants to set the Church's course for the coming third millenium must expect to be punched in the face, as I myself have discovered, even though I have always escaped with no more than a black eye."

Now the angel changed his tactics. He stopped fighting and rubbed my forehead caressingly, as if he wished to heal my black eye, and without speaking he communicated to me the following insight through a kind of telepathy: "You've fought well. Keep at it. I'm with you, as I'm with the Church too. Consider: historical processes don't happen through miracles, but through human confrontation, through laborious evolution. Time will show that you are right. There is no way to predict the creative inspirations of God's Spirit. He can suddenly find new solutions and make what is impossible possible, what is hardened supple and moldable. Even if you had to perish with your ideas, your cause, the cause of Jesus will survive, and the freedom of the children of God will shape the picture of the Church in the future.

Now the angel gave me a piercing look, and his garments suddenly became flooded with blinding white light as if at the coming of Christ in judgment. He said: "Meanwhile, you must take the Church as she is, with all the harsh legalism and the old traditional clericalism at the top, with all the usual routine habits among the masses, with all the offense taken at that by the people who fancy themselves good. But are they really good? Are *you* really good? Isn't everyone subject to sin and deprived of God's glory? Don't we all have to begin church reform with ourselves? So long as the Church walks along in her pilgrim's robe, we have to put up with all her dust and wrinkles. It remains the face of the Church, more, the face of Christ, bathed in sweat and blood, even covered with sin, that the Lord has taken upon himself. A mystery Church, not only in the coming glory, but also in the present wretchedness. Do you understand?"

Suddenly I was frightened by the talking and laughing and gesticulation of a crowd of young people, which called me back from my reverie to reality. The whole vision appeared to have vanished, too beautiful to be true. Or had it? I believe that this is the path we must go with the Church, a path fraught with difficulty, between confident statement, "On the third day he will rise," and hesitating supplication, "If it is possible, let this cup pass from me." Yet the last word goes not to wavering, but to God's confidence, his surprise, his solution.

2. THE POPE SELLS THE VATICAN

The Apostle Peter had to realize in a dream vision that things and customs that were sacrosanct to him could be seen otherwise and therefore could be changed. We read in the Acts of the Apostles 10:9-35:

> The next day, as they were on their journey and coming near the city, Peter went up on the housetop to pray, about the sixth hour. And he became hungry and desired something to eat; but while they were preparing it he fell into a trance and saw the heavens opened, and something descending, like a great sheet, let down by four corners upon the earth. In it were all kinds of animals and reptiles and birds of the air. And there came a voice to him, "Rise, Peter; kill and eat." But Peter said, "No, Lord; for I have never eaten anything that is common or unclean." And the voice came to him again a second time, "What God has cleansed, you must not call common." This happened three times, and the thing was taken up at once to heaven.

> Now while Peter was inwardly perplexed as to what the vision which he had seen might mean, behold, the men that were sent by Cornelius, having made inquiry for Simon's house, stood before the gate and called out to ask whether Simon who was called Peter was lodging there. And while Peter was pondering the vision, the Spirit said to him, "Behold, three men are looking

for you. Rise and go down, and accompany them without hesitation; for I have sent them." And Peter went down to the men and said, "I am the one you are looking for; what is the reason for your coming?" And they said, "Cornelius, a centurion, an upright and God-fearing man, who is well spoken of by the whole Jewish nation, was directed by a holy angel to send for you to come to his house, and to hear what you have to say." So he called them in to be his guests.

The next day he rose and went off with them, and some of the brethren from Joppa accompanied him. And on the following day they entered Caesarea. Cornelius was expecting them and had called together his kinsmen and close friends. When Peter entered, Cornelius met him and fell down at his feet and worshipped him. But Peter lifted him up, saying, "Stand up; for I too am a man." And as he talked with him, he went in and found many persons gathered; and he said to them, "You yourselves know how unlawful it is for a Jew to associate with or to visit any one of another nation; but God has shown me that I should not call any man common or unclean. So when I was sent for, I came without objection. I ask then why you sent for me."

And Cornelius said, "Four days ago, about this hour, I was keeping the ninth hour of prayer in my house; and behold, a man stood before me in bright apparel, saying, 'Cornelius, your prayer has been heard and your alms have been remembered before God. Send therefore to Joppa and ask for Simon who is called Peter; he is lodging in the house of Simon, a tanner, by the seaside.' So I sent for you at once, and you have been kind enough to come. Now therefore we are all here present in the sight of God, to hear all that you have been commanded by the Lord."

And Peter opened his mouth and said: "Truly I perceive that God shows no partiality, but in every nation any one who fears him and does what is right is acceptable to him."

The journalists of the world press were puzzling over what headlines to run for New Year's Day, 2000, when the TELEX machines typed in what they wanted, a sensational announcement: "The pope is selling the Vatican."

In fact Pope John XXIV had convened a consistory on December 30. But instead of merely accepting the congratulations of the cardinals, and giving the usual review of church and world politics, which at bottom said nothing and, above all, changed nothing, he had presented a future model of Peter's service, developed entirely on his own and in secret, that made the world sit up and take notice.

He had argued in his speech:

The Second Vatican Council changed the historic image of the charge and gave impulses that won approval on the theological-theoretical level, but on the pastoral-structural level have not yet been translated into practice. I am very anxious to say a bold yes to certain results of the Council. . . . Not only do clothes make the man, but buildings shape the people in them. For centuries the Baroque and Renaissance milieu of the Vatican has helped to create in this center of church administration a style and a mentality that are hard to change within the walls of these buildings. All this quite apart from the fact that these premises have proved to be very expensive to keep up and impractical for work. On the threshold of the third millenium, therefore, it seems to me that the time has come to jettison our historical ballast. . . .

For this reason I have decided to put the Vatican, along with its museums, up for sale to a European institute of culture. With the proceeds I shall have a modest, functional central administration building put up somewhere else for the Latin Church. I emphasize, for the Latin Church. I mean by that the Church of the old Christian countries of the western world, which grew from the soil of Roman culture and shaped the Church, as it concretely lives, in its historical form. With regard to the other continents it has pleased the Holy Spirit and myself to cooperate with their own particular cultural sensibilities, not to impose the "western" Church upon them, to let them have a large amount of autonomy and authority, so that the Gospel can take flesh and form with them, and begin its new history, and in this way it may become Latin American in Latin America, African in Africa, and Asian in Asia. . . .

When the Vatican is sold, that will mean that the papal state no longer exists, which means that the function of the nuncios will likewise be at an end.

I myself will transfer my residence to Jerusalem, in order to serve the world at large there, unencumbered with all the historical animosities that are bound up with the name of Rome. Since all the churches long for unity, but—rightly—do not wish to fall under the power of the Roman Curia, I felt that Peter's successor should offer a new, evangelical model of the "sign of unity" that all churches could accept. In this way they could finally stand before the world of the non-Christian religions and of unbelief once again as one Church with a common witness to Christ. I shall, therefore, get into touch with the other Christian churches as soon as possible, to ask if they are ready to attend a joint Council—call it Jerusalem II—in order to lay the foundations on which would, without prejudice to our different traditions, recognize each other as the one Church of Christ. That is, only the different continental Catholic churches, together with the Orthodox and Protestant churches, *jointly* exhaust— to some extent—the being of the Church. Only this whole group makes the "Katholike" (universal Church) appear. Furthermore I would like to try to bring together in Jerusalem the three great religions that are represented there—Christianity, Judaism, and Islam— into a sort of ecumene, even including the other great religions. For I am convinced that all men and women who seek and love God must be close to one another, and, like all churches, so too only all religions together can express the fullness of the workings of the Holy Spirit.

I know that I cannot yet foresee all the consequences of this decision, just as John XXIII, when he announced the Council, could not foresee its outcome. But I believe I have acted in the spirit of Jesus and the Council, and I ask all sisters and brothers in the churches to accept it in this spirit and to cooperate readily in carrying it out. So help me God and his holy Gospel.

Thus G. Morselli had, in a certain sense, been vindicated. In 1974 he had written a futuristic novel called *Roma senza Papa* (Rome without the pope). He was a Catholic rightist.

What John XXIV had only planned was, of course, something altogether different and was the response not to a defeatist panic but rather to a prophetic vision. People from all over reacted to it with surprise and enthusiasm. Now, they thought, the dossier on the "Donation of Constantine" (based on a forged document), according to which the Emperor Constantine had provided the pope and the Church with titles and territories and privileges, would finally be laid away in the archives, that the page of the second millenium, with its churchly triumphalism and exclusivism and, because of that, its schisms, would turn, and now a new chapter of church history would begin with the third millenium.[41]

3. WHITHER THE CHURCH?

It makes little difference whether Peter saw the resurrected Lord in the flesh, touched and spoke with him, as if the Risen One had once more been as he was before, or whether he experienced that only in an inner vision, in a dream, or whether it was not an authentic saying of Jesus at all, but only an expression of apostolic tradition. In any event the early Church was convinced that Jesus had three times put an intimate question to Peter in a mysterious fashion, and on the strength of his unshakable love three times given him the commission that we read about in John 21:15-17:

> When they had finished breakfast, Jesus said to Simon Peter, "Simon, son of John, do you love me more than these?" He said to him, "Yes, Lord, you know that I love you." He said to him, "Feed my lambs." A second time he said to him, "Simon, son of John, do you love me?" He said to him, "Yes, Lord, you know that I love you." He said to him, "Tend my sheep." He said to him the third time, "Simon, son of John, do you love me?" Peter was grieved because he said to him the third time, "Do you love me?" And he said to him, "Lord, you know everything; you know that I love you." Jesus said to him, "Feed my sheep."

The year 2000 was rung in with more feeling than usual. Among great and small more speeches were delivered, more champagne bottles popped open. In other ways, however, it was a quite ordinary succession of day and night in the long course of time. The moon took no leaps in its orbit, the sun stayed put. And no cosmic catastrophes occurred, as had been prophesied years and months before.

Nevertheless, every thinking person sensed that with the year 2000 a new epoch had begun. The third millenium will not simply be the prolongation, much less the repetition, of the second millenium, with its repugnant national, colonial, religious, and world wars. To that extent contemporary history *is* decidedly making a qualitative leap forward. The breakthrough, which the previous decades have paved the way for, from the age of the western Church to that of the World Church, from the age of authority to that of human dignity and freedom of conscience, will produce its full effects only in the third millenium. He who has eyes to see, let him see.

As far as the Church goes, the speech to the consistory by Pope John XXIV stirred up an enormous sensation, and gave the Church fresh impetus and the whole world new hope. Among the other major events the bishops' synod in May was outstanding. It was to be the last of its kind, because the synods had petered out all by themselves, crippled as they were by the principle, "Stet lex, dum volvitur orbis"—freely translated, "Never mind the synod, so long as canon law remains intact." Now the pope had already made it known that in the course of decentralization (postulated by the synod of 1985, though naturally with no palpable results at that time) there would be continental synods. And then these synods, within the framework of a fundamental law which would obtain for all Catholic and Christian churches wishing to live in unity, could draw up their own codes of canon law. The "Roman synod of bishops" in a new form would remain a superior authority, designed to serve the cause of information exchange and mutual inspiration and to celebrate the feast of unity.

The pope wished to give this synod for the year 2000 the fresh and revolutionary character of a brain-storming session. No resolutions were to be passed for the World Church, but new horizons were to be opened up, new interpretations sought, new directions given.

To begin with, situation reports by each continental Church were scheduled for the first few days, to be given in alphabetical order. This meant that Africa was the first to have the floor, Europe the last. There was no need to be concerned with the jesting commentaries this evoked among the participants.

Now it was Europe's turn. The symposium of the European bishops' conferences had nominated as its spokesman Cardinal B. Hume, who of course had been president of this symposium for many years. For all his modesty he had played a great role as an outstanding leader, and he enjoyed an unprecedented prestige, even in the Anglican Church. When the archbishop's throne of Westminster became vacant, the Apostolic Delegate, B. Heim, had discovered (not through a lucky stab, but by a popular referendum) and supported him. All the people in the archdiocese had been given an opportunity to name their candidate. Out of the roughly 6,000 letters received, a great wave of sympathy had welled up for the Benedictine abbot, B. Hume. People knew that he was a genuine European, speaking English, French, and German; that he was on good terms with high-ranking politicians and with leaders of the Anglican Church; and that he said little, but what he said was telling.

As archbishop and cardinal he continually furnished evidence of this style. At the bishops' synods his votes always carried great weight. At the 1980 synod on marriage and the family he spoke of the Christian consensus that precisely on questions of marriage, celibate bishops should not be the only ones passing judgment on married lay people, but rather that they had to listen to good Christians led by the Holy Spirit, so as to learn what would do and what would not, in the light of the Gospel and the individual conscience. This "sense of the faith," he said, constituted an authentic source of theology, with the help of which we must ask probing questions, even about the so-called "eternal truths." In 1987, on the subject of the laity, he had the courage to press for the idea of "tested men" as candidates for the priesthood, even if they were married, although he knew that would not sit well with the Vatican. He wanted to remedy the growing shortage of priests in Europe and the other continents, and to stop the Church's law of celibacy from holding back so many people from participating in the Eucharist, as God's command would have them. Finally in 1990, when the Second Vatican Council (despite the synod of 1985, which had fully and firmly backed the Council) was still being very restrictively construed by many churchmen, Hume had emphasized that the point was not simply to give the conciliar texts as such the right interpretation, but to go beyond the Council and to be open to the further evolution of life. Just as there is development in the gospels, from the first gospel, Mark, to the last gospel, John, and development in dogma, which can be shown throughout all of church history, for the same reason there is development in the Council: We must leave the conciliar texts open-ended and in so doing be true to the Council, so that in its spirit we may always respond afresh to the signs of the time.

Cardinal Hume was now 77 years old. Twelve years before he had insisted on being released from his post. Since then he had lived in his erstwhile Benedictine monastery and dedicated himself to prayer and study, and above all, to his main concern, ecumenism. On this topic he remained the tireless admonisher, who could not be worn down by setbacks and opposition. Now the symposium of the European bishops' conferences had asked this man to present in their name, as a sort of prophet, an analysis of the subject, "The Church of Europe at the End of the Millenium" at the bishops' synod of 2000.

And now this pale, gaunt figure, with his St. John's aquiline nose symbolizing his keen scent, rose and began to speak:

"The last will be the first, and the first will be last" (Mt 20:16). Providence has seen to it that it is not always the same people who must stand in the sunlight and the others in the shade. Here at the synod is not the only place where Europe has drawn the last place in the row. In world history, too, it has had to withdraw from its centuries long political, economic, and religious hegemony over the world and give precedence to other peoples. With all the crises that Europe is going through because of this, I am amazed that when it was dismissed from its leadership role it did not suffer the usual post-retirement "fold" and then collapse. It regained its composure rather well and faced the new situation. We should not, therefore, speak of "Europessimism" or "Euro-sclerosis." We do not have to write the epilogue to European history, much less its obituary, but the prologue for the new phase of its history that stands before it. This era will find its meaning and its greatness in the fact that it no longer makes the world revolve around Europe, but makes Europe serve the world with its technological superiority.

Not only Europe, but the Roman-western Church, must make the adjustment. It is no longer *the* Church. It has become part of a greater Church, the World Church. The closer the various continental Churches get to obtaining their relative autonomy and evolving their legitimately pluralistic style in theology, liturgy and discipline, the more we need a sign of unity to hold everything together. The pre-eminence of the Roman Church cannot be challenged. The question is only how it makes use of its mandate. Over the course of the centuries and into the modern period it has strongly exercised a central power that made it unpopular. It must now find a new mode of leadership. It must go from being a Church of Law to a Church of Love, not as an alternative but as a priority. If Vatican I taught that the bishop of Rome "has the precedence of regular authority over all other churches," and indeed "the full and supreme competent authority over the entire Church," Vatican II developed this doctrine forward and completed it with the idea of collegiality. In so doing it was being faithful to its origins and keeping abreast of the current situation, because human beings, including today's Christians, will no longer let themselves be dominated—despite all the totalitarian systems—but will accept only inspiration that they find meaningful. The Council was on the right track also because Jesus at the very beginning, with his triple question to Peter, "Do you love me more than these?" clearly conferred on him the primacy of love, not of law. Thus the charismatic element should predominate. That does not exclude structure, order, authority, or love, but places them under the more important claim of love. A prevailing legalism and forced uniformity are incompatible with charisma.[42] We are very much obliged to thank Pope John XXIV for drawing upon these ideas in his promise not only to liquidate the palace but also radically to restructure the Roman Curia.

Now let me speak from the heart and remind you of the reunion of the Anglican and Roman Churches, which took place last year. It was a long road to travel. The theological commissions did very good work, and the official Churches had more trouble keeping up with them. We had to visit so many of the authorities and continually insist on their rethinking the situation. But finally the result fell like a ripe fruit from the tree.

As far back as the 1920's, in the dialogues at Mechlin, Cardinal Mercier had said that it ought to be possible for the Anglican Church to be united with but not absorbed by Rome. Then, in 1977, Pope Paul VI declared to Dr. Coggan, the archbishop of Canterbury and primate of the Anglican Church: "These words of hope from Cardinal Mercier are no longer a mere dream." And now we have moved from the dreaming phase to reality. The Anglican Church has remained itself and yet become different, changing from a Church divided from Rome to one united with Rome. At the same time King Charles III renounced his right to be the supreme head of the Church, since, in the light of contemporary ideas on the separation of church and state, this office had long since become obsolete. The state should cease interfering in the Church's affairs, both in the Marxist states of the East and, still more, in the free states of the West. We are lucky that this reunion, which was still a bit of a shotgun marriage, could take place last year; and so we did not have to drag into the third millenium the fatal calamitous split that characterized the second. We hope that this model, this prototype, in which so much faith, hope, and love had to be invested, will also give the other Reformation churches and the churches of the East the courage to take the same step, so that the Christian churches can bear common witness in the face of the other religions and the atheistic world.

Here I must correct myself at once. We are accustomed to speaking of the "atheistic world" of the present. I find that the world has never been so very much a world of God as it is in our days. For God is:

—more than ever present in the Eucharist. Since Vatican II, receiving communion on Sunday has become a matter of course, in the good sense, for churchgoers. There have never been so many people going to communion as there are today. As the worthy heir of the former 'Christian West,' the Church of Europe can boast that it has helped build so many churches in the Third World, and that this help continues. These are nobler monuments than those erected to the heroes of our past, who were honored for having fought and conquered neighboring nations;

—more than ever present in the Holy Spirit. There have never been so many Bibles in so many of the world's languages as there are today. Since Vatican II, the zeal of the Protestant Bible societies has been

joined by similar activities on the part of the Catholic
Church. Europe is providing a great deal of help in
disseminating the Bible in the Third World and in the
Eastern countries. The men and women in those countries are grasping hungrily for it, because in their bad
situation they yearn for good news;

—more than ever present in the non-Christian religions. Hitherto we had limited God's saving work to
the Catholic Church. For centuries those other religions were considered the doing and the service of the
devil. The Second Vatican Council, for the first time,
spoke well of them. Since then post-conciliar theology, first in Europe, and later increasingly in Asia has
further developed the theology of the non-Christian
religions, and discovered in them the power of God
and his Spirit and the cosmic presence of the Logos.
This powerfully extends the scope of God's action, that
is, we have finally seen and acknowledged what was
always there. If the second millenium was marked
by the sign of the Christian West, the third will be
marked by the world religious community, by universal
religion, for all the legitimate differences in individual
convictions. But we Christians have the first task of
being interpreters for this all-embracing work of salvation by God. We call that "evangelizing," spreading
the good news to the world;

—more than ever present in the poor. Awareness
of the poor and the powerless as a privileged site
of Jesus' presence has never been stronger than it is
today. The "option for the poor" has never been
stronger in widespread circles of the Church than it
is today. The pressure of these groups, it is to be
hoped, will continue to increase, so that finally even
the European-American economy will have to yield
and become more flexible and humane in the North-

South dialogue, in the negotiations for justice in the world marketplace. This could be called "shalom-izing"—not simply speaking fair words to the world about God's love, but making it capable of experiencing God's salvation here and now in a life that is worthier of humanity.

—present, too, in the secularized world. I now come to the specific religious situation of the western world. The earlier reports by the continental churches have shown that Latin America sees the liberation of the poor as its most urgent problem, for Africa it is inculturation or the Africanization of Christianity, for Asia the dialogue with non-Christian religions. Our most pressing task in Europe is the confrontation with secularism. Depending upon the country and region anywhere from 50 to 95 percent of Europeans no longer go to church. Should we simply write off the mass of people who are alienated from the Church, ignore them, and be content with the 'little remnant' of churchgoers? Once it used to be said that here in Europe we have the Church, over there in Africa and Asia they have the missions. Today there are six continents, but there are also missions on every one of them, that is, the Church is everywhere in a missionary situation. I do not hesitate to call Europe the most difficult missionary country of all. We have to get into dialogue with these people—I call them religious nomads, who have abandoned the sedentary life of religious institutions and now go their own way. They find this liberating, fascinating, but at the same time frustrating. I do not believe that they can be simply called non-religious. They are all burdened with questions that no one can avoid, questions about the meaning of life and death—questions that are religious in the profoundest sense. In this secularized world we Christians are called to perform a threefold task:

1) of interpretation: We are not to write off those secularized persons, not even the atheists. God doesn't write them off either. They remain, now as ever, human beings, which is a great deal. They belong, now as ever, to the race of Jesus, who accepts and loves them. They have left the Church, but they still live in the Kingdom of God, in the grace and love of God. No one can fall beyond God's love. Even if he gives God up, God does not give him up. He remains true to him, and he knows ways and means to catch up with him and bring him home; 2) of representation: As a small minority, we are not to live merely for ourselves, to try to sanctify ourselves and save our souls, but we are constantly to keep in mind the whole human race and to pray and celebrate the Eucharist in their name and for them, in the same way that Jesus himself does in our midst; 3) of vocation: We are to wander together with those nomads and to say the right word of salvation to them at the right time and in the right way, and perhaps to win one or another of them back, so that once again they too may share with us in this wonderful mission of the Church in the world. For the Church is not there to burden people with laws and nuisances, as the ancient synagogue did, but, as Vatican II said, to be a "sign of salvation for all." She has to attest to this divine salvation and tell everyone about it. She also has the mission for the third millenium of proclaiming the Good News to the world so that everyone whose "soul is naturally Christian" may hear it and rejoice in it.

For the other continental churches, meanwhile, we wish and implore that they, like our common source, the early Church, may be driven and led by the Holy Spirit. We pray that in this way the 20th century Acts

of the Apostles, a history marked by so many meaningless individual events and yet not quite "lost" as a total
process, may find its dramatic continuation in the third
millenium Acts of the Apostles, for the Spirit is never
weary, never exhausted.   In its power the churches
too, like Jesus, remain a sign of the presence of God
amongst humanity, indefatigable with ever fresh inspiration.

Still somewhat shaken, the old man stood there in front of the
microphone. A long burst of applause roared up to him. When it
quieted, just as the moderator was about to address the assembly,
the clock in the belfry of St. Peter's tolled the hour with majestic
serenity, as it always has, as if to remind everyone that history
has always had its highs and lows, as in a natural rhythm. And
the whole audience noticed that as the millenium came to an end
the Church was heading not for a low but for a new high, if only
she understood the challenges of the time and always held herself
open to the surprises of the Spirit of God.

Abbreviations

AG = *Ad Gentes*, Decree of the Second Vatican Council on the Mis-
       sionary Activity of the Church

EN = *Evangelii Nuntiandi*, Apostolic Admonition of Paul VI on the
       Duty of Proclaiming the Gospel

LG = *Lumen Gentium*, Dogmatic Constitution of the Second Vati-
       can Council on the Church

OR = *Osservatore Romano*

RH = *Redemptor Hominis*, Encyclical of John Paul II on the Dignity
       of the Human Person

SC = *Sacrosanctum Concilium*, Constitution of the Second Vatican
       Council on the Sacred Liturgy

SKZ = *SchweizerischeKirchenzeitung*

Notes

[1] See the instructive book by C.M. Martini, *Von seinem Geist getrieben: Dynamische Gemeinde nach der Apostelgeschichte* (Freiburg im Breisgau, 1985).

[2] K. Klinger, *Ein Papst lacht: Die gesammelten Anekdoten um Johannes XXIII* (Frankfurt, 1963).

[3] W. Bühlmann, *Weltkirche: Neue Dimensionen—Modell fur das Jahr 2001* (Graz, 1984), pp. 146-7.

[4] H. Jedin, *Lebensbericht*, ed. by K. Repgen (Mainz, 1984), pp. 201, 227.

[5] Based on the statement of one of the most committed bishops of Brazil, Pedro Casaldaliga. See T. Cabestrero, *Mystik und Befreiung. Ein Portrait des Bischofs Pedro Casaldaliga* (Wuppertal, 1981), pp. 113-14.

[6] L. Boff, *Kirche. Charisma und Macht* (Dusseldorf, 1985).

[7] G. Caprile, *Il Concilio Vaticano II* (Rome, 1969), V, 415.

[8] This sentence was struck from the German edition by the publisher, but is retained in the seven other languages into which the book was translated.

[9] Cf. the book by T. Schneider (ed.), *Der verdrangte Aufbruch. Ein Konzils-Lesebuch* (Mainz, 1985).

[10] See W. Bühlmann, *Weltkirche*, pp. 172-266. This is an exposition of the lines along which such a renewal would have to run. See further W. Bühlmann, *Wandlung zum Wesentlichen. Der Sinn der Evangelisierung* (Munsterschwarzach, 1976), especially pp. 147-57.

11 See H. Vorgrimler, *Karl Rahner verstehen* (Freiburg im Breisgau, 1985), p. 117.

12 1 Celano 33.

13 *Spiegel der Vollkommenheit*, German trans. by W. Ruttenauer, Book III (Munich, 1953), p. 117.

14 2 Celano 30. F. De Beer, *Francois, Sue disait-on de toi?* (Paris, 1977), pp. 66-111, based on the Chronicle of Jacques de Vitry.

15 "La Congregazione di Propaganda Fide e l'Ordine Cappuccino," in *Vita minorum* (Rome, 1972), pp. 47-55.

16 J. Metzler (ed.), *Memoria Rerum. Storia di Propaganda Fide* (Freiburg im Breisgau, 1976), III/2, 578-612.

17 In the German edition of the book, *Wo der Glaube lebt* (Freiburg im Breisgau, 1974), pp. 155-58.

18 With regard to these two specific great figures, it must be noted—if we are being honest and critical—that, unquestionably zealous for souls as they were, they were also swayed by considerations of political power, Fidelis for Austria, Massaia for Italy.

19 Amalorpavadass, the blood brother of Archbishop Lourdusamy, was for twenty years the driving force for reform in the Church of India. He built and directed the National Liturgical-Catechetical Center of Bangalore, led seminar after seminar for lay people, nuns, priests, and bishops, and published many books. But he also had difficulties with certain bishops and with Rome, so that he finally left the Center and is now professor of Christian spirituality at the state university in Mysore.

20 Further elaborated and substantiated with bibliographical references in W. Bühlmann, *Wenn Gott zu allen Menschen geht* (Freiburg im Breisgau, 1981), pp. 76-119.

21 He was afterwards called as a professor to the seminary at Roermond (Holland), well known for being very conservative.

22 At the time Karl Rahner bluntly pointed to the fact that in the course of the last hundred years the Roman authorities have defended the faith in an admittedly real but also purely sterile fashion, without striving for a positive integration of the new problems. That sort of solution had to be sought by the people

who were placed under suspicion in Rome for seeking it. "Practically everything said by the Roman authorities on biblical questions in the last one hundred years before Vatican II has become obsolete, no one pays any further attention to it" ("Glaubenskongregation und Theologenkommission," in *Schriften zur Theologie* X, 338-57.

23 In Part I of this book I presented the reasons that have now "compelled" me to publish these documents.

24 In *Schweizerische Kirchenzeitung* (Lucerne 1982), 118-22, 134-36. Printed at the same time in the magazine *Theologie der Gegenwart*.

25 This is a large-format magazine that lives on advertising and so is delivered free, carrying extreme right wing theological supplements, to rectories and convents. In 12 of its long columns my "optimism about salvation" was presented as contrary to the statements of the Council, and condemned.

26 The letter to Cardinal J. Villot of November 5, 1974 (p. 89). The letter to Archbishop Martinez Somalo of May 23, 1980 (pp. 84-5). The letter to Archbishop G. Benelli of May 10, 1975 (p. 105).

27 The very harsh encyclical by Pius XI against communism (1937), which says: "Communism is bad in its innermost being, and whoever wishes to save Christian culture may not cooperate with it in any area."

28 Currently president of the Pontificia Accademia Ecclesiastica in Rome, formerly for many years Apostolic Nuncio in Cuba, who managed to obtain a great deal from the regime there through his good relations with it. Before I went to Mozambique I met with him to get some good advice for missionaries in Marxist countries. In the Secretariat of State itself, before the political upheaval, we had been advised only to recommend to the missionaries "to preach the Gospel and not get mixed up in politics."

29 He was named archbishop of Lubango in 1977 and then became a cardinal in 1983.

30 Later, it is true, he took a turn for the better and gave, for example, a very courageous speech on inculturation at the

bishops' synod of 1980.

31 There is journalistic report on this Congress in W. B¨ uhlmann, *Alle haben denselben Gott. Begegnung mit den Menschen und den Religionen Asiens* (Frankfurt am Main, 1978).

32 I could not locate this letter, so I am citing it from memory.

33 The long series of articles later also appeared in book form: J. Beckman, W. Bühlmann, J. Specker, *Die heilige Schrift in den katholischen Missionen* (NZM-Verlag: Schoneck-Beckenried, 1966).

34 Cf. note 31.

35 *Wenn Gott zu allen Menschen geht. Fur eine neue Erfahrung der Auserwahlung* (Freiburg im Breisgau, 1981).

36 P. F. Knitter, *No Other Name?: A Critical Survey of Christian Attitudes Toward the World Religions* (Maryknoll, 1985).

37 With this brief, Pope John XXIII tried to keep the use of Latin alive in the Church, as he had been urged to by certain traditionalistic groups. The brief had no effect at all, and the pope himself is said to have smiled at it afterwards."

38 A group of young people that has a center near the church of Santa Maria in Trastevere. They lead a very intensive prayer life, but also go out in the evenings to various parts of the city to help old, lonely, sick, and neglected men and women.

39 Fr. Junipero Serra (d. 1784), a Franciscan who worked in Mexico as the "Father of the Indians," also traveled to California, and is considered the "Apostle of California." Some of his Indian settlements grew into great cities, such as San Francisco.

40 In my book *Weltkirche*, I have discussed further the path this reform might take. For the kenosis of the Latin Church, see pp. 172-76. For the place of Rome in the new understanding of the Church, see pp. 197-206.

41 Already printed in *Publik-Forum*, Jan. 11, 1985; and in *Luzerner Neueste Nachrichten*, Feb. 23, 1985.

42 On these ideas cf. H. Fries, *Fundamentaltheologie* (Graz, 1985), pp. 420-38.